# The
# German-Jewish
# Legacy in America,
# 1938 – 1988

To my mother, Anna Kolton Peck, z"l, survivor of Auschwitz, who provided me with a legacy that I somehow lost but which I now have found.

# *The German-Jewish Legacy in America, 1938–1988*

## From *Bildung* to the Bill of Rights

Edited and Introduced by Abraham J. Peck

 Wayne State University Press/Detroit 1989

**Library of Congress Cataloging-in-Publication Data**

The German-Jewish legacy in America, 1938-1988 : from Bildung to the
    Bill of Rights / edited and introduced by Abraham J. Peck.
          p.      cm.
        Reprinted from American Jewish archives, v. 40, no. 2, Nov. 1988.
        ISBN 0-8143-2263-8.—ISBN 0-8143-2264-6 (pbk.)
            1.   Jews, German—United States—Intellectual life.    2.   Jews—
    United States—Intellectual life.      3.   Immigrants—United States—
    Intellectual life.      4.   Judaism—United States.      5.   United States—
    Intellectual life—20th century.      I.   Peck, Abraham J.
    II. American Jewish archives.
    E184.J5G38 1989
    973'.04924031—dc20
                                                        89-16561
                                                        CIP

"Dachau: Lest We Forget" by Hans Juergensen from *The Ambivalent Journey,* 1986, p. 45
reprinted by
permission of American Studies Press. Inc.

# *Acknowledgements*

This book would not have been possible without the advice and cooperation of many individuals. I am especially grateful to Professor Alfred Gottschalk, the president and *rosh yeshiva* of the Hebrew Union College-Jewish Institute of Religion. The idea for this volume emerged from numerous discussions with Professor Gottschalk about the nature of the German-Jewish legacy in its American context. I also acknowledge with pleasure my indebtedness to Professor Michael A. Meyer of the Hebrew Union College-Jewish Institute of Religion for his comments on and criticisms of the guidelines which were sent to the numerous contributors of the book as a means of focusing their insights into the nature of the German-Jewish legacy in America. I am most grateful to Alice M. Nigoghosian of the Wayne State University Press for her many technical suggestions and for the thoroughly professional manner in which she helped bring this book to its intended reading audience. Eleanor Lawhorn and Ruth L. Kreimer devoted many hours of painstaking toil to organizing, typing and retyping countless pages of the manuscript and the vast correspondence associated with its completion. Rick McGowan of the Rosenthal Printing Company was a great help in assuring that the manuscript would be free from as many typographical errors as possible. Also of great value to me was the brilliant copyediting done by Robert Milch who also completed the index. The final responsibility for this book, naturally, rests with me.

My greatest thanks must go to my father, Shalom Peck and to my mother of blessed memory, Anna Kolton Peck and to my wife, Jean, and children, Abby and Joel. They have each given me that which together makes me an American, a Jew and a human being.

April 1989                                                              A. J. P.

# Contents

# Introduction

It has now been more than five decades since Rabbi Leo Baeck concluded that "the end of German Jewry has arrived."[1] Baeck spoke these words not long after Adolf Hitler came to power at the beginning of 1933.

Perhaps his conclusion was premature because the precise meaning of Leo Baeck's words was demonstrated to German Jewry with a furious and destructive finality over five years later on the night and day of November 9 – 10, 1938 during a vicious national pogrom. The end of German-Jewish life had indeed arrived.

If German Jewry's physical presence had been all but eliminated, what about the spirit that defined more than a century of German-Jewish existence? And what of its transfer to numerous places of refuge, especially the United States of America? These are two of the more important questions which this book hopes to address.

Initially, of course, one must define that spirit. In its modern form such a spirit was centered in the concept of *Bildung*, a post-emancipation notion that included character formation, moral education, the primacy of culture and a belief in the potential of humanity. *Bildung* was an important, perhaps the most important, secular concept which fueled the extraordinary transformation of German Jewry between the years 1780 to 1840 as it struggled for social and political emancipation.[2]

For German Jewry, the aim and the mission of *Bildung* was to create a new German Jew, one who would be accepted by his Christian neighbors. This would be achieved by a process of reeducation—the acquisition of civility through improved manners and morals.[3]

But German Jewry had a second aim. It would use its notion of *Bildung* to secure a common ground with non-Jewish Germany. Above all, it would create an environment where the universal would be more important than the narrowly patriotic, where German history—which the Jew could not fully share with the German—would be less important than art, culture, or the humanistic ideal.[4]

In theory, such aims might work. But reality in nineteenth-century Germany was another matter. In seeking, first of all, to maximize the process of political and civic emancipation on the path of assimilation into the mainstream of German culture, German Jewry created a clearly definable, if not yet visible, subculture.[5]

Second of all, even though the ideal of *Bildung*, channeled through the *Gebildeten*, or educated people, could be traced back to Martin Luther's universal view that all human beings were created in the image of God, German history had changed that ideal beyond recognition. The nineteenth-century gave rise in Germany to emotions that had little room for notions of the universal. Patriotism, romanticism, and pietism narrowed the German concept of *Bildung*, and made it forever unacceptable to German Jewry.[6]

One can already see, from the very creation of the German nation-state in the 1870's, the growth of an environment essentially hostile to the Jewish idea of *Bildung*. Indeed, the "Ideas of 1789," of the French Revolution and the Enlightenment, the foundations upon which the German-Jewish concept of *Bildung* were based, became the code word (along with anti-Semitism) for all that was thought to be in opposition to "true" German ideals. As one German nationalist wrote before the start of World War I, "the old terms have to be changed: instead of religion, language and artistic intuition; instead of humanity, the race."[7]

The outbreak of the First World War solidified the anti-1789 feelings into a coherent philosophy. The "Ideas of 1914," as this philosophy came to be known, was a direct rejection by the German nation of Jewish *Bildung*. With one quick stroke, the "Ideas of 1914," would sever all alien influence from the German people. What the "Ideas of 1789," with their notions of humanity and democracy, had done to make Germany morally and intellectually impure, the new concept, with its uniquely "German" vision, would readily undo. The spirit of the Enlightenment and its legacy to German Jewry, *Bildung*, with its accompanying concepts of democracy and humanity, would finally be broken.

And yet, the Jews in Germany, after the end of the war, continued to believe in an ideology that was accepted by nearly no one else. And despite the external appearance of the Weimar Republic as a triumph of the Jewish idea of *Bildung*, a place where art and culture did indeed seem to prevail over the spirit of nationalism, the illusion was soon played out. Weimar culture became, as George Mosse characterizes it in the pages of this volume, "an inner-Jewish dialogue to which few gentiles listened."

The Nazi triumph in 1933 and the events of November 1938 finally destroyed the belief that *Bildung* could be used as a means of creating in Germany a more modern and democratic environment. Quite obviously the idea of *Bildung* as defined by the Nazis, linked as it was to racism, nationalism, and the "German" idea of truth, beauty, and culture, could not and would not have anything to do with an ideology created by Jews.[8]

Even sizeable segments of the Jewish community began to abandon a completely middle-class idea of German-Jewish *Bildung*. Left-wing Jewish intellectuals had, especially in the early Weimar years, attempted to reach out to the German masses, despite fears of the irrationalism associated with that segment of society.[9] And German Zionists, while sharing the humanistic interpretation of *Bildung*, showed disdain for an old-style notion that failed "to take into account the prerogatives of the [Jewish] *Volk*" or nation.[10]

After 1938, most German Jews found themselves leaving the Third Reich for places which would be more suitable environments for their particular ideas. Less than two months before the November pogrom, the leading German Zionist newspaper, the *Juedische Rundschau*, paid tribute to those who had already left: "We are represented abroad by those who represent a people who cannot do anything else than institute the ideas of humanity and historical consciousness."[11]

In its transatlantic crossing from Europe to (primarily) America, the German-Jewish spirit, as represented by the notion of *Bildung*, became the German-Jewish legacy. But how would this legacy and its individual ingredients fare in an America so unlike the country where it was shaped and yet so potentially conducive to the basic presumptions of the German-Jewish spirit? John Kosa, in a symposium on the immigrant scholar in America, described the possible encounter of that spirit with the American idea. "One cannot live in America without being carried away by her," Kosa wrote. "That very puritanical spirit that has been so helpful to the persecuted ones has a strong persuasive power and molds everybody in accordance with its gentle design."[12]

The objective of this book, then, is to try and understand the German-Jewish legacy in its American context. The distinguished contributors to *The German-Jewish Legacy in America*, over forty in number, have considered a number of questions, among them:

How may one interpret the German-Jewish legacy?

How has that legacy expressed itself in the author's values as an American and a Jew?

What does the legacy mean for our time and what happened to it in its American context? Has it found a home in America or does the German-Jewish spirit remain in exile?

Is this legacy important to the continuation of a democratic American society? To the future of American Jewry?

Which elements of that legacy are worth preserving for the next generation and which are not?

I am particularly pleased to have given a large number of "second generation" North American Jews, whose parents either fled Nazi Germany or who, as German Jews, survived the Holocaust, the opportunity to examine the German-Jewish legacy. Such an opportunity to examine their legacy has been available to the children of Holocaust survivors, mostly of East European background, for well over a decade,[13] but few of the former group have been able to do so in print.

It is my hope that this book will be a useful addition to the history of the German-Jewish experience and to that of American Jewish life. Most important, it is an effort to commemorate the end of one of the greatest communities in Jewish history and to explore those elements of that greatness which may still be relevant and useful in insuring that our own Jewish community remains a vibrant and productive part of a free, human-oriented, and democratic American society.

## Notes

1. Quoted in Leonard Baker, *Days of Sorrow and Pain. Leo Baeck and the Berlin Jews* (New York, 1978), p. 145.

2. For a first-rate analysis of this transformation, see David Sorkin, *The Transformation of German Jewry, 1780–1840* (New York, 1987).

3. Ibid., p. 36.

4. George Mosse, "Jewish Emancipation: Between *Bildung* and Respectability," in Jehuda Reinharz and Walter Schatzberg (eds.), *The Jewish Response to German Culture* (Hannover, N. H. and London, 1985), pp. 14 ff.

5. Sorkin. *The Transformation of German Jewry,* pp. 6 ff.

6. George Mosse, *German Jews Beyond Judaism,* Bloomington and Cincinnati, 1985) pp. 12ff. Mosse, "Jewish Emancipation: Between *Bildung* and Respectability," p. 13.

7. Quoted in Abraham J. Peck, *Radicals and Reactionaries: The Crisis of Conservatism in Wilhelmine Germany* (Washington, D. C., 1978), p. 134.

8. Mosse, *German Jews Beyond Judaism,* pp. 71 ff.

9. Ibid., pp. 55 ff.

10. Jacob Boas, "The Shrinking World of German Jewry," in *Leo Baeck Institute Yearbook xxxi* (1986), p. 254. The most impassioned plea for the continuation of *Bildung* as the foundation of German-Jewish culture was made by Heinz Kellermann in a *CV Zeitung* article entitled "*Bildung am Ende?*" (The End of *Bildung?*) published shortly after the passage of the Nuremberg laws, Boas, "The Shrinking World," p. 258.

11. Quoted in *Juedische Rundschau,* September 16, 1938.

12. John Kosa (ed.), *The Home of the Learned Man* (New Haven, 1968), p. 38.

13. See Abraham J. Peck, "The Lost Legacy of Holocaust Survivors," in *Shoah* (Fall/Winter 1982/3): 33-37 and "The Children of Holocaust Survivors," in Allan Schoener, *The American Jewish Album, 1954 to the Present* (New York, 1983), pp. 309 – 310.

# The End Is Not Yet: A Personal Memoir of the German-Jewish Legacy in America

*George L. Mosse*

As I have given my own definition of the German-Jewish legacy in *German Jews Beyond Judaism*, I want to confine myself here to some personal observations of how its spirit seems to have survived in the United States when it had long been pronounced dead in Europe. I will have to reach into my own past in order to explain how I came to experience this revival of the German-Jewish legacy in America, and what I think it meant to those who have continued its history. It may seem odd in retrospect that it was the rediscovery by young Americans of this legacy which led me back to some of my own intellectual roots. But I had been educated at a boarding school which did not particularly nurse that heritage, and left Germany at a relatively young age in order to continue my education in England and America. Still, in some manner this German-Jewish legacy did pervade my family setting in Germany and in exile, centered as it was upon the so-called "mission of Judaism" with its emphasis upon *Bildung* as self-cultivation, cosmopolitanism and a rational attitude towards life. Yet because of my education I never experienced that depth of the German-Jewish heritage which, for example, made it difficult for refugee parents to understand their American children, who seemed to grow up without any culture or proper comportment. For the German ideal of *Bildung*, which required self-cultivation as a process of inward development and the acquisition of aesthetic taste, was unique—after all, the word *Bildung*, representing the moral universe itself, has no equivalent in any other language.

When I started teaching at the University of Iowa, directly after the war, I first came face-to-face with the differences between a European and an American education and outlook upon life. Here I shared an experience with many much-older refugee professors, who had been educated in Germany, and who often commented upon the ignorance of their students, their lack of aesthetic judgment and sophistication, and at the same time their freshness, their eagerness to learn. At that point I had little interest and almost no knowledge of a German-Jewish legacy, and instead pointed to the lamentable state of the American high school and of departments of education devoted to the notion that school was not an instrument of learning or of personal development but an engine for socialization. Many U.S.-born colleagues joined the fight in order to save so-called subject matter from being drowned by the emphasis upon method, upon "how to do things," then the staple of teachers' training.

Perhaps such conflicts with American educators were a preparation for things to come, for they can be seen in retrospect as a struggle against an American pragmatic tradition which had worn thin. While originally *Bildung* had served to help integrate German Jews into the educated German middle class, in America it led to their isolation from the mainstream of educational and intellectual thought. It was the attack upon the dominant system of thought from an entirely unexpected direction which was to bring about change and to awaken my own consciousness to the lasting importance of the German-Jewish intellectual tradition. The student generation of the 1960s threw down the gauntlet as part of their unease about the promise of American society, and this before the so-called student revolt turned into mindless rage and the use of force. I was then teaching a course on European cultural history at the University of Wisconsin which necessarily emphasized different social theories and approaches to life, such as those deriving from Marxism, liberalism, or the German philosophers. There was no special emphasis upon the German-Jewish legacy, and courses in modern Jewish history, where this heritage could be displayed, had not yet been introduced into most universities. And yet, whenever certain ideas closely related to part of this legacy were discussed, the students, most of whom were not Jews, felt a new excitement of discovery, and this, in turn, led me to reconsider my own heritage.

Why students searching for new approaches and meanings in life should have felt a special attraction to ideas which derived from this legacy is difficult to say. The failure of high school or even the university in transmitting a meaningful American heritage is important here; students turned to Lukacz, Gustav Landauer, the Frankfurt School, or the left-wing intellectuals of the Weimar Republic rather than stand on a native ground which had never been made relevant to their needs.

Marxism was central, at first, as a means of protest and as a theory which explained and put order into the totality of their lives. But Marxist orthodoxy was rejected as a straitjacket and the Soviet Union held no attraction at all. Teaching European cultural history to ever larger classes (by the mid-sixties some 500 students took this course), interest peaked whenever attempts to loosen Marxist orthodoxy were discussed, theories which emphasized the use of a critical mind within a revolutionary dynamic. It was the search for a left-wing identity which led back to the German-Jewish tradition.

In *German Jews Beyond Judaism*, I saw such a left-wing identity as a climax of the German-Jewish legacy, for it emphasized the ideal of a common humanity based upon *Bildung* and the Enlightenment as essential for the autonomy of the individual. The primacy of culture as an instrument of social change, based upon individual consciousness, suited the actual situation of these students, and at the same time exemplified one thrust of the German-Jewish tradition. This meant seeing life as a totality in which aesthetics as well as learning had their place. Men and women's lives were not merely determined by class struggle or governed by the liberal division between politics and life which seemed to perpetuate alienation. Students at the time seemed especially taken by the aesthetic dimension of this worldview as over against American mass culture, which came to symbolize manipulation and domination. Herbert Marcuse was important, passing on a culture-oriented view of society in which the combination of *Bildung* and Enlightenment would lead to social equality. Even so, though the students liked Marcuse's (and my own) German accent, there was no one to link theories which had such a great appeal to a German-Jewish legacy which had managed to preserve the original link between Enlightenment and *Bildung* without the distortion of modern nationalism. Nor did the students realize that these views might have a much greater liberal than Marxist potential.

That this was not merely a chance revival became clear when it seemed to appeal to students regardless of whether they were Jewish or not or where they were born, and when a philosopher like Juergen Habermas became its champion (conscious of the German-Jewish tradition involved), whether or not one had personal ties to the German-Jewish past. However, some more years were to pass until I finally decided to write the book. The students made me think about the implications of this tradition, but political concerns led me to undertake this task. From 1969 onwards I had taught at the Hebrew University in Jerusalem as well as at Wisconsin and had taken part in the lively debates about the nature of nationalism. There it seemed obvious that former German Jews were overrepresented in peace movements as well as in the movement for a binational state. Perhaps there was a certain German-Jewish tradition at work, which, if it could be rediscovered and articulated, might yet help to rehumanize modern nationalism.

What does this have to do with America? Such a heritage, as we saw, filled a need for young Americans ignorant of or disillusioned with their own heritage. The apparently lasting interest in Weimar—the many books which appeared in America on this subject—is closely related to the German-Jewish legacy. Indeed, what is generally regarded as Weimar culture has little bearing upon what the average middle-class German read or thought, but was (to quote the late George Lichtheim) an inner-Jewish dialogue to which few gentiles listened. The term "left-wing intellectual" current during the Weimar Republic not only described men and women in the past who had combined *Bildung*, Enlightenment, pacifism, and the quest for greater equality, but provided a new inspiration for young Americans who feared isolation and atomization and wanted to embrace the totality of life.

The hunger for totality was important here, and the dead-end of a world where war had become almost a way of life. Here also the optimism which the German-Jewish heritage retained from the Enlightenment had great appeal—not the American optimism about the future of society but that which emphasized the potential within each individual. Yet there was actually a great deal of American patriotism among such students, not connected to an American past, but to the United States as the nation which could build a new culture and therefore a new society upon the principles I have discussed.

But what of the present and future? Not only in Germany, but to a certain extent even in exile in the United States, German Jews had identified with this legacy. But such traditional support is vanishing with the passage of time. Nor could this heritage any longer address social needs as it had done in Germany. With its emphasis upon *Bildung* for all, the potential of each human being, it had suited a minority reaching out for greater equality. Not only had the German-Jewish tradition become counterproductive as an instrument of Americanization, as I have pointed out, but in a society where anti-Jewish discrimination is at such a low ebb it can no longer fulfill any social need. Instead, it has found the kind of support it never had in Germany, from Jews and gentiles alike—articulate intellectuals regardless of their place of origin.

The specific consequences of this heritage in America are difficult, perhaps impossible, to trace, for they combined with various other influences. Perhaps the integration of aesthetic taste into a general outlook of life is one such consequence, and the increased interest shown in theoretical questions in the social sciences another. The notion that theory is not a useless ornament invented by Germanic professors has been gaining ground—indeed, that without a sound theoretical base any intellectual activity remains one-dimensional.

Many books have been written about the contribution of German-Jewish refugee intellectuals to the United States. My own observations lead me to provide a slightly different emphasis. One of the basic attractions of their intellectual outlook was that it could provide a congenial alternative to the existing order, based upon changed minds rather than class struggle, on the thesis that culture must be taken seriously. As such—irony of history—ideals once meant for integration with the establishment became directed against it.

Like all traditions, the German-Jewish legacy did not and will not remain intact, though bits and pieces will be taken up and combined in different ways as fits the need of the age. Yet more and more intellectuals, both in Germany and the United States, recognize that the heritage German Jews made their own still has a role to play as an attitude towards life, as a prism through which to view and humanize society. That it took young Americans to recall at least one German Jew to this legacy should itself testify to its strength and capacity for survival.

# The German-Jewish Legacy—and I: Some Personal Reflections

*Peter Gay*

This invitation to submit some autobiographical thoughts on the German-Jewish legacy in the United States, of which I am a beneficiary and (I suppose) a representative, is at once flattering and disturbing. The flattering quality is obvious, the disturbing one requires some explanation. What I mean to say is that for me, at least—and I am speaking only about, and for, myself—the very idea of a German-*Jewish* legacy contains something of an irony. I strongly suspect that among the wide diversity of responses you are likely to get to your invitation, mine will be something of an exception, though hardly unique, and will stand at one end on the spectrum of the German-Jewish experience. That spectrum included numerous Germans of Jewish ancestry for whom Jewishness was invisible and who accordingly, after living in the United States, have judged the "German-Jewish legacy" quite differently from most of their fellow refugees.

## I

For a closer look at this irony, I must begin with my German childhood. My parents saw themselves as wholly assimilated into German society. Both were principled, and in the case of my father, aggressive, atheists. The earliest "information" I got about religion was anticlerical humor, and since the only religious people my father, who had grown up in a small town in Upper Silesia, had known were Jews, his stories were anti-Jewish stories. Indeed, I recall the very first time I heard the name of Karl Marx: my father told me that there was someone named Marx who had once said, "Religion is the opium of the masses"—and added that Marx had been right. Not surprisingly, my parents had officially left the Jewish faith, and lived in the Weimar Republic as "*konfessionslos.*" So, of course, did I, and without difficulties. Only Hitler made me into a Jew and, it turned out, not a very good one.

It is true that while we had gentile friends, most of our social life revolved around our large family—my father and my mother each had four siblings, and a number of them lived in Berlin, or came to visit us there. Two of my cousins, Hanns and Edgar, were my intimate companions, especially on Sundays, when we went to cheer our soccer teams. But this did not make me Jewish. Now, since on soccer hangs more than one significant tale—significant to me—I shall stay with this apparently trivial theme for a while.

My cousin Hanns, three years my senior, was like me a supporter of Hertha B.S.C. while his younger brother Edgar, who was my age, stuck loyally with Tennis Borussia. Anyone who knows anything about the history of German *Fussball*—and I suspect that it is likely to be mainly other contributors to this symposium who do—will recall that some half a century ago, Berlin was a respectable soccer city. The principal local rivalry was between the two teams that my cousins and I supported, and while Tennis Borussia never really achieved national prominence, it proved an interesting, at times upsetting, competitor to "my" team. On the other hand, Hertha B.S.C. was in the nation's eye. It fielded a sensational team in the late 1920s and early 1930s, when I was growing up. Four times, from 1926 through 1929, Hertha had managed to fight its way into the finals, only to be defeated. And then twice, in 1930 and 1931, they broke through and became German soccer champion. I listened to these last two triumphs on the radio, and then, from about 1932 on, as the glory somewhat faded but the team remained fairly competitive, I attended Hertha B.S.C.'s home games at the Hertha Platz, in the north of Berlin—attended them faithfully.

This fidelity did more than just provide entertainment for me. For one thing, it tied me to my father. All of his adult life, he had been an enthusiastic sports fan, both of soccer and of track and field. As a young man, when he had lived in Frankfurt for a time, he had supported the Frankfurter Eintracht, which in the years I followed the sport, boasted several players regularly called upon to represent Germany in the national team. I vaguely recall more than one visit from one of these players, none of them Jewish, in our apartment in Wilmersdorf. After marrying and settling in Berlin, my father had shifted his allegiance to Hertha B.S.C. In those years, when amateurs were amateurs, teams depended on voluntary helpers who could be counted on to do small chores for the club, and to accompany it as a welcome cheering section, on away games. My father did all that, and by adopting his interests—and his team—I came closer to this undemonstrative man than I could have in any other way. Mine was a liberal, which is to say cool, rationalistic, German upbringing.

Soccer did even more for me than this. My parents and I did not finally manage to get out until April 1939, and during the six insane years I spent under the Nazis, my regular attendance at the Hertha games contributed, I am convinced, to my sanity. My father subscribed to not one but two weeklies wholly devoted to soccer, *Der Kicker* and *Fussballwoche*, and I studied these magazines thoroughly every Monday, obsessively fastening on their statistics and their exhaustive reports of games all across the world. This rather mindless reading helped me to escape to a playful reality by taking me, even for a few hours each week, away from the harsher reality of Nazi broadcasts, Nazi posters, Nazi teachers, Nazi fellow-students.

I attended these soccer games with my cousins, I said. But there were times in the fall when a high Jewish holiday would fall on a Sunday. What to do? It was understood that I would go to "important" games, but then I had no trouble proving to my parents that every game was important. In any event, my father and mother had no qualms about my going to see Hertha play on Rosh Hashana. My cousins, though, did not enjoy quite that much freedom. *Their* parents were what German atheist Jews used to call "three-day Jews." Wholly ignorant of Hebrew or of the Jewish religious tradition, they still felt obliged to buy tickets for the high holidays and attend synagogue three days in the year, understanding nothing. My parents poured scorn on such hypocrisy, and I was allowed to go to my game, if necessary alone.

But once, probably in 1935 when I was twelve, Yom Kippur fell on a Sunday, when there was another important game, probably a match between those archrivals, Hertha and Tennis. So my cousins conspired with me that they would go the synagogue while I waited for them outside, have their tickets stamped at the entrance and, pretending that they had forgotten their prayer books, come out again. To the important game we went. The episode caused a family crisis because my lovable and indiscreet cousin Edgar, who could not keep a secret, revealed our adventure on Sunday night. His parents were furious, but not mine. We three had no intention of having Hitler tell us who we were—or my aunt and uncle tell us what to believe.

Our alienation from Judaism, then, was absolute, and nothing the Nazis said, or did, changed that for my parents—or for me. We despised the Nazis as barbarians who had somehow taken power in Ger-

many and destroyed its culture. I know now, and need hardly be reminded, that this is a rather shallow view of the German past. Plainly,
there was a good deal of denial in my view of things. But that is how I
was brought up, and enjoyed being brought up. I found it gratifying,
but not particularly remarkable, that in the desperate days of late
1938 and early 1939, when we needed help in every way (whether to
hide our family silver or to obtain coveted passage on a ship that
would get us out of Nazi Germany), it was several of my father's
gentile friends who came to our rescue.

## II

Coming to the United States from Cuba early in 1941, after more than
a year and a half of waiting, I kept what I have called my alienation
from Judaism firmly intact. There could be no question for me of
converting to any branch of Christianity, for which my respect was no
greater than it was for the Jewish religion. At the same time, though,
there could also be no question of denying my Jewish origins. Too
much had happened, too many had been murdered in the extermination camps, including my father's two sisters, to permit me such a
craven evasion. But an acknowledgment of my origins was as far as I
was willing to go. When I switched my "national" allegiance, I switched from being an atheist German to being an atheist American.

Again I proved my father's devoted son: he was vocally critical of
those refugees who condescended to what they were pleased to call the
thinness of American high culture, or had petty grievances against the
country that had been willing to take them in. My father called such
exiles, derisively, *"Beiunskis"*—that is to say, complainers who kept
saying that *"Bei uns* in Frankfurt, or Breslau, or Cologne, things had
been better." Under his guidance, I made my transition to being an
American quickly—more quickly than he in important ways, for he
never learned English very well. When, in 1976, I was asked to write a
short autobiographical account for the *American Scholar* to celebrated the Bicentennial, I titled my contribution "At Home in America."
This was not hyperbole.

Since my mother had a virulent case of tuberculosis, my father and I
decided to migrate with her to Denver. Once there, I found associates
outside the Jewish community. It seemed not without significance that
while my mother was confined to the "National Jewish Hospital," the

principal donor to the hospital, whose picture hung prominently displayed in the front lobby, should be a gentile, William Randolph Hearst. In this spirit, the National Jewish Hospital conspicuously advertised its fundamental integrationist policy with a slogan proclaiming that it took patients who were unable to pay, regardless of race or religion. It was an attitude I could fully understand, and endorse.

Soon I had an opportunity to practice it. After two years of working at menial jobs as a shipping clerk and as an office clerk, I finally managed to attend the local college, the University of Denver, living at home and on a generous fellowship. It was not long before I made friends there—Christian friends, in fact Methodists. One day the closest of these friends invited me to come along to a meeting of like-minded young Methodists who gathered regularly every Sunday evening with their pastor, a young, civilized, philosophically inclined minister, for good conversation and good music. I went, was made to feel at home, and rapidly became a regular member of the group—to the chagrin of the editor of a local Jewish weekly, who, hearing about me from the pastor, wrote a long column in his paper denouncing me for forgetting my experiences under the Nazis. As though I could forget them!

My parents met some of my new friends and were greatly pleased with the company I was keeping. Indeed, when my father died prematurely in January 1955 at the young age of sixty-two, he left a letter of instructions asking that he be cremated and given a secular send-off. And he listed two men either of whom he thought suitable to preside over the ceremony—one was a Reform rabbi (who, it turned out, was out of town), and the other the Reverend Harvey H. Potthoff, the Methodist minister with whom I had become good friends by then. Up to this point in my life, the idea of the German-Jewish legacy in the United States was abstract, anticlerical, and a little self-serving. I have already observed that, far from identifying myself with Germany, I promptly became a good American. But if there was any content in the very idea of cultural transmission enforced by Nazi barbarism, it was simply that we, the refugees, had taken artistic, academic, literary, musical culture with us when we went into exile, leaving our former homeland a wasteland.

### III

It was not until 1946, when I moved to New York to attend graduate school to study political theory at Columbia University, that the idea of a German-Jewish legacy in my new country began to acquire some concrete outlines for me. I began to meet refugee intellectuals, read books by refugees, above all observed refugee professors at work. Not all of these were Jews, though most of them were. I delighted in them and their ideas; I shall never forget, for instance, the excitement with which I read Erich Auerbach's great historical study of literary realism, *Mimesis*, in the summer of 1954. But I welcomed such scholars as scholars, not as refugees; it would take me years before I could begin to notice, let alone assess, the particular contribution—both to clarity and to confusion—of these exiles from Hitler's Europe.

I say "clarity and confusion," for I discovered that it was a mistake to sentimentalize the refugees whom I was meeting and reading. No doubt, some of them like the remarkable art historian Erwin Panofsky transformed American scholarly life beyond cavil, and indeed beyond compare. I first heard him lecture in 1955, and met him a few years after that, when he was a very old man, though still full of life and brilliant puns—two unforgettable experiences. It was only appropriate that the friend who took me to visit Panofsky should have been another great refugee scholar, the historian's historian Felix Gilbert. No doubt, the influx of emigres of this caliber proved an exhilarating force in American cultural life. There were others like them, who were leaving the United States different from, and more interesting than, the way they had found it. But others, no less prominent, aroused my skepticism. I recall that while I was at Columbia, both as a graduate student and young faculty member, the Frankfurt School, with its representatives on campus, was all the rage. But I found its heady mixture of aristocratic cultural conservatism and schematic Hegelian Marxism in the end uncongenial to me, and became somewhat troubled even about its intellectual honesty.

I came to know one of the "Frankfurters," Herbert Marcuse, a most amusing and good-natured companion, fairly well during the 1950s and 1960s. He lectured at Columbia often and was my teacher Franz Neumann's best friend. I liked him, but I had very mixed feelings about his work. No question, the first half of his well-known study of Hegel, *Reason and Revolution*, was a salutary influence on me, and on others who had, like me, naively identified Hegel's worship of the state with Nazi political ideology. But in the second half of his book, which followed upon the persuasive demonstration that Hegel was not an ancestor of Goebbels or Rosenberg, Marcuse tried to make European positivists like Comte into proto-Fascists instead. And here I could not follow him.

Still, it was a pleasing discovery that there were German-Jewish refugees with whom one could disagree and yet learn from—immensely. I am thinking particularly of my teacher Franz Neumann, who exercised such a powerful influence in what used to be called, a little grandiloquently, the department of public law and government. Almost everybody studied with Neumann. My official thesis adviser was the eminent political theorist Robert Morrison MacIver, with whom I was supposedly writing a dissertation on the political thought of the revisionist German Social Democrat Eduard Bernstein (another German Jew who had left Judaism behind). But MacIver was indifferent, even lazy, and gave me virtually no advice. Neumann was my man. He did not care for Bernstein, for he struck Neumann, a rigid philosophical left-wing Marxist, as too feeble, too accommodating a thinker. At the same time Neumann, who, with his bald head, hooked nose, and severe look strongly resembled a Roman senator—one could easily visualize him in a toga—was an intellectual democrat. If I wanted to work on Bernstein, and show him that Bernstein was indeed an interesting thinker, why not?

Neumann's impact, then, was marked even on those who, like me, did not share his political orientation. He was a gold mine of bibliography. His lectures were sprinkled with references to Max Weber or Wilhelm Dilthey, and it was virtually law among the graduate students in the department that if Franz mentioned a writer, we would have to read him. Here was an instance of what refugee scholars could do for Americans: bring to bear the legacy of European culture in American universities.

Yet it was a most varied legacy. While in the public law department Neumann was disparaging positivists from his particularly European perspective, in the sociology department, the Austrian refugee Paul Lazarsfeld was brilliantly presenting European positivist social science to *his* students. Another refugee, Hajo Holborn—not a Jew—would come down from Yale to offer exciting seminars in the history department, from a viewpoint different at once from Marxism and positivism. It was an electric atmosphere.

This kind of teaching was by no means a strictly one-way affair. One cannot read the often touching and always informative little book by refugees, *The Cultural Migration: The European Scholar in America* (1953), with autobiographical essays by Franz Neumann, Erwin Panofsky, Paul Tillich, and others, without recognizing that America's teachers were also America's students. Their assertions were more than mere politeness. Neumann, Panofsky, Tillich, and the others cheerfully acknowledged that the German academic tradition, while it held much of value for empirical, practical-minded Americans, also suffered from grave defects: a certain arrogance, remoteness from experience, what a later generation would learn to call elitism. Indeed, it was this fruitful interchange between the newcomers—to repeat, not all of them Jewish—and their American hosts that I first witnessed and learned to value at Columbia University. Those of us not born in this country dare not slight this symbiosis between two cultures, however partial, as we reassess the German-Jewish legacy in the United States. That legacy, impressive as it was on its own, did not survive without some drastic alterations.

## IV

These observations, I am aware, offer a highly personal, hence necessarily somewhat restricted, perspective on the German-Jewish impact on the United States. Late in the 1960s, I had an opportunity to widen that perspective. I was invited to write a long prefatory essay on Weimar culture for a collection, edited by Donald Fleming and Bernard Bailyn, *The Intellectual Migration: Europe and America, 1930 – 1960* (1969). The editors collected fascinating reminiscences by great physicists like Leo Szilard and controversial social theorists like Theodor Adorno, no less fascinating memoirs about modern sociology by Paul Lazarsfeld, and illuminating papers on German and Austrian psychologists and psychoanalysts, literary historians and literary critics, architects, art historians, and philosophers at work in the United States. The volume, though bulky, does not pretend to be an exhaustive account, and it is grounds for a measure of pride, though not of complacency. Not all the legacy was, as I have noted, a productive one, but much of it transformed American culture, did America lasting service, and we all know the names of those who performed them. It gives me much poignant pleasure to think of them. In one matter, though, they failed, regrettably. They never managed to persuade Americans that soccer is a sport worth watching.

# German Culture, Jewish Ethics

*Guy Stern*

German-Jewish artists, facing certain extinction, grafted their agony with make-shift materials onto the painterly style of German Expressionism. Poets, established as well as amateur, recorded death-camp dirges dedicated to themselves and to their fellow victims in heart-wrenching German lyrics. Exiled writers from Madagascar to Manhattan entombed voluminous novels, often autographical, within a language all but unpublishable in their country of asylum. As you look mesmerized at a stamp-sized watercolor in Sybil Milton's and Janet Blattner's stunning book *Art of the Holocaust*, discover a hitherto unpublished poem in the new edition of Manfred Schloesser's *An den Wind geschrieben (Writ upon the Wind)*, or leaf through unpublished fiction at the New York Leo Baeck Institute or at one of half-a-dozen archives in Germany, you are likely to ask yourself: Was a cultural tradition ever put to a more terrible test or did it produce within its collective representatives a more desperate dying/undying commitment?

Such unswerving—some would add quixotic, even blind—loyalty calls forth a search for its origins. What made us, the majority of German Jewry, so enwrapped in and enraptured with the German and German-Jewish culture? What made virtually all of us, including even most Zionists, so attentive and responsive to all its manifestations? Growing up in that milieu, nurtured by it, observing for a while its progressive strangulation and, finally, lending a hand in its transplantation in a new soil, I can draw on some random perceptions, first-or second-hand, in trying to arrive at a practical answer.

Many of the contributors to this anthology will argue that the Jewish devotion to German culture, the perceived or real symbiosis with it, was predicated on an identification with the German precept of *Bildung*, perhaps mankind's last attempt to aim for an *Uomo Universale*. The concept of *Bildung* as a well-rounded education, resting on a knowledge of modern and ancient history, philosophy, and the sciences (both natural and social), indeed had a magnetic attraction for us, and we identified it, even as we read the classics—*nota bene* in

German translation—*in the* German tradition. But there was a difference in our, Jewish, reception of *Bildung* in comparison to that of gentiles.

Ours was an idealistic subgroup within the German cultural realm, a utopia that was a heritage of the Jewish ethic and ethos. True, most of us had turned away from Orthodoxy, and that departure had resulted in stages of belief or nonbelief that ranged from Reform Judaism to apathetic synagogue attendance to an occasional apostasy. But all of us of high school age, growing up in the medium-sized North German town of Hildesheim in the twenties and early thirties, came together in biweekly after-school religious classes, mandated by the state as surrogate for the religious instruction at Protestant or Catholic high schools. And what our teacher, *Herr Landrabbiner* Dr. Abraham Lewinsky of Hildensheim, tossed at us in rapid-fire dictation were not exegeses of the Pentateuch or Haftarah, but the ethical teachings of Hillel, or the *Pirkei Avoth*, or of Moses Maimonides or, occasionally, of Moses Mendelssohn or Martin Buber. And these we debated in our Saturday afternoon youth group meetings conducted by our beloved, boyish-looking cantor, Josef "Seppl" Cysner. As I found out, this totally enjoyable concentration on the Jewish ethic was widespread in the increasingly secularized German-Jewish communities. Jewish ethical humanism and humanitarianism, especially as it had been reshaped during the eighteenth-century Age of Enlightenment, became the filter, the detoxifier and, to change mood and metaphor, unfortunately also the rose-tinted glasses through which we viewed German *Bildung*. It is that aspect of the German-Jewish relationship which this essay addresses.

I remember the effects of that filter, implanted by my parents in my childhood, in full and paradigmatic operation as early as age six. They took me, as my introduction to opera, to the Hannover Opera House for a performance of Wagner's *Lohengrin*—conducted, by the way, by a Jewish guest conductor, Karl Schuricht, whom I met forty-odd years later in Cincinnati. On the train ride home, I hero-worshipped Lohengrin's chivalric championing of wronged Elsa and filtered out his desertion of her under the terms of a trivial and inhumane prior condition. Today, I am convinced that the German-Jewish Wagner-mania and patronage of the grownups of that and previous decades rested on a similar predisposition. If one looks through the rose-colored glasses of Jewish humanitarianism, one will focus on the noble self-sacrifice of Senta, the altruism of Hans Sachs, the paean to compassion in *Parsifal*. But those lenses also obscure Wagner's rival-bashing through the figure of Hunding, his mythophilia in many of his libretti, and his egregious anti-Semitism in his essays. One will revel then in his music while ignoring the pernicious side of his texts.

When one views German culture through a Jewish filter, other examples come to mind. The libraries of my parents and of the parents of my Jewish friends—all of them impressive collections—differed subtly from those assembled by the elders of my Christian friends. No, there was no strict "confessional" segregation on either side. My parents owned a novel by Stehr with a Christ-like figure as hero and a fictionalized biography of Nicholas of Cusa; and all "non-Jewish" libraries included books by such German Jews as Stefan Zweig and Jakob Wassermann. But only Jews, even before the arrival of the Nazis, owned the works of the Jewish Expressionists, though I also caught a glimpse of them in the house of a friend whose father was a newspaper editor. And there were books, prominently displayed on the bookshelves in gentile homes, which my parents would not let into our house, the folk novels, often with anti-Semitic plots or subtexts, of Gustav Freytag, Hermann Loens, and Willibald Alexis. In fact, I recall how my parents, tactfully but uncompromisingly, insisted that my aunt and uncle exchange the latter's slightly anti-Semitic *The Trousers of Mr. von Bredow* "for a present somewhat more suitable." I ended up with a German-begotten Wild West story—and with the opportunity to observe how my parents (like many other middle-class German Jews) beheld German *Bildung* selectively.

In short, the widely shared Jewish ethos spawned, in conjunction with the best elements in German culture, a German-Jewish mood of considerable optimism and an idealistic philosophy. We dismissed the opportunists, materialists, and scoundrels in our own ranks with ostracizing aphorisms and the Nazis and anti-Semites, whom we routinely encountered, as antediluvian curiosities to be studied under the microscope.

The Jews of Germany frequently fell short, of course, of their self-imposed ethos, yet they never failed to uphold and to canonize it. It is therefore a canard that needs refuting from time to time that the Jews, perhaps aside from a few demented individuals, would have embraced

Hitler if they had been given the chance. As Franz Werfel has his hero Jacobowsky declaim as a credo: "No, I could never be a Hitler—not until the Last Judgment Day."

The danger of extremism lay elsewhere for us. We strove to be Germans as good, patriotic, and cultivated in the best eighteenth-century sense as the non-Jewish *Bildungsbuerger*. Here lay the challenge constantly before us. We were not to be deterred from that goal even when our admired culture heroes, Thomas Mann, for example, maintained for a good while, before he became a spokesman for exiles in America and an advocate and helpmeet of German Jewry, that acculturation was beyond our grasp.

That unfulfilled challenge became, to my mind, another mainspring in the Jewish quest for acculturation. Obviously it spurred on German-Jewish artists and writers: few painters rivaled Max Liebermann in his landscapes and portraits of Imperial Germany; few poets commanded a more powerful, evocative vocabulary than Karl Wolfskehl; few critics were better judges of German usage and style than Karl Kraus. But the challenge also was driving the average German-Jewish citizen with equal force. My grandfather, a small businessman, said very quietly to my mother, when being serenaded by his fellow volunteer firemen upon his twenty-fifth wedding anniversary: *"Wir haben's geschafft!"* ("We have made it!") An impulse, communally so deeply imprinted, may sustain—or delude—a person till the very end.

My own utopia was no different, and my idealistic and idealized vision of German culture did not immediately break down with Hitler's seizure of power or with my arrival in the United States, in 1937, as the sole survivor (as it turned out) of my intimate family. The last sparse fibers of that comforting filter were finally swept away on April 12, 1945. I had returned to Germany via the Normandy beachheads and in the khaki uniform of the U.S. Army and with the six stripes of a master sergeant.

That day in April, beyond marking for me the death of a revered president (Roosevelt had died that day), also dealt me the interrogation of one Dr. Schuebbe who, under the shock of capture and the torpor of a self-administered morphine injection, conversationally admitted to a fellow interrogator of the U.S. Military Intelligence and me that he had killed or supervised the killing of 25,000 people during a two-year tour of duty in occupied Kiev.

Our intelligence report of that week, widely disseminated by the media until overshadowed by horrors even more grisly, reflected, as I remember, less our sense of outrage and contempt for one individual than the monstrousness of a totally dehumanized system. Hundreds of individuals—not only party officials or paid butchers but average citizens—had cooperated and connived, so that Dr. Schuebbe and his henchmen in Kiev could wield their syringes. There were many among them, as I was later able to confirm, who like me listened to Beethoven, enjoyed Goethe, or admired the woodcuts of Albrecht Duerer.

Yet today, forty years after my encounter with Dr. Schuebbe and my traumatizing visit to Buchenwald the day after its liberation, I teach and lecture about all three of those German cultural luminaries, write often about eighteenth- and twentieth-century German literature, and have assumed, at various times, professional leadership positions in the United States and guest professorships in the Federal Republic of Germany. Have I, members of my family and friends have asked me, if in different words, returned to past ideal or idyll, or tried to resurrect a shattered utopia? I have attempted to answer that question, for the sake of my friends as well as for myself and my American-born wife, in a variety of ways, mostly orally, and once in the pages of *Columbia Magazine*, published by my alma mater. I argued then, and continue to argue, that to forego my particular heritage would constitute an act of intellectual self-mutilation, that my expertise on the writers expelled by Hitler and on earlier German-Jewish artists and writers may help rescue them from an oblivion the Nazis had intended for them. But in the context of this essay a different, more sweeping rationale must be invoked.

In times past, as I have contended above, we distilled from the German cultural heritage what was good and valid while ignoring its ignoble aspects, both in keeping with the spirit of an ennobling and creative, if secularized Jewish ethos and, let it be said in retrospect, with the unquenchable, sometimes unpardonable optimism wrenched from a dolorous diasporic history. Our inability to see the flaws in the German cultural tradition, our misplaced optimism were, however, sloughed off in transit to the American asylum; the adherence to the Jewish ethos stayed with the Jewish exiles.

The immense contribution of the German-Jewish cultural confluence, once it was diverted by *force majeure* to America, will continue to fill volumes, recording achievements in fields ranging from music to physics and medicine, from Jewish theology to art and art history. In fact, many essays in this anthology enlarge upon just such achievements. My focus, however, remains with the implantation of Jewish ethos upon German culture and with how that combination became manifest in America.

Shorn now of its utopianism, this configuration became all the more effective. Whereas German-Jewish intellectuals of the Weimar Republic, with some notable exceptions, often ignored or suppressed the illiberalism, latent hypernationalism, and autocratic thinking in the German heritage (a case in point: the Austrian-Jewish editor of the prestigious journal *Der neue Merkur* [1917 – 25] allowed only two mentions of National Socialism in its pages), once in America they or their younger successors became far more conscious of these flaws. What was said of one American-exiled Jewish writer, Alfred Polgar, applies to many intellectuals: "The misery [of exile]," observed the German literary and cultural historian Paul Stoecklein, "imparted to him the profound insight that ethics—and ethics alone—can lead to an understanding of the world's condition."

After the war, when I was allowed to sit in on the heady, often night-long debates of one of the exile circles, I was struck by the acuity and fairness with which they separated the gold of German culture from the dross, the dross from the dirt and the toxin. The novelist Hertha Pauli, the translator and historian E. B. Ashton, the poet Walter Mehring, the biographer Karl Frucht, the dramatist and historian Paul Frischauer: they were not, of course, a noble breed apart (though I idealized them at the time), but never did they allow themselves to espouse an autocratic thought or to lapse into the jargon of the Nazis. They watched themselves and each other in their speech and their writing, which, of course, was still largely German. One evening Paul Frischauer chided me because I had used a word that had become mildly trendy during the Nazi years. And they followed, if not always, a kind of ethical imperative. My friend Hertha Pauli, the "half-Jew" from Vienna, who had never seen a black before coming to America, undertook out of a moral impulse and in recognition of a parallel minority fate, to write the first, ultimately widely acclaimed, biography of Sojourner Truth, the black woman who fought for her people's emancipation and equality.

In fact, the German-Jewish refugees in America have been consistently in the van as detoxifier of the corrosive poison made in Germany. Outstanding philosophers, psychiatrists, and historians such as Hannah Arendt, Bruno Bettelheim, Fritz Epstein, Peter Gay, George Mosse, Fritz Stern, and Herbert Strauss, each in his or her own way, have traced the origins and early manifestations of Nazism and modern dictatorships, and they have alerted their new homeland, America, "that the lap is fertile yet from which those sprang," to quote Bertolt Brecht. Ruth Angress (together with the American-born scholar Sander Gilman) has sounded the alarm against lingering anti-Semitism in recent West German fiction; I also have pointed out similarities between German literary anti-Semitism in the past and its counterpart in contemporary American literature. But the element common to all these writings, no matter how different their approaches and conclusions, is their philosophy. A rationalistic Jewish ethic, brought over from Germany in the spiritual luggage of these scholars and now applied more realistically, is being set as a foil against its illiberal antithesis.

The filter of Jewish ethics has been applied, in short, to a great many questionable German cultural exports. In a remarkable speech before an international congress of Germanists, Richard von Weizsaecker, President of the Federal Republic of Germany, thanked the foreign scholars of German literature and culture for keeping both undefiled by the propagandistic exploitation practiced by the Nazis. The heroization of Germany's classical authors, particularly of Goethe and Schiller, which prevailed in many German schoolrooms even in the postwar period, and which has alienated countless German schoolchildren from their most celebrated authors, gained little ingress to the United States, because here, too, German-Jewish refugee scholars celebrated the humanity of Goethe and the love of freedom of Schiller in their teaching and writing. Many scholars, such as the late Oskar Seidlin, helped set the standards which were to secure the German classicists an accurate, if small, echo in the United States. And progressive German authors of our times have received a fair hearing among American intellectuals because of the brilliant reports that the English-based German-Jewish critic and author George Steiner has filed for the *New Yorker*.

In a modest way I can retrace, I believe, the conscious or subconscious impulse which motivated such scholars to rescue the German heritage from its Fascist adulterators. In 1970, while at the University of Cincinnati, I approached my colleague Gottfried Merkel with the following argument: "No one in the history of German literature has fought as hard and consistently for human equality and mutual toleration as Gotthold Ephraim Lessing; no one was a better friend to Moses Mendelssohn; no one in Germany argued more persuasively for the equality of the German Jews." The *Lessing Yearbook*, which we, in consequence, founded at the time and which is now published by Wayne State University Press, has become an international forum for the study of the German Enlightenment and has helped to spread on this continent Lessing's political philosophy, which is strikingly like that of our founding fathers.

The spirit that imbued many of the German-Jewish scholars, that particular interpretation of two heritages, will likely endure in America. Care has been taken that the testimony of its existence, its remaining cultural artifacts, its printed, handwritten, and oral documentation will be preserved. The Leo Baeck Institute, founded by Max Gruenewald and Martin Buber, and now directed by Fred Grubel with the help of a board drawn largely from three generations of German-Jewish refugees, is commanding ever wider attention from an American intellectual lay public. Other archives and institutes devoted to German-Jewish individuals, such as the Lion Feuchtwanger Archive and the Kurt Weill Foundation or the pages and files of the fifty-year-old German-Jewish newspaper *Aufbau,* serve a like purpose. The last-named resource, if read consistently, also reflects German culture filtered by a Jewish ethic. All of these repositories have come now to the attention, at ever more frequent intervals, of America's most prestigious newspapers and magazines. That fact may also help ensure the permanence of the German-Jewish impact on America.

Is there further evidence of such lastingness? Believing in the dictum of *scripta manent* or that literature has been and will continue to be the least ephemeral of written human records, I would like to cite a curious literary phenomenon as additional testimony. American writers have discovered the German-Jewish exiles and have set them down in their fiction and dramas. Susan Sontag discovered the Austrian-Jewish writer Hermann Broch, Christopher Hampton presented a whole galaxy of refugees in his drama *Exiles,* which he premiered in America, Elly Welt created a "half-Jewish" survivor who finds peace at last in the United States when he says *Kaddish* for his dead. Ernest Hemingway, in his foreword to his Civil War film script *Spanish Earth*, celebrates the humaneness of a German-Jewish physician; Erica Jong's disturbed heroine receives caring treatment only from a Jewish psychiatrist. The list could be continued. But all the fictional or fictionalized German-Jewish exiles I have been able to identify in American literature embody the best of their dual German-Jewish heritage.

Of course they have no monopoly on being the purifying conduit for imported German culture. The "other," better Germany was represented in the United States as well by such German Christians as Dietrich von Hildebrand, Paul Tillich, Thomas Mann, and Erwin Piscator, to mention just a few. Someday their story, the motivation behind their humanity and acts of altruism must be recorded. This essay is meant to pay tribute, of course, to the German-Jewish cultural life as it once existed, and its continued impact on the United States.

At one of the last religious classes I attended in my hometown, Rabbi Lewinsky dictated one more saying to us: "The world rests on three foundations: truth, justice, and peace. To bring these three into harmony," he added, "is our constant task." I believe that admonition was upheld and applied by the rabbi's contemporaries and his spiritual progeny who succeeded, as he could not, in reaching the United States.

# An Autobiographical Approach to the German-Jewish Legacy

*Georg G. Iggers*

I believe that it is difficult to reduce the "German-Jewish legacy" to a common denominator and therefore would like to take an autobiographic approach which will illustrate what aspects of this legacy affected me most directly.

We tend to identify the German Jews in the nineteenth and twentieth centuries too generally with the *Bildungsbuergertum*. My family, like very many German-Jewish families, laid claim to being cultured *Buerger* without being able to justify this claim either in terms of education or income. Our bookcases were lined with the German classics, which my father had received as Bar Mitzvah gifts in 1907, but I was the only one in my family who read them, and there were original paintings by little-known artists on the wall. My parents rarely went to a play or a concert. They were proud of the fact that they had completed their schooling to the *mittlere Reife*. Religiously, they were Jewish but came from two different directions. My father came from a practicing Orthodox family. He received his entire formal education in the schools of the Orthodox Breuersche *Gemeinde* in Frankfurt, but after his marriage to my mother, who had come from a very secularized family, gradually ceased practicing Jewish ritual.

I entered public school in Hamburg in April 1933, at the age of six, on the Monday after the Boycott. For the next several years until our emigration to the United States in October 1938, German and specifically Jewish impulses were important in shaping my consciousness, impulses which even in this period were closely interwoven. In contrast to many of my German-Jewish contemporaries with whom I have compared notes, I was fortunate to be in a school where both my teacher and the children, who came for the most part from working-class families, shielded me against the growing official anti-Semitism. Still in October 1936, when my parents transferred me to the Talmud Torah, at a time when I wanted to attend a Jewish school, the teacher tried to persuade my parents that I was perfectly safe in the school as long as he was there. At the same time, he was an ardent nationalist. I do not know whether he was a member of the NSDAP, but he inspired his pupils with a good deal of the spirit of the *Jugendbewegung*, including enthusiasm for nature, hiking and singing, the return to the countryside and the crafts, and a nostalgia for the comradeship and heroism of the First World War, which he—he was born in 1904—had experienced only as a child. At the school I felt like a German. At the same time, in part undoubtedly as a reaction to the anti-Semitism of the Nazis, I became increasingly aware of my Jewish, not only my ethnic but also religious identity. At the age of six, I began to have private Jewish instruction, which must have been much more meaningful and imaginative than that which my father had received. In 1934 I for the first time went to a Jewish summer camp. I began to accompany my uncle to religious services and joined the Bar Kochba athletics club. In the Jewish youth circles I found a good deal of the idealism and the enthusiasm of the youth movement culture similar to that which I had experienced in the German school. I became Orthodox, a Zionist and, without knowing the term, a communal socialist who saw the synthesis of his ideals in *aliyah* and in the *kibbutz*. All this caused problems with my parents, who shared none of these ideals. The fact that I insisted on *kashrut*—which at this time in Nazi Germany meant vegetarianism—and wanted to observe the Sabbath created an awkward situation for my parents. Secretly, against the wishes of my parents, I joined a Jewish *Bund*—it must have been Mizrachi—and participated not only in hikes but also in study groups. All this at the age of ten. In December 1937 my parents sent me to the Juedische Waisenhaus und Erziehungsheim in Esslingen since they did not know how to cope with me, a remarkably progressive school for the time, where I stayed until a few weeks before our emigration.

The transition to America was therefore probably more difficult for me than for many of my contemporaries. After three months in and near New York City, I came to Richmond, Virginia, in January 1939, a city which at that time was still very Southern in its attitudes. There was a good deal which I welcomed in this new environment, the democratic ideals which I immediately accepted and the relative openness in the school and generally in human relations, which contrasted with the rigidity and tensions which marked much of German life. Yet almost immediately I became painfully aware of the stark contrast between democratic pronouncements in Virginia and the racial policies and practices, which even as a twelve-year-old reminded me of anti-Semitism. I found it difficult to accept the consumerism which appeared to me so much in conflict with the attitudes I had acquired in Germany and was taken aback by the lack of intellectual sophistication of my teachers. I was also very much aware of myself as a German and a Jew, or more specifically a German Jew. The fact that I continued to practice my Orthodoxy throughout high school and college in Richmond marked me as someone who was different, although it did not isolate me. Incidentally, despite my Orthodoxy, I had no close Jewish friends but several very good non-Jewish ones. With my American friends I shared a concern with contemporary social problems—we were already then involved in the civil rights movement—and an interest in literature and philosophy. Much of the instruction in school seemed very simple to me; thus I was able to complete high school, which at that time in Virginia ended with eleventh grade, by the age of fifteen and received my B.A. from the University of Richmond at the age of seventeen. At the same time philosophy, literature, history, social studies, and social science classes provided much greater freedom for critical discussion than had been possible in Germany. I majored in French in college but at the same time read extensively in German literature and philosophy. I subsequently completed an M.A. in German literature at the University of Chicago. From 1945 to 1946 I spent the most fruitful year of my career as a student in the Graduate Faculty at the New School, where I studied with Horace Kallen, Albert Salomon, Felix Kaufmann, Carl Mayer, and Frieda Wunderlich. Thus I was thoroughly steeped in the German intellectual heritage, with a particular interest in the German Jews.

By now I had given up my Orthodox practice without, however, feeling less Jewish, even in a religious sense. The aspect of the Jewish religious legacy which now appeared important to me personally was the universalistic, ethical note which I believed expressed itself in a long tradition from Isaiah, Amos, and Micah to the secularized social reformers of recent times, although I recognized that this was only a minority current in Judaism. I viewed Judaism less in ethnic terms than as a cultural heritage which existed not apart from modern culture but as a part of it, as it had in post-Enlightenment Germany. My attitude towards Zionism changed too. I basically agreed with the Brit

Shalom movement. I continued to believe that Jews were entitled to a national home but was disturbed as early as 1948 about attitudes among Zionists which insufficiently acknowledged the needs of coexistence between Jews and Arabs.

I believe that my German, and specifically my German-Jewish, experience very deeply affected my career as a citizen and as a scholar in America. At graduate school at the University of Chicago I met my wife, Wilma, who came from a Jewish farming family in western Bohemia, also emigrated in October 1938, and took her Ph.D. in German in Chicago with a dissertation on Karl Kraus. In 1950, while we were in the final stages of our dissertations, my wife and I went to Little Rock, Arkansas, to teach in a small black college. Almost immediately we became involved in the NAACP and did a good deal of the research and planning which went into the suits challenging legal segregation in Arkansas. Arkansas demonstrated to us not only one of the negative sides of America, the racism which permeated Southern and to an extent American society, but also the strength of voluntary associations, the undogmatic interchange of various segments of the population, black and white, in which unfortunately the Jewish community played very little of a role in Arkansas. In 1957 we went to Dillard University, a black university in New Orleans, where with the exception of a two-year leave of absence in Europe from 1960 to 1962, we stayed until 1963 and also were active in the NAACP. Beginning with the Cuban missile crisis in 1962, we became increasingly active in the peace movement, first in New Orleans, then briefly in Chicago, and after 1965 in Buffalo, where both of us have been teaching since then, I at SUNY, my wife at Canisius College, and where, since early in the Vietnam War, I began to counsel conscientious objectors, first civilians and after the end of the draft men and women in the military.

My wife's scholarship increasingly turned to Central European Jewish themes; mine to the political context of the German tradition of historical thought. Her extensive studies of the German- and Czech-language literature resulted in 1986 in a book, *Die Juden in Boehmen und Maehren*, published in West Germany, which seeks to recreate the life and culture of Jews in the Czech lands from the Enlightenment to the present, not only of the Prague intellectuals but also of the Jews in the small towns and the countryside. My work has always had a broad international and comparative scope, but in the years after 1960 I began to examine the role which historical scholarship played in the formation of anti-democratic attitudes in Germany's democratic and humanistic legacy. The resulting volume, *The German Conception of History*, which appeared in several paperback editions in West Germany, was intended as a contribution to the critical discussion then taking place in West Germany on the German historiographical tradition. Since our first lengthy stay in Germany in 1961 and 1962, my wife and I have established close contacts with scholars in West Germany, and since 1966 in East Germany as well. Goettingen, where we have spent several sabbaticals and many a summer, has become in a sense a second home to us. We have increasingly published in German. In both West and East Germany we have had close contacts with groups interested in a Christian-Jewish dialogue. In Buffalo, I have been instrumental in organizing an interdisciplinary program of modern German studies. This has been accompanied by an extensive student exchange with West Germany and most recently with East Germany.

Once more, in conclusion, I remain cautious about defining the German-Jewish legacy or its expression in American life in abstract terms. The legacy has been as multifaceted as has been its impact on America. Therefore I have chosen the autobiographical approach. Until now studies of German Jews have largely concentrated on the elites. There is a good deal of justification for this because of the tremendous impact of persons of Jewish background or at least ancestry on German thought. This thought in turn has had a tremendous influence not only on thought and culture in America but in the world generally. But in America this influence, transmitted by the post-1933 emigres, was greatest. One should, however, be careful in attempts to define the importance of the German-Jewish legacy to the "continuation of a democratic American society." Politically Jews in Germany have represented the entire spectrum of opinion from monarchists to Marxists, although their intellectual and cultural heritage, which is very difficult to define, contributed to their being frequently more often associated with critical and humanitarian positions than other groups of the population. The German-Jewish legacy in its many expressions deserves to be studied as one of the creative highpoints of modern culture. Increasingly it is being studied as such in America, Israel, West Germany, and in most recent years East Germany and elsewhere. All this is encouraging. So far it has been largely the study of elites. German-Jewish society and culture should, however, be studied more broadly than it has been until now, to include a much wider segment of German-Jewish life, including the more humble settings from which many of those who made names for themselves were only one or two generations removed.

# German Jewry as Spirit and as Legacy

*Harry Zohn*

It would be a pity if readers discounted the following remarks as made merely *pro domo* and perceived their author as the mouthpiece of certain vested interests. It is true that I write as a sort of guardian and professional purveyor of the German-Jewish heritage, for its spirit is very much in evidence in the thinking, teaching, and writing I have done during my nearly four decades on the faculty of Brandeis University, and my scholarly, pedagogical, and personal orientation has been aided, refined, and reinforced by the numerous distinguished colleagues from the German-Jewish orbit who have been associated with my university. Suffice it to mention Ludwig Lewisohn, Nahum Glatzer, Alexander Altmann, Simon and Esther Rawidowicz, Aaron Gurwitsch, Herbert Marcuse, Rudolf Kayser, Erwin Bodky, Kurt Wolff, Marianne Simmel, Leo Treitler, Frank Jacoby, Claude Vigée (Strauss), Erich Heller, Edward Engelberg, and Egon Bittner. Several courses I have given at Brandeis have been dedicated in part or in their entirety to an exploration, distillation, and presentation of the German-Jewish cultural legacy: "The Literary Harvest of the German-Jewish Symbosis," "Vienna at the Turn of the Century," "The Culture of the Weimar Republic: Berlin in the 1920s." When one considers that such broadly cultural courses include such dissimilar Jewish spirits—from Vienna, Berlin, Prague, Czernowitz, and elsewhere—as Suesskind von Trimberg, Moses Mendelssohn, Heinrich Heine, Arthur Schnitzler, Theodor Herzl, Richard Beer-Hofmann, Otto Weininger, Karl Kraus, Gustav Mahler, Sigmund Freud, Franz Kafka, Paul Celán, Joseph Roth, Alfred Doeblin, Jakob Wassermann, Max Liebermann, Martin Buber, Franz Werfel, Walter Benjamin, Max Brod, Friedrich Torberg, Elias Canetti, Walther Rathenau, Else Lasker-Schueler, Kurt Tucholsky, and Nelly Sachs, even a very liberal definition of what has been called the German-Jewish spirit may not be sufficiently comprehensive. There are, after all, enormous differences between Beer-Hofmann, the only *homo judaicus* in the "Young Vienna" circle of mostly Jewish-born writers in *fin-de-siècle* Vienna on the one hand and Felix Braun, who became a Catholic writer, and Otto Weininger, the prototype of the self-hating Jew, on the other. What all those mentioned above and many others shared was the typically Jewish (and perhaps unholy) fascination with the German language and the cultural values embodied in it, which makes the much-discussed German-Jewish symbiosis the most tragically unrequited love affair in world history.

*Fin-de-siècle* Vienna, to whose culture Jews made such imperishable contributions, has been very much in the consciousness of today's American intellectuals, who near the turn of another century are searching for the roots of modernism and parallels to our troubled times, for the guidance and wisdom of a period of tremendous political, social, and cultural change through a better understanding of the problems and solutions (or non-solutions), the insights and ideas that have shaped the modern world—in literature, music, psychoanalysis, art, and architecture. Weimar Germany, which in its arts and politics was decisively shaped by Jews, has been of equal fascination. Contemporary critics like Walter Laqueur and Gordon Craig have faulted its greatest satirist, the lapsed Jew Kurt Tucholsky, for stunting the growth of the weak reed of German democracy with his satiric sniping—and yet present-day America, which has produced no satirist of the stature of Tucholsky or Kraus, is precisely in need of the "Tucholsky syndrome," the radical criticism which Laqueur is sorry to see proliferating in some American-Jewish circles.

In his stimulating book *German Jews Beyond Judaism,* George L. Mosse attempts to define the German-Jewish spirit in terms of a fervent faith in *Bildung*—the kind of moral education, character development, and buoyantly optimistic, humanistic mode of thought and feeling that was intended to validate Judaism as a religion and protect the Jews' wholehearted participation in German culture. As Mosse points out, for the critic Walter Benjamin "the road to a knowledge of Hebrew and to Zionism passed through the study of German culture," and Buber's Hasidism had close ties to German mysticism. In light of the sad failure of the German-Jewish symbiosis, particular poignance attaches to the reflection that Friedrich Schiller (and, to nearly the same extent, Goethe and Wilhelm Humboldt as well) became the "rabbi" of German and even Eastern European Jews as far as their egalitarian, libertarian, humanitarian, and assimilationist aspirations were concerned. German Jewry increasingly became a *Bildungs-buergertum* that clung to the noble ideals of the Enlightenment and German Classicism long after other Germans had abandoned them. The utopian vision expressed in Lessing's play *Nathan the Wise* sustained generations of German Jews and, ironically, the play became their sole property, as it were, when the Nazis banned it from the general German stage.

The German-Jewish legacy has been extensively studied and interpreted in recent decades, and such important books as *The Intellectual Migration: Europe and America, 1930 – 1960* (Donald Fleming and Bernard Bailyn, eds.), *Jews from Germany in the United States* (Eric Hirshler, ed.), *The Legacy of the German Refugee Intellectuals* (Robert Boyers, ed.), *The Refugee Intellectual* (Donald Kent), *German Exile Literature in America, 1933 – 1950* (Robert Cazden), *Exile in New York* (Helmut Pfanner), *Exiled in Paradise: German Refugee Artists and Intellectuals in America from the 1930s to the Present* (Anthony Heilbut), and *Refugee Scholars in America* (Lewis Coser) have been devoted to it. It is difficult to conceive of a time when the scholars, thinkers, teachers, and artists discussed in these and other studies will no longer influence and inspire new American generations. In connection with a modern polymath and rare spirit like Erich von Kahler one thinks of Schiller's words *Denn wer den Besten seiner Zeit genug getan, der hat gelebt fuer alle Zeiten* ("a person who has lived up to the best of his time has lived for all times"). If a Viennese-born singer and actress like the late, lamented Martha Schlamme can inspire her pupil Belle Linda Halpern to bring to life the fabled Berlin cabarets of the 1920s and interpret the chansons of Brecht-Weill and Tucholsky for American audiences, one need not fear that the German-Jewish heritage is in imminent danger of becoming merely historical.

As a teacher, lecturer, writer, and translator I have long regarded myself as a cultural mediator, and in this orientation and such endeavors I have been guided principally by Stefan Zweig, the subject of my doctoral dissertation, and his first wife Friderike, my beloved mentor during her decades of residence in Connecticut. In a centennial talk delivered at Beersheva, Israel, in 1981 I raised the question whether cultural mediatorship may be regarded as an eminently Jewish trait and answered it with a qualified yes. In his autobiography *The World of Yesterday* Stefan Zweig discusses the mediating zeal of Jews eager to be active among their host nations in an effort to improve their position by increasing the store of understanding, tolerance, and humanitarianism in the world. Certainly the ethical rigorism of Judaism was an inspiration (albeit, alas, one that could not sustain him in dark times) to Zweig as he strove to translate in a wider and higher sense across national, literary, and personal boundary lines and struggled to maintain his integrity and artistic freedom in a world out of joint. Raphael Patai has pointed out that in the process of cultural transmission Jews played "a crucial role as mediators between East and West, especially in medieval Spain and in pre-Renaissance and Renaissance Italy." In the past two centuries this tradition has been strengthened by Goethe's concept of *Weltliteratur*. When Moses Mendelssohn translated the Hebrew Bible into German, he enabled his fellow Jews to take the giant step from the ghetto into Europe. Heinrich Heine was almost forced to become a mediator between his native land and his country of exile, France. Martin Buber not only collaborated on another Bible translation but also felt impelled to introduce his host people to the *Kalevala,* the Finnish national epic.

In his study of German-Jewish leftist intellectuals, Paul Breines views Woody Allen's character Leonard Zelig as a prime example of Jewish self-surrender and self-alienation for the sake of an ideal of *Bildung* and humanitarianism and goes on to say: "In their reckonings with the dialectic of universal (human) and particular (Jewish, German, emigré), the Tollers, Einsteins, and their scattered kindred spirits recognized that self-surrender cuts several ways; that just as the consistent assimilationists repressed their Jewish particularity, the more Jewish Jews who opted for the synagogue or for Jewish statehood repressed some of their universal humanity." Lucy Steinitz, the daughter of the Berlin-born former editor of *Aufbau*, reports (in *Living After the Holocaust: Reflections by Children of Survivors in America*) that her father reacted to Emil Fackenheim's statement that one can't give Hitler posthumous victories by giving up one's Judaism by saying that one can't give Hitler the credit for having changed our lives, for *making* us Jewish. I, for one, have not minded letting my experience of expulsion, flight, and exile increase and enhance my Jewish awareness and identification. I feel that American Jews ought to heed this adaptation of Terence's celebrated dictum: *Homo judaicus sum; judaici nil a me alienum puto.* If they do, the rather unsavory and unproductive conflict between *yekkes* and *yiden* will finally come to an end. As a counterpoise to the selfishness, careerism, and crass materialism rampant in our age, Goethe's words *Wo ich nuetze, ist mein Vaterland* ("My fatherland is where I can be of service/do some good") should supplant the ancient Roman adage *Ubi bene, ibi patria* ("One's fatherland is where one is well off").

Anthony Heilbut has pointed out that Freud's assertion that Jewish identity was discovered not in religious ritual or folkloric custom but in sustained critical resistance matched the attitude of many emigrés, who evinced no desire to return to the faith of their fathers but wanted to belong in the line of Heine, Marx, Luxemburg, and Einstein. In his discussion of both left-wing intellectuals of the Weimar Republic and more traditional academicians, Mosse discerns a "process of intellectual questioning and debate that is still with us." What Mosse says about German-Jewish intellectuals of the 1920s surely applies to American-Jewish scholars of the 1980s as well: they "sought to use scholarship and their intellectual authority as a weapon to stem the tide which threatened to engulf all rational and cultivated minds."

In the final analysis, I believe that the most important and most enduring legacy of the German-Jewish spirit, as refined in the light of decades of experience and altered conditions, will or should be, in addition to the mediatorship, criticism, and Jewish rededication and self-assertion delineated above, an insistence on excellence and the highest intellectual and moral standards, a concern with purity of language in what Karl Kraus has described as a "language-forsaken" age, a principled opposition to mediocrity, a refusal to yield to the blandishments of panaceas or facile solutions, and—last but not least—an informed vigilance.

# The German-Jewish Legacy After Auschwitz

*Norbert Wollheim*

As a survivor of the Holocaust as well as a Jew from Germany I find it somewhat difficult to discuss the concept of a German-Jewish legacy. If by legacy we mean the act of passing on certain values to people, whether they deserve them or not, then I have difficulty recognizing the continuation of that legacy in America.

There are several reasons for such a feeling. I must admit that I have been critical of the German-Jewish establishment in this country for failing to pass on that legacy with consistency or success. I found this to be the case when I came to this country in 1952 and I find it more or less the same today.

I do not mean by this that German Jews who came here from Nazi Germany have not made individual contributions of an important nature to the life of America, but they have not done it as a collective group.

There are reasons for this as well. America is a melting pot society. German Jewish life in Germany was based on strongly ideological grounds. That is hardly the way in which our American Jewish organizational life works today, a life that is based on American pragmatism and the ability to pull strings.

I have been told that German Jews did not make contributions to American life as a group because we did not enter the United States on the Lower East Side. Perhaps there is some truth to this. Our Yekkishness is a recognizable trait, and perhaps not a trait that fits into the American Jewish style, which, after all, was developed by an East European Jewish community, at least since the end of World War I. And that style is not our style.

And yet I do not find such answers totally convincing. I still struggle with the question of why our German-Jewish refugee organizations and their successors have made little or no contribution to American Jewish life. Rabbi Joachim Prinz, one of the great German-Jewish rabbis of the 1920s and 1930s, was president of the Conference of Presidents of Major American Jewish Organizations but not as a leader of German Jews in this country. Indeed, our organizations have never even joined the Presidents Conference.

There is yet another problem with regard to this German-Jewish legacy. That involves the psychological gulf and the historical gulf that separates those German Jews who left Germany before the implementation of the Final Solution and those who did not. That of course is understandable. For those who were not there it is not easy to understand, perhaps we can call it a kind of mental barbed wire between those who survived Auschwitz and those who did not have to.

And one of the great ironies of the Holocaust is that such a difference cannot and does not exist between the German-Jewish survivors and those from eastern Europe, the *Ostjuden,* who always made us so uncomfortable in our pre-Holocaust German existence. But what we German-Jewish survivors learned from Auschwitz has remained. Whatever prejudices we had against the *Ostjuden* were burned out at Auschwitz. Today we form with them a survivor community of fate based on love and on tears.

Have we Jews from Germany really done enough to transmit the darkest part of our legacy, to educate our children and grandchildren and to bring to them the message of those who went their way *al kiddush hashem* together with the six million we mourn? Has enough been done to bring into the consciousness of German Jews, of American Jews, the legacy of our martyrs, for which names like Otto Hirsch, Julius Seligsohn, Heinrich Stahl, Paul Eppstein, Hannah Karminski, Cora Berliner, and others are the symbols of the sacrifice of all the victims of German Jewry?

Our grandchildren, the grandchildren of Jewish refugees from Germany, are now part of the American experience. And I think, despite our legacy, we will have to settle for that. We German-Jewish survivors talked to them, tried to make them aware of their past and ours. But I do not know if we have been successful.

We German Jews understand that America is not a country of continuities. We know that America is a different part of the world and is not suited to continue our heritage. That is why I do not believe that the concept of *Bildung* can offer very much in its American environment.

*Bildung* flourished among German Jewry in that special environment that allowed it to blossom. It was a certain attitude, a certain approach to life. It included a sense of *Herzensbildung*, to have a responsibility for the community, for those who were in need. It also meant that Jewish parents saw to it that their children became *gebildet*.

For German Jews *Bildung* meant both an acceptance of what was good in German culture and what they possessed as Jews. I, for example, was proud of the library at my parents' home. It contained books by Heine, Goethe, and Schiller but also books by Dubnow, Graetz, Buber, and Franzos.

Those of us who tried to live Jewish lives lived according to what was good in Jewish tradition and what was good in the German tradition. It was a life based on education and knowledge. We thought that sticking to our own religion and our own holidays would make us different but not separate. We lived for the idea that because of the Enlightenment and its teachings, we German Jews could live in Germany on the same basis as non-Jews but with our own values.

It took me a bit longer than others to believe that all of this was in vain.

When I saw synagogues burning in Berlin on November 9, 1938, I asked myself: Is this being done by the people of Goethe and Schiller?

The day before I reached Auschwitz I did not believe that such a place could exist and be built on scientific principles to destroy a people, my people.

All of this, too, is part of the German-Jewish legacy. It, too, is part of the history of German-Jewish life and of its death. It is the most tragic part of our legacy as German Jews, but it may serve to save humanity from having to experience that which we human beings, Jews or otherwise, should never have to endure again.

# A German-Jewish Legacy

*Manfred Jonas*

In order to speak meaningfully about a German-Jewish legacy and its presumed impact on either the American Jewish community or the United States as a whole, we must posit the existence of a definable "German-Jewishness." We must further assume that this German-Jewishness consists of more than some common attitudes, perceptions, and values of Germans who also happen to be Jews, or of Jews who also are, or at least have been, Germans. In short, we must consider the German Jews as a distinct religio-cultural group which could have a definable impact on its original environment and retain its identity sufficiently to have an impact even after transplantation. Such assumptions are debatable. But only if they prove true can studies of German Jews as a religio-cultural group yield a definition of a German-Jewish legacy.

My contribution to such a process must, perforce, be a modest one: to use my personal experience as a partial definition of German-Jewishness, and to consider its possible impact from this micro-perspective. Since my experience may well not have been remotely representative, this approach is certainly open to challenge. But it can, perhaps, add a small reality-based element to a highly speculative enterprise.

* * *

My parents and paternal grandparents lived in a small town in western Germany, my maternal grandparents, whom we visited often, in a small city less than 100 kilometers away. A substantial part of the family had earlier come from rural villages, where its members had been tradesmen. Those relatives of whose existence I had any great awareness were largely "in business," in some fashion. My father was part-owner of a small winery, my maternal grandfather dealt in scrap metal and animal products, one of my uncles in shoe leather. Others I knew were shopkeepers, or salesmen of some description. One not too distant relative was a "banker," though in what capacity I do not know. All were literate and, except for some in the very oldest generation, had completed some sort of secondary education. Most had cultural interests—literature, the theater, music, art—and considered themselves both educated and cultured, but none had attended a university. My mother, who had wanted to study medicine, had been denied the chance by her father.

To the best of my knowledge, everyone thought of himself as both German and Jewish: German in nationality, Jewish in religion, acculturated in both. I certainly did. At the time of the 1936 Olympics, I could still be found rooting for the "home team" and collecting pictures of its heroes, though by that time I had reason to know that Jews were not Germans in the Third Reich. My mother still read Schiller and Thomas Mann (but also Shaw and Stendhal), and admired Wagner's music.

Not until after we had emigrated to the United States did we encounter persons who, to our astonishment, identified themselves as Jewish in the same fashion as those from County Cork called themselves Irish. We did not do so even then. Our nationality remained German, though we used the term "refugee" to suggest that we had none at the moment. Jewish it was not.

Being Jewish in religion and, especially, in culture was very much part of my consciousness, however. No one whom I knew well could be described as a fully observant Jew. Even my maternal grandfather, chairman of the local congregation, kept no kosher house and did little more than put in obligatory appearances at synagogue functions. Outward signs of Jewishness were limited to "family traditions," such as the lighting of Sabbath candles, annual seders (one), synagogue attendance on the High Holy Days, and the consumption of various "ethnic" foods (German-Jewish, to be sure, not "Eastern-Jewish"). And these limited observances were more prevalent with my grandparents and their generation than with my parents' and my own—at least until 1933.

Despite this, my parents always regarded themselves as Jews, and in that sense somehow different from most of their neighbors. They occasionally had a gentile friend and knew more than a few non-Jews quite well. My mother reminisced, on occasion, about non-Jewish boyfriends (my grandparents would surely have been aghast), and my father about gentile schoolmates, but the vast bulk of their associations were with Jews, inside the family and out. Much the same was true for me, even before 1933. Since the small town in which I grew up had only a handful of Jewish families with small children, most of my playmates were, in fact, cousins of some description. Two of these had non-Jewish neighbors with children of their respective ages. They knew these children, of course, but were not friends, and rarely played together. After 1933, they did not play at all.

Jewishness, while not considered *the* central element of existence, was certainly accepted as a given. Passing or converting were steps which no one in the family considered. Others who did, or tried to, were regarded as weak, dishonest, or even sick. We were in some ways quite proud of being Jews, and felt culturally and, indeed, morally superior to "goyim." But we also distinguished between ourselves and East European Jews in these respects, and thus our cultural Jewishness was German-Jewishness.

Hitler's accession to power in 1933 brought some changes in behavior. On the theory that if we were to be ostracized and persecuted for being Jews we should at least understand our Jewishness better, my parents became active in the synagogue and began to promote my Jewish education. My mother collected money for tree planting in Palestine, and my father thought seriously about emigrating there. We became more Jewish—but not more religious.

For me, school began in April 1933. As one of only two Jewish children (the other was my cousin) in the first grade of the town school, I suffered both from a teacher who was a prominent local Nazi and whose son (also in the class) was one of the earliest *Jungvolk* recruits, and from classmates who had been encouraged to believe that beating up Jews made one a better German. A sympathetic principal advised my parents to take me out of the school, and by the following year I was in the newly established Jewish school of the nearest major city, an hour's train ride away. At age seven, my cousin and I now lived during the week with two unemployed Jewish teachers, and enjoyed the freedom of the big city, where nobody knew us and where our streetcar passes were passports to adventure.

The school we attended was itself a product of the events of 1933 and of German-Jewish consciousness. Staffed by teachers fired from the public schools, it was Jewish in its personnel more than its curriculum. It had a Zionist orientation and required us to study *Ivrit*, presumably as practical preparation for emigration to Palestine, but the course of study was certainly secular and decidedly German, with some "Sunday School"—Jewish history and Jewish ethics—added for good measure.

My father had thought of emigrating soon after Hitler came to power, but had been dissuaded, primarily by his brother. A World War I sergeant (rare rank for a Jew), and member of the *Reichbund Juedischer Frontsoldaten* (a quintessentially German designation that reflects both the extent and limits of assimilation) who treasured his Iron Cross, my uncle could not believe that Hitler's attacks on good Germans like us were anything but a temporary aberration. He held to this theory until 1938, when he was temporarily imprisoned in Dachau. My father never shared that view, and by 1936 was determined to leave. Our destination was to be the United States, to where a visa could be obtained. But when an emigration inspector went through our baggage prior to departure and questioned the source of the World War I decorations he found, my father not only produced the citations which had accompanied them, but added with some bitterness that he still awaited the promised "thanks of the Fatherland."

The United States, where we arrived on Armistice Day 1937, certainly had greater impact on us than we had on it. And in various ways it altered not only our perceptions of ourselves as Germans, but also as Jews. Thus clearly our German-Jewishness was transformed.

First and foremost, of course, we became Americans. We had come not to find a temporary refuge but a new home, away from the Germans who had betrayed us. (My parents, who traveled widely in Europe after the war, never visited their old home again. I did so several times, but then I had grown up as an American.) Though we lived for years in a neighborhood inhabited largely by other "refugees," and socialized mainly with them, we—and they—were not as interested in building a German-Jewish community in America as in assimilating to the larger surroundings. English became our language of choice in short order, and application for American citizenship was made at the earliest possible date. And we sought—and found—American (largely American-Jewish) friends.

If America as a whole replaced most of our Germanness, our Jewishness was affected by contact with an established Jewish community comprised largely of Jews from Eastern Europe. Less assimilated than we had felt ourselves to be in Germany, more self-consciously Jewish than we were and, on the whole, more observant as well, the nature of our initial contacts with them was most clearly symbolized, perhaps, by our amazement that they spoke Yiddish, and theirs that we did not. Our prejudice against "Eastern Jews" did not evaporate at once, nor did their reciprocal one. But over time a degree of mutual adjustment took place which reinforced, as it reshaped our Jewishness.

* * *

On the basis of such considerations, what can we say about the possible impact of German-Jewishness in the United States? The most accurate answer is, of course, "not much." The German Jews who came to the United States became only a very small drop in a very large pond—even of Jews. They were not entirely homogeneous, their "German-Jewishness" was almost immediately altered, and the primary aim of most became adjustment to the new surroundings, not changing them. But that may not be the whole story.

If, as my experience would suggest, German Jews brought with them a nationalism (German—but transferable) created by assimilation, a partially secularized religiosity which put knowledge, understanding, and morality (not unlike George Mosse's concept of *Bildung*) at the core of their Jewishness, and a cultural sensibility which placed them squarely within the Western tradition, they may well, by their existence as well as by their actions, have made an impact in their new home.

The fact that the German Jews were a relatively educated and assimilated group helped, without question, to focus American attention on the plight of the Jews everywhere, to lead—however slowly and inadequately—to American policies which sought to alleviate this plight (including, ultimately, the prompt recognition of the State of Israel), and to create a better climate for Jews, even in the United States. For the same reason, both the example and the practice of the Jews from Germany probably speeded up the already ongoing process of assimilation for American Jews, which peaked in the war and postwar years.

Because many came with some professional qualifications, because most sought to reproduce in America the assimilation they thought they had achieved in Germany, because they did not, on the whole, carry their Jewishness like a badge and, to be sure, because they were relatively few in numbers, German Jews were able to penetrate American society more effectively and more rapidly than many other immigrant groups. They were aided by world events which conferred upon them the status of innocent victims, but that too owed something to their German-Jewishness. They quickly appeared in respectable numbers in the arts, the media, and the universities, and they joined social, cultural, and even political associations in surprising numbers.

Such activity translated itself into influence—not directly, for German Jews had little power, but indirectly through the process of acceptance and through the relevance of German-Jewish concerns to the events of the time. That influence was probably slight. But both the United States and the American Jewish community moved in the direction in which that influence was exerted. The greater openness of the society to "Jewish concerns" and the greater assimilation of all American Jews followed.

Can that be regarded as a legacy? Indeed it can, for the changes that German Jews helped promote were both significant and beneficial. But to speak of a continuing legacy seems to me far more problematical. The "German-Jewish spirit," whatever that may mean, has found a home in this country, has helped to make this country more congenial to itself, and has thereby lost much of its distinctiveness. Though it may not have fully disappeared, it is now so much a part of an American, and indeed an American Jewish, amalgam that to search for its future impact would be an exercise in futility. Many of the ideas and values which it encompassed are, of course, enduring values that can and should be nurtured, but at least in the United States, something definable in significant ways—i.e., in ways likely to have an impact— as German-Jewishness seems to me a thing of the past.

# Bildung: Was It Good for the Jews?

*Henry L. Feingold*

Memories of my German boyhood are composed of a series of very concrete images which do not encompass an abstraction like *Bildung*. That can only be derived by interpreting those memories from hindsight. Happily as a boy I recall almost nothing of the Jewish obligation for *Bildung* which so impresses Professor Mosse. I recall parades in which I could hear the sound of hobnailed boots on cobblestoned streets long before I could see the columns of uniformed men. To me it was stirring, the kind of *Bildung* I most appreciated as a boy. I remember the interim period of freedom when the Jewish children were no longer able to attend regular school and the Jewish school had not yet been organized. Such happiness could not have come from a child much concerned about *Bildung*. I recall my father's twice-weekly sessions to teach my sisters and me to read Hebrew. Surely that was not part of the *Bildung* process, because I couldn't wait for them to end. Yet I do recall hearing the word *gebildet* even *sehr gebildet*. It was usually spoken with awe by my mother to describe someone she greatly admired.

I think I can be more helpful describing how that reverence for *Bildung* worked itself out among us children in America. I was about nine years old when we arrived in Hoboken. My father, who was among other things a good Hebraist, enrolled me in a yeshiva, I think less for religious reasons than to keep me out of my mother's hair. In Germany the ban on *shechita* served as a kind of final blow to their fragile Orthodoxy. Few families in Ludwigshafen could afford the kosher meat imported from the Saar, and my family was particularly hard-pressed. Unlike Chaim Potok, I found the world of the yeshiva alien and difficult to adjust to. It was automatically assumed that as a German I was a good fighter, which gave me a full year of unearned peace. It ended when someone sought to test the proposition and found me vulnerable. It may be those rounds of trouncing in which each classmate needed to separately prove his mettle which turned me to things cultural. I may literally have been beaten into it.

There is no precise one-word English equivalent for *Bildung*. The term "educated" or "cultured" does not yield its precise meaning, which relates to a process of cultural and educational self-actualization, of becoming, morally, culturally, and professionally, what one ought to be. My sisters and I were raised with such an "adoration" of culture and education, but I am not at all certain that it stems from our early German-Jewish background. We share none of the Middle European pretentiousness regarding *Kultur*. We are better educated, and so are my colleagues and friends who are the children of East European parents. They are quite as *gebildet* as we, although we had a headstart. It was in the air we breathed. We knew the works of various cultural carriers, instrumentalists, writers and thinkers, the way the others knew baseball statistics. But somewhere there was a great catching up, and today Jewish "culture vulturism" has no national label. It convinces me that the *Bildung* concept is not exclusively a German-Jewish value but is historically linked to the urban/urbane cosmopolitan "high" culture which developed among post-Emancipation Central European Jewry. Its principal nexus was in the remarkable cultural axis anchored in Berlin, Vienna, Prague, and Budapest which spun off cultural heroes like Freud, Einstein, Kafka, and Herzl. (My parents' litany was much longer.) These represent only the tip of the iceberg. Today that Jewish cultural effervescence can be as readily located in New York or Washington (perhaps Moscow and Jerusalem too) as it once was found in the cities of Central Europe.

Even if it were possible to assign such a specific character to German Jewry, I would still be hard-pressed to discover to which segment it belongs. If one learns anything from a recent study of Washington Heights in New York City (Steven Lowenstein, *Frankfurt on the Hudson*) it is how dangerous it is to generalize about German Jewry. It was in fact a multilayered Jewry. On one level there were the Jewish scientists from Central Europe who made such a notable contribution to the Manhattan Project, on another there was the Breuer community, which became even more pious in America. In between there were thousands of ordinary people, many of whom, like my parents, had been declassed by a precipitous uprooting. If the children of such parents were ambitious, I suspect that the spirit of "catching up," of recovering lost status, had as much to do with it as the spirit of *Bildung*.

Withal, there was something distinctive about the comparatively small Central European immigration coda of the thirties. In short order it furnished itself with a relatively complete organizational infrastructure which included a full complement of religious congregations, and social work and philanthropic agencies. It has done well in recording the history of a splendid lost community. But one should take note that the new president of the Leo Baeck Institute is the son of eastern Jews who specializes in the history of Sephardic Jewry. Amalgamation has been the order of the day, and it has become increasingly difficult to identify a separate German-Jewish subculture.

The German-Jewish immigration of the thirties enriched the nations which received it, the United States, Britain, and Israel (Palestine). It gave them a population supplement uniquely equipped to handle the problems of modernity. Everywhere German Jews became, in disproportionate numbers, members of the existing modernizing elites without whom no complex modern society can operate. Some go as far as attributing the postwar American explosion in technology and culture to the intellectual capital carried in the baggage of the refugee scientists, scholars, and sundry cultural agents, most of whom, at least according to the Nuremberg Laws, were Jewish. Germany's loss was America's gain.

There may be some measure of truth in such self-aggrandizing assessments, but I suspect that the contribution was made after the German-Jewish spirit was altered so that it could work in America. It is only in that sense that we can think of it as still being alive in America. I find discomfort in speaking of the "German-Jewish spirit in exile." It gives that spirit an autonomy and particularity it did not possess in reality. For me German-Jewish civilization marks a moment in the millennial history of the Jews, a particularly brilliant one, although Jewishly not untroubled. It was another diaspora in a history full of diasporas. Its spirit does not vanish when that community is extirpated. It rejoins the larger stream of Jewish history, carried by survivors who bring those new ideas and behavioral modes which they have internalized. The host Jewish communities with which they have amalgamated do well to incorporate these ideas and modes as they have. They were learned at a terrible price.

Finally, we are all prisoners of history and do not have the power to choose which elements of a cultural legacy to bring forward. My parents, who adhered to a German-Jewish *Kulturgebiet* but were not German Jews, would nevertheless have been quite certain that there was a distinct German-Jewish culture whose assets they could have enumerated with pride. They would have spoken of their version of *Bildung*, self-discipline, will, energy, the crucial ingredients to gain mastery of a skill and complete the self. But alas, their son musters no such certainty. He is uncomfortable standing on the spongy ground of national character and detects an unhappy Teutonic ring to what they find so commendable. Discipline and "stick-to-itiveness" become in his Americanized mind identified with rigidity, humorlessness, and over-intensity.

I note among the survivors of my father's generation that they are a distinct, recognizable type, similar values, walks, inability after more than four decades to distinguish between the *v* and *w* sounds. But the children are virtually indistinguishable from their American-born peers. Most remain intensely achievement-oriented but are somehow more comfortable in their skins.

They are "looser," less German, and often more Jewishly Jewish. That brings us to the crucial question of whether *Bildung* was good for the Jews or Judaism. Professor Mosse may be on to something when he suggests that *Bildung* had become a normative and, in some measure, a central expression of the Jewishness of German Jewry. But I am uncertain whether that is "good for the Jews." In my mind *Bildung* is related to Jews in that they cherished it. It was normative but not necessarily related to the traditional Jewish culture, which had its own aspiration for *lernen*. What we see is a new form of basically secular identity formation which gives high priority to intense individuation, autonomy, and the internalization of controls. That kind of person does not easily perceive himself as a member of a flock of which God is the shepherd. *Bildung* may yield civic virtue, but can it accommodate pious, believing tribalized Jews? Can the study of Jewish texts be accommodated? Can a demanding *Halacha*?

Finally, we need to come to terms with German-Jewish history. It was a community that was compelled prematurely to depart from the historical stage, so that we will never know whether the values on which it based itself, like *Bildung*, were sufficient to sustain a viable Jewish culture. Because of the tragic nature of its demise there may be a tendency to idealize what was, to write a history which makes German Jewry in death what it was never in life. That would be a disservice to all, the living and the dead.

The cultural incubator which produced German Jewry no longer exists. Those fortunate to survive have had to adjust to other cultures. For some that adjustment has been full of pain. Many, like my parents, never again were able to live at ease in the world. But from a historical vantage, the greater tragedy is the destruction of a centuries-old cultural ambiance which produced a remarkably productive humanity. But before we berue what was lost in the transplantation, we do well to remember that it was a character fashioned by a host culture which also produced values which ultimately proved lethal to the Jewish enterprise. It places our loving talk of the German-Jewish symbiosis in limbo.

There is good reason to believe that the American Jewish achievement, which is based on an Americanized version of *Bildung*, will generate much more for both the host culture and for world Jewry and at a lower price. It does not require that the Jewish dimension of culture be so radically refashioned, although in some ways the solvent produced by an open American society is even more challenging for Jewish continuance. An easier America speaks, not of *Bildung*, but of pluralism. I think it offers a more workable principle on how Jewish life might be carried forward. *Wirklich, Amerika hat es besser* ("America is really better").

# *Bildung* and the Dilemma of Hyphenation

*Herbert Pierre Secher*

The Vienna of my childhood during the late twenties and the thirties until the year of the *Anschluss* did not provide the necessary cultural milieu for the care and protection of my Jewish legacy. As a totally assimilated third-generation Jewish family living in the heart of *Mitteleuropa*, we were sufficiently aware of being of a different religion; but as the once "supranational" people of the now fragmented Austro-Hungarian empire, Viennese Jews especially cherished the cosmopolitanism of their city's distinctive culture, preferring to identify closely with the ideological currents of the time. Depending on their degree of assimilation Jews, therefore, could be found supporting a whole spectrum of ideas and movements ranging from the very conservative to liberal and/or radical ones. Still it was generally recognized that the large majority of Vienna's Jews felt very comfortable within the progressive liberalism of the Social Democratic party, which in 1922 had succeeded at the polls in making Vienna peacefully the first socialist-governed city outside the Soviet Union. My family, comfortably middle-class, could be heard to complain occasionally about new city ordinances designed to give domestic help the same rights and benefits as other employees, yet on the first of May, they joined happily in the festivities celebrating the achievements of this Social Democratic administration. As well they should; not before, and, of course, never again were Jews in Europe able to enjoy such complete equality and the opportunity to consider themselves an integrated part of the community. As has been documented and commented on by observers at that time and scholarly treatises later, Jews could be found at all levels of the city's government and administration, dominant in its social and professional life, outstanding in its arts and sciences. Many of these achievements were the result of the open-minded, pragmatic, and innovative policies pursued by the Social Democratic party. Small wonder that the first of May brings back to me childhood memories of such joy and tranquility that normally might have been reserved for religious holidays. There was no religious observance in my home other than the annual trek to a grandparent's home for the sumptuous breaking of the fast at the end of Yom Kippur; the day itself being spent, except for a short attendance to listen to the Kol Nidre or participate in the memorial service, in leisurely walks in the Viennese Woods or in one of Vienna's many beautiful public parks. Seders were observed only infrequently; there was, after all, that ritualistic bother, but my services as "the youngest" were occasionally called for by one of the many childless or one-child families of my parents' generation.

Youngsters of my parents' circle of friends joined the *Roten Falken*, the youth organization of the Social Democratic party, or, if less politically inclined, the Boy Scouts, and somewhat less frequently the Jewish sports club *Hakoah;* personally, I joined all three at one time or another. *Hakoah* by the way also fielded a team in Austria's national soccer league; it was not a very outstanding team, yet it had its solid group of fans who probably never thought of this as some outstanding Jewish cultural achievement! It was simply accepted by my generation that in Social Democratic Vienna Jews were not a "tolerated" minority but very much part of the establishment. Most likely, class identification—social and/or economic—preempted religious solidarity. Nobody I knew ever talked of religion as a defense against a strange or even hostile environment. The very fact that "religion" was taught in school made us even less aware of any special status; we treated it just like any other subject and without much reverence. I recall that my first instructor in religion during elementary school was a poised, friendly, soft-spoken young woman, in all likelihood a member in good standing of the Social Democratic party (how else could she have obtained this municipal job?), who in an easy, noncommittal manner informed us about the Old Testament. To this day I view this as a major component of my Jewish legacy, since I do not recall ever learning about the Old Testament from any other source at that time. Later, in the *Gymnasium*, the process was repeated, with some Hebrew lessons thrown in to help us read the prayer book. We were taught by a rather dry, scholarly, bearded type who could be distinguished from other faculty only by virtue of his keeping on a hat during class. He was replaced eventually by a younger, more modern but also openly Zionist teacher whose dedication to discipline probably further accelerated our secularization process. At least it did mine.

My Bar Mitzvah brought in a rabbinical type who drilled me for six months in the phonetics of the Torah passage but otherwise provided no inspiration to explore further the meaning of Judaism. Later, at the party at home following my uninspired reading of the Torah passage, I recited enthusiastically one of Schiller's classic poems which I had committed to memory with a lot less difficulty than the prescribed passage. In short, in the free-flowing, emancipated secular, cosmopolitan atmosphere of post – World War 1, pre-*Anschluss* Vienna, "there was no importance in being Jewish"; one could cultivate one's Jewishness or one did not—most of the young people I grew up with chose not to!

What "Jewishness" there was, however, did not manifest itself in faith but rather in the recognition of a cultural bond that expressed itself primarily in the Yiddish language, with its own set of values which, whether humorous, critical, or lyrical, always provided some trenchant insights into the human condition. My circle of young friends experienced no crisis in self-perception with respect to their role as Jews and/or as citizens of Vienna; we all spoke the leveling Viennese dialect affected by both aristocrats and proletarians, liberally sprinkled with Yiddishisms (just as today *chuzpah* and *maven* find their way into American usage). For us Yiddish was truly a lingua franca that seemed well suited to a Social Democratic ethos of internationalism, progress, and respect for a humanist tradition. We read, in German translations, Sholem Asch, Shalom Aleichem, and occasionally saw films such as *The Golem* or *The Dybbuk* without feeling that such preferences imposed some inescapable choices on us. The Jewish bourgeoisie accepted Yiddishness with the same nonchalance it reserved for anti-Semitism; both conditions were a fact of life but one had overcome them somehow, *man muss sich darueber hinwegsetzen*, that is, neither fact was important enough to get in the way of a normal, rational, orderly, and upwardly mobile way of life! Obviously, those of us whose early socialization took place in the Vienna of the 1930s considered ourselves neither flawed nor particularly discriminated against and shared in the uneventful, yes, happy, childhood of middle-class children everywhere in *Mitteleuropa*.

When Hitler happened, he reminded us rudely that we were different, but it was our social status rather than our religion that became the target of initial Nazi violence in the first months following the *Anschluss*. During those early uncertain months some Jewish "working-class" families were not molested by marauding bands of freshly uniformed, formerly illegal Nazis if they were known to them as neighbors (which happened frequently in workers' housing projects erected by the Social Democratic party). Nor were these months particularly tragic ones for myself and friends who were in the process of enjoying the unfolding of teenage exhilaration. We continued with our dances, listened to the latest hit records (paradoxically "Bei Mir Bist Du Schoen" was sweeping Europe then), went hiking, swimming, and waited with rather joyful anticipation for the day of emigration. We also were more than ready to bid farewell to the dreary classical education, which, as the events of that year seemed to prove, could no longer serve to orient us in the modern world that lay beyond the borders of this small, inland country.

So that when I arrived eventually in New York and went to register at George Washington High School on Audubon Avenue and 185th Street in Manhattan, the last thing on my mind was how to nurture my Jewish legacy. What did reassert itself, with a vengeance I might say, was that very "classical" education we had so gladly left behind. For the hundreds of German-Jewish refugee kids who passed through GWHS, the great bond was not their Jewishness but the very solid *Gymnasialbildung* most of us had been exposed to. Our teachers loved us for the seriousness and dedication we brought to our studies. Less so our American, whether Jewish or not, contemporaries, with whom we very soon acquired the reputation of "grinds". During those early years I do not recall any discussions of Judaism and/or Jewishness, and the idea of belonging to a congregation or simply visiting a synagogue on High Holidays was very far from our concerns. If we were undergoing some kind of cultural transition, it would never have occurred to us to view this as leading from a German-Jewishness to an American Jewish identity! On the contrary, at the time we had little doubt that we were the bearers of a venerable European tradition of true intellectual knowledge that put us way ahead of the greedy commercialism around us. In that respect also, our future was always very clear to us; as writers, artists, and professionals would we make our mark in this crassly materialistic culture. In principle we were not different from any other immigrant youths who had come before us, wanting to make something of themselves, shedding their ties to the old culture and become "Americanized". Only we were steeped in the chauvinistic intellectualism of *Mitteleuropa,* and the characterization *er amerikanisiert sich* (He is becoming American) was reserved for those who had lost their intellectual *Drang* (fervor). Not that we didn't work hard at some very nonintellectual occupations, e.g., laundry sorter, messenger, delivery boy, etc. Only the thought of entering some business or other practical occupation rarely, if ever, entered our minds. I recall how surprised I was, together with my group of friends, when we learned that the pharmacy clerk in the local drugstore had actually gone to college! "Going to college" carried entirely different connotations for us. We gloried in our intellectuality, the result of that *Bildungsdrang* that had been drilled into us since early childhood. We did not regard our being foreign-born as a handicap; most of us were conversant with at least another language other than English, very likely French, which many had picked up while waiting for American visas in France or Belgium. I don't doubt that we were perceived as arrogant by our American peers. Some native-born Jewish students made the effort to get to know us better but eventually drifted away, unable to find some common ground between us, least of all our Jewishness. In what direction our expectations would have led us without the war and the subsequent G.I. Bill is impossible to say; but there is no doubt in my mind that without these two key events many doors would have remained closed to us. Henry Kissinger, one of GWHS's more famous graduates, can easily serve as a prototype for that purpose. Together with other refugee youths he graduated with an outstanding record that did not carry one much further than CCNY, but once the war came, those with education and a fluent knowledge of German soon made it into more interesting jobs in the military, possibly in intelligence first, later with the occupation authorities in the European theater. From there, talent and ambition could carry one as far as hard work and good luck would permit. Most of us went to Ivy League or Big Ten universities, and though Henry is probably the only one who made it to that stage where he merited being addressed as "His Excellency," many of us joined the ranks of successful professionals, academics, scientists, and government bureaucrats. In the course of this socioeconomic ascent it was not uncommon also to acquire a non-Jewish spouse and, in a rather curious way, this could be interpreted as making that part of a German-Jewish legacy complete!

Only by the time we had reached those plateaus of our success about which we could only dream during the intense years of the immigration, Jewishness had lost its confining character. The war had also socialized a new generation of Jewish-American youths out of their ghetto mentality and into a more positive attachment to Judaism. Israel had become a flourishing state, the Holocaust provided the blood-bond, and the menace of "atheistic Communism" left little room for the secular kind of Jew who was indifferent to his religious heritage. Even those children who had been brought up in an atmosphere of bland, tolerant, liberal secularism began to show their dissatisfaction with the draining off of their religious roots. Some literally turned away from the diluted Judaism of their parents to an altogether new religion or they found a spiritual home in a more orthodox Judaism.

In my own case the desire to escape the ghettoized existence among German-Jewish refugees in New York was overwhelming. I wanted to know about life in the "interior," discover America on that other side of the Hudson, and when the opportunity came I chose a college in the "distant" Midwest. It was easy enough during the forties not to feel the need to be Jewish in America; the war against Nazism had ended in victory, the world of higher education had been opened up completely to all regardless of color or creed, so what reasons could there be to renew one's religious bonds? I was part of an intellectual consensus that viewed religion as an antiquated form of absolutism no longer suitable to the conditions of a modern age. Progress meant to jettison it as an unnecessary ballast that only served to impede the further evolution of liberal democratic ideas and practices. Even the choice of political science as the centerpiece of my academic career was an idealistic one motivated by a desire to help in the building of a better post-war world. Today such an attitude might have probably led me in the direction of a more religiously oriented movement. At the time neither Zionism nor any other kind of ism held my interest, and for thirty years I pursued my professional goals without the slightest urge to confront my Jewish heritage. Then an abrupt change in my personal life brought me to a small midwestern college town where my family found refuge and comfort in the circle of about a dozen Jewish families. When we gathered in the small, simple, yet tastefully constructed synagogue on the edge of the prairie to celebrate holidays and rituals that I had either long forgotten or never experienced, it brought to me a reawakening, literally, of the meaning of the "temple community."

There in the heartland I felt as if I were experiencing the joining of the original American tradition of simple religiosity with the unadorned faith of the "world of my great-grandfathers!" Without the services of a rabbi, but with complete and dedicated participation by everyone in the community, I was able to discern again some fundamentals of the Jewish faith that had gotten lost somewhere in the pressure of solicitations for the obligatory trips to Israel.

I have long since departed the atmosphere of that small Jewish community, but the infusion of Judaic spirit which it gave has stayed with me. All the magnificence of our suburban synagogue will not suffice to nurture that spirit unless it is accompanied by a willingness to confront basic ethical questions that transcend the narrow interests of the State of Israel, or for that matter, those of the United States of America. Maybe that is the lesson of the "German" or "Viennese" Jewish legacy; to find and renew our faith apart from national, ethnic or, heaven help us, racist considerations!

We already know that Yiddish and Yiddishkeit are in the process of disappearing; we have left behind the stigma of the wanderer or pariah, no doubt as a consequence of the creation of the State of Israel. But even Israel's existence has not been settled in a way that will continue its character as a Jewish state rather than a state for Jews. If it will be no longer possible to validate one's Jewishness in "the world of our fathers" or in the identification with Israel—where and how can Jewishness acquire the necessary strength that will assure its survival into the next century and beyond? There is a point beyond which even affluence and the respectability that comes with being absorbed into a national community may not be sufficient to sustain a faith. Wasn't that the point reached by the German-Jewish community when Hitler came upon the scene? Doesn't the mere replacement of German-Jewishness with Jewish-Americanness carry with it the same risks that were part of the very German-Jewish experience?

It does not take any great leaps of imagination to visualize a time when a change in the configuration of world politics—a much closer rapprochement between the USSR and the United States in certain regions of the globe—no longer identifies Jewish-American goals and issues with new policies and strategies of the United States. This need not be the result of a rise in anti-Semitism, the appearance of a racist demagogic leader, or of a decline in the importance of Israel—but

simply the outcome of change in the ever evolving relationship between nation-states in general and the two superpowers in particular.
Then it must be possible to remain true to one's Jewish faith without
having to worry about the significance of hyphenation or dehyphena-
tion.

# Reflections on the *Kristallnacht* and the End of German Jewry: Some Transcendent Thoughts

*Curt C. Silberman*

For Jews in Germany emancipation was a slow, painful process. It proved to be a rather lopsided love affair. Whether there was ever a symbiosis, whether Jews ever had equal rights or just a license, will remain an academic question. The fact is that during the 150 years of emancipation, the Jews in Germany used the opportunities of liberalism to give free rein to the creative forces accumulated and suppressed in ghetto life. It is to the credit of Germany Jewry that the vast majority refused to pay the price of conversion for the privileges and enticements of emancipation. The greatest contributions of German Jews in all sectors of human endeavor were made during the fourteen-year period of the Weimar Republic, in the face of the ever growing confrontation with the growth of racial anti-Semitism, the *voelkische Bewegung*. Just as it reached its height, emancipation came to an abrupt end, and with it all the achievements of emancipation. There followed the years of systematic deprivation of property and civil rights, of humiliations and persecution, of the creation of the torturous institution of the concentration camps and of the degradation to pariah status under the Nuremberg Laws. The end of German Jewry was finally sealed by the bestial government-organized pogrom of November 10, 1938, whose flames destroyed the synagogues of Germany, and at the same time signaled the beginning of the *Endloesung*, the destruction of the majority of European Jewry. While those German Jews who escaped to the United States did not come as a political unit, they came here endowed with a great Jewish and European cultural heritage. They came with the conviction and appreciation of democracy as the only form of government where Jews as individuals and as a group could live, thrive, and exist; where the concept of pluralism permitted them to immediately take their place in the community, to become part of the mainstream of American life and—after the difficult task of settling down—to begin again making their contributions towards and for the benefit of society out of their rich cultural heritage and sad political experience. True, they came here deprived of their worldly goods; but their spirit and their will to rebuild had not been broken. They were not satisfied just to survive, they were determined to find new roots. Once they had learned to take care of basic necessities, they unpacked the only valuable luggage they had been able to bring along: their heritage. And as these lines are concerned with the contributions made to the American community and especially to American Jewry, the following is the author's attempt to describe some of them in a summary fashion:

It was the Jewish philosopher Professor Julius Gutmann who, in his book *The Philosophy of Modern Judaism*, stated that Germany had become the birthplace of modern Judaism. He advanced the view that all religious, cultural, pedagogic, scientific, and even political problems and concerns facing world Jewry today have their origin, their basis of discussion, their orientation, in the German-Jewish creativity of those years of emancipation. German Jewry, in particular, opened new avenues for Jewish religion, away from the strict rabbinism and rabbinical talmudic adherence, thus paving the way for the modernization of Judaism:

- The liberalism which led to the Reform movement.
- The modern Orthodoxy where Samson Raphael Hirsch had found a way to combine the authority of Jewish Law with the progress of social and scientific development of the outer world, a synthesis between the religious law and secular culture.
- The Conservative movement, represented by the Breslau Rabbinical Seminary.
- The Hochschule fuer Juedische Wissenschaft, emphasizing the Science of Judaism.

Even the German Zionist movement—though prior to Hitler shared only by a minority of the German Jews, yet led by an elite of Zionist thinkers—participated effectively in paving the way for the Jewish state. It should be noted that the important literature on Zionism of the time was published in the German language, and the *Juedische Rundschau* in Berlin was a strong voice for Zionist hopes and aims.

Through their own example and experience, these Jews from Germany brought along a historical message in our time—and, if you so want—a variety of lessons:

The Weimar Republic failed; democracy needs an educated citizenry; the Germans were not prepared for it. Hitler's rise to power—achieved without revolution and in a pretended parliamentary procedure—has proven that democracy can be undermined by its own tools. Democracy must be guarded against abuse. It is the only form of government protecting the individual and providing an atmosphere in which Jews can live and prosper.

Culture and civilization are no safeguards against barbarism and human madness, as has been shown in Germany, the land of poets and thinkers.

The Jews from Germany have proven that there can be *Bewaehrung im Untergang* (Reaffirmation in Destruction). Flames may destroy physical structures, they cannot, however, extinguish the spirit to survive and to rebuild.

Hitler has taught marginal Jews—as paradoxical as it may sound—that there is no escape from one's identity. Awareness of Jewish values, learning, and education as prerequisites for self-respect is the most effective shield against Jew-hatred. Jewish defense organizations are important; their program cannot, however, be the core of the Jewish agenda. We have experienced that anti-Semitism is a problem for the Jews. It is not a Jewish problem, however; the others must solve it.

When crimes against humanity are committed, when millions of human beings are slain, the silence of governments and church becomes a sin of omission.

The synagogue is the symbolic center of Jewish life. The *Kristallnacht* has taught this truth. Even the most remote Jew, the one who had not or had only rarely made use of the synagogue, felt that something important was taken away.

For the sake of Jewish continuity there must be unity in our midst and no divisiveness. No guarantee for the diaspora without Israel, but also no guarantee for Israel without a loyal diaspora.

Auschwitz should have done away with any discrimination in our midst. Any walls which once may have existed between Western and Eastern Jews must be removed.

The Holocaust is not the unique experience of any singular Jewry. German Jews were the first to experience the humiliations and the destruction; they were the first victims of Hitler's barbarian innovation: the concentration camp. Therefore any attempt to advance the beginning of the Holocaust to the year 1941 appears to be a distortion of Jewish history.

The world and humanity have a short memory; later generations assign the most tragic events to history as a matter of fact; emotions are quickly forgotten and only historical knowledge and understanding protect against intentional and unintentional forgetfulness. In the interest of the self-preservation of present and future generations, we must never allow the Hitler period to be written off as an episode.

And finally, when Hitler's dream of a 1000-year Reich came to an end after twelve years, leaving death and destruction to an extent the world had never experienced before, for a moment the conscience of humanity became moved. Israel's creation is largely the result of the world's guilty conscience. We must never allow that conscience to fade.

Throughout history we Jews have played the role of the monitors of world conscience, too often at great sacrifice. Let us keep our own house in good order so that we can effectively continue our role as monitors with conviction and dignity, for the sake of the world and all mankind.

# The Less Than Total Break

*Wolfgang Holdheim*

I remember *Kristallnacht* very well.

The consciousness of something wrong, something sinister, had come to me only quite gradually. My parents had kept me sheltered as best they could, concealing their growing worries about the evolution of events. During the first few years, for that matter, the deterioration of the atmosphere was not so obvious in Berlin, that sarcastically sophisticated capital where the Nazis never really felt at home. My great youth also helped; chronologically, my natural period of dawning awareness corresponded almost embarrassingly to the years of growth of the regime. I entered elementary school in 1933, when Hitler came to power. I never heard anything about either the Reichstag fire or the Night of Long Knives, and only remember the Saar referendum as a joyful occasion that made me engage in enthusiastically patriotic conversations with other children in the street. True, there were disharmonies in that best of worlds. The uniformed bands of the Nazi party were vaguely conceived as unpleasant, and I realized early that somehow they were not my friends. And in 1935, my mother told me with precautionary discretion that she was going to send me to a Jewish private school, where I would have more in common with my comrades. However, I initially failed to grasp the significance of this move. I did know that my parents were troubled by the unspeakable Berlin cockney in which I had come to express myself after two years in public school, and considered it only natural that they would turn to a Jewish school to steer me back to the use of New High German. All this cast few shadows on those early years, during which I still spent idyllic weekends at my uncle's Wannsee estate—my own garden of the Finzi Contini. As for the 1936 Olympic Games, I distinctly recall them as a time of cheerful excitement.

In 1936 I was ten years old, and the fall from grace began soon thereafter. The Games were the regime's propagandistic apotheosis; the ensuing deterioration was rapid and ominous. I took private English lessons because it was increasingly obvious that our future, if a future there was, could not lie in Germany. The possibility, then necessity of emigration arose, moved to the foreground, finally became paramount. At the same time, I sensed growing problems and harassments surrounding the family business. By 1938, that parallel process of historical development and personal education had reached a climax (though only a provisional one, as we were to find out). My memories of that year are very clear. The *Anschluss* no longer enthused me, as the Saar referendum had done: a sure sign of heightened insight and maturation. The war scare in the Sudeten crisis stands out in my memory, with the installation of anti-aircraft guns on rooftops. My father, on a business trip in England, hurriedly tried to rejoin us in Berlin but got only as far as Holland, where friends and relatives forcefully put him on a plane back to England: he, not my mother, was the Jewish member of the family who had everything to fear. That crisis passed, and my father returned to the Continent, to his ultimate undoing. Then, in November, came *Kristallnacht*—not yet, as we now know, the culmination of that diabolical course of events, but a symbolic and traumatic breaking point.

We did not witness any depredations in our residential neighborhood. We stayed indoors, and in the late afternoon, after everything was over, went on an exploratory walk. We came upon a sizable crowd of people reading a notice posted on a wall. It was Goebbels' manifesto, commending the German people on their healthy and natural anger but asking them to desist from further demonstrations so as to avoid the destruction of German property. The readers' faces were stony, the quiet was absolute—we heard no reaction, not a word. (We already knew that in Berlin, there had been nothing spontaneous about the outbursts that had been organized by party personnel and joined by other riffraff, avid for plunder.) As we turned away, we ran into one of our neighbors, a retired official of the old Prussian school. I will never forget his clenched fists, the hissing whisper in which he spoke to us: "This is scandalous, abominable; Red Spain and Soviet Russia are nothing compared to it!" My father's business had remained undamaged (factories do not lend themselves to the pettier forms of plunder), but he did not return there for some time, spending the nights (together with his brothers) at a sister's home: there were arrests, the fathers of several of my school companions were taken away. But it was still a hit-or-miss affair, and for unknown reasons the

Holdheim brothers seemed not to have made the blacklist as yet. A relative normalcy returned thereafter, but the screws were being drawn ever tighter, especially in the economic domain. Our factory was forcibly "aryanized" to a Turk who specialized in "buying" Jewish businesses for next to nothing. Our attempts at leaving became desperate. A Melbourne tycoon, a business friend of my father, repeatedly tried to bring us to Australia, guaranteeing everything, including employment—in vain: Australia wanted only Anglo-Saxons. At last in April 1939 we left for Holland, our fortune reduced to the permitted 10 marks per person, with the support of an aunt who had settled in Amsterdam. The refuge proved too close by, the Nazis were to follow us thirteen months later—but that is the beginning of a much more horrible story which here I do not have to tell.

How, under such circumstances, could I be expected to relate to my cultural heritage? My family had its "patristic" antics: the Reform rabbi Samuel Holdheim was my great-granduncle; but he had been an extreme liberal for his time, a nonconformist—and it was this aspect of his legacy that has come down to me. As for the religious side, the family was completely secularized and assimilated. Our particular branch had consisted of businessmen for several generations, but my father (like Thomas Buddenbrook) was sometimes a reluctant businessman. He loved literature above all else, read voraciously, and was a gifted (although inevitably an occasional) writer and poet. He stood entirely in that German tradition which had been so astonishingly internalized by the German Jews: Goethe and Schiller, Heine and Lessing; the ideals of *Bildung* and of the Enlightenment, in whose capital, after all, we lived. It might have been expected that I would reject this all-too-German background, which seemed barely to be mine in any case; my secondary schooling was Dutch, my university education American. My feelings in 1945, understandably, were far from Germanophile. And there were indeed attempts at rejection. I ended up in the field of French literature in my studies, undoubtedly to counteract what I felt to be German in myself. On the other hand, I had abandoned philosophy largely because its study, in America, did not sufficiently concentrate on the German tradition. And in my new field, I could hardly fail to encounter the distinguished tradition of German *Romanistik*. I soon expanded into comparative literature, coupled with an increasing emphasis on the hermeneutic tradition in philosophy, from Schleiermacher via Boeckh and Dilthey to the present day. In a broader and professionally intensified way, I had rediscovered and rejoined my father's cultural background; I am even teaching a course on the *Bildungsroman*. This development was experienced by me as a veritable process of self-discovery and self-elucidation. I do not know why this should be so. The German I speak is (thank heaven!) no longer Berlinian cockney, but I am told that it is strongly reminiscent of the Berlin of the Weimar Republic. This as well, considering that I was six in 1932, is somewhat odd.

I know, however, that such things cannot be seen in exclusively personal or psychological terms. One is not an isolated individual but a representative, the carrier of a tradition—even when one seems to have been totally uprooted. What I have acutely experienced, as I now realize, is the peculiar intensity with which the German Jews were grounded in the German cultural and intellectual tradition, and precisely in what is best in it. The question is not self-elucidation but elucidation: can this heritage furnish it, can it contribute to American culture; specifically, can it help to illuminate and advance the field of humane studies which I have chosen as my own? Of course it can— which does not necessarily mean that it will. Few would deny the importance of the German intellectual tradition, and of the Weimar period in particular. In my specific domain, that of literary studies, there has been a feverish philosophical, epistemological, and methodological activity in the last fifteen years. My background has enabled me to evaluate this development without surprise and (I believe) correctly. For one thing, it has helped me to recognize, sometimes with considerable amusement, how many of those supposedly revolutionary insights rested on inspirations that go back to the German philosophical tradition, and how many of the problems that were raised had occupied German thinkers long ago. There are some signs that the awareness of these German roots is growing; if so, this will help to place the entire phenomenon into a better perspective.

Perhaps more importantly, my heritage could also serve as a counterweight to some less desirable present-day tendencies. I am here thinking, above all, of the ideal of *Bildung* or cultivation, which George Mosse has singled out as the very crux of the German-Jewish heritage. In this late twentieth century (as indeed already in the Germany of the 1930s), the notion tends to be viewed as hopelessly outmoded and bourgeois. But it has remained active for some of us, and one hopes that it can be reactivated in a more universal context. Not of course in its older, often naively idealized, overly aestheticized form, and surely not as the reflection of a supposedly existing state of affairs—but very definitely as an ethical postulate. The continued strength and value of the concept lies in its creatively *temporal* character. Contrasting the all-too-widespread modern proneness to view reality either in terms of chaotic dynamisms or of manipulable staticities, *Bildung* calls for a creative effort of coherent growth, an intelligent marshaling of the flux of time. As against contemporary tendencies literally to wallow in psychological insights into the discontinuity and the threatening fragmentation of the subject (an attitude that reflects ethical fecklessness and *laisser-aller*), *Bildung* would stand out as a volitional effort of personal identification and responsibility: the self, after all, is not a given fact but a demand. And finally, in its expansive openness to dialogue, to the recognition of otherness, *Bildung* counteracts that urge towards ideological reductiveness which is perhaps the most potent expression of the ethical feebleness that besets our age. I do not know whether my commitment to such views is still realistic. All I can say is that it better be.

# The German-Jewish Legacy: A Question of Fate

*Alfred Gottschalk*

"The end of German Jewry has arrived." Those words were spoken by Rabbi Leo Baeck, in 1933, a short time after Adolf Hitler became the leader of Nazi Germany.

And while those words may have brought sudden shock and surprise to a German Jewry whose base was in the large cities of Berlin, Cologne, Hamburg, and Frankfurt, and whose cultural orientation embraced the concept of *Bildung* and a failed effort at interfaith dialogue,[1] they were not so much of a shock to the Jews of Oberwesel.

My Oberwesel (although I have never really thought of it in those terms) was a Rhineland town whose essential claim to an affinity with *Bildung* was its nearness to the community of Bacharach, the setting of Heinrich Heine's famous story, *Der Rabbi von Bacherach*. It was a Jewish community that had never even debated Heine's famous comment about conversion as a passport to civilization. It was a community that did not and would not entertain intermarriage. The only scandals concerned certain Jews, who from the 1850s and 1860s onwards began to disappear to a far-off and crazy place called America.

As a child (I was born in 1930), until I was six or seven, my playmates were mostly Christian, since there was but one other Jewish child of my age in the town. Prior to public school, I attended a Catholic kindergarten run by an order of nuns who showed me inordinate kindness. As hostility toward Jews became increasingly unpleasant under the Nazis, some of these nuns came by our house from time to time to show their concern for the Jewish families. Many of my immediate neighbors were Catholics, and although they knew about Jewish custom and ritual with an intimacy hardly imaginable in today's world, that knowledge did not keep some of them from joining in the burning and the ravaging which marked the destruction of our synagogue and stores in November 1938. It also did not keep them from evicting me, six months earlier, from Oberwesel's public school. On that day a Nazi official suddenly entered our classroom and shouted,

"All Jewish children out." A little girl, Ruth Lichtenstein (who would later survive Auschwitz), and I, the only two Jews in the class, were unable to understand this sudden expulsion and were shouted out of the classroom while jeers of "Christ-killers" and Werner-scourgers" followed us.

We were called "Werner-scourgers" because Oberwesel had been, during the Middle Ages (1287 to be exact), the site of a ritual-murder accusation. For over six centuries the supposed scourging and murder of a little boy, Werner, by Oberwesel's Jews had haunted every Jew in the region.

Little Werner was canonized and in the neighboring town of Bacharach a church was built over his remains, while his memory was kept alive through local catechetical teachings with the story of Werner often enacted.

His purported crucifixion was linked to that of Jesus. "Holy Werner's" Chapel, with its relief sculpture depicting the story, became a tangible and permanent invitation to anti-Jewish sentiment.[2]

The Jewish reaction in Oberwesel was to make certain that we would never use red wine during Passover, because when we opened the door for Elijah we might have to let a non-Jew come in and he might become infuriated at the sight of red wine or "Holy Werner's blood."

The Christian reaction in Oberwesel was to beat me up on Saint Werner's Day, even though neither I nor those who hit me really knew the reason for the beating.

Hence, in Oberwesel, physical closeness and intimate knowledge of Judaism did not generate either the search for a German-Jewish dialogue or the belief that we Jews were simply "German citizens of the Jewish faith." I do not mean to imply that we ever felt less German because of the Werner libel. My own identity as a German Jew was formed as a young boy when I was told that I had been named for my uncle Alfred, who along with his twin brother, Berthold, had been two of the twelve thousand German Jews who died fighting for the "Fatherland" in the First World War. My own grandmother had, at one time, been president of Oberwesel's town council. But certainly the all-pervading intensity of the centuries-old Werner legend had kept our self-consciousness as Jews at the highest possible level.

There was an intensity in this Jewish consciousness which was demonstrated by the Jewish life in our community. A marvelous description of this life has been provided by Hugo Mandelbaum, although his description was meant for Jewish life in southern Germany:

> "The Jewish families of the village were close-knit. They shared each other's joys and sorrows, and a helping hand was readily extended whenever necessary. All the men who were home at the time attended the daily *minyan*. If someone failed to put in an appearance on Shabbath morning he was surely ill, and everyone would visit him. They also felt obligated to pay a visit to anyone who had a guest from outside the village over Shabbath. On these occasions visitors were received in the *gute stube*. It was better furnished and had an aura of dignity and festivity. It was . . . "the home's Shabbath suit."[3]

This comfortable and spiritually beautiful world ended for me on November 10, 1938. As I have written elsewhere, I remember running with my grandfather to the synagogue in Oberwesel in the hours after the great devastation had been visited upon every Jewish community in Germany. It was something the Nazis would call the "Night of Broken Glass," but that Germany's Jews would ultimately refer to as the "November Jewish Pogrom."

There, at the Oberwesel synagogue, I found a blackened, destroyed synagogue interior whose ark was violated and whose *bimah* had been hacked to pieces. My grandfather and I found the sacred scrolls of the Torah in the freezing waters of a nearby brook. They had been desecrated into shreds.

In December 1940, the great Austrian novelist Franz Werfel, newly arrived in the United States, wrote the following words in an *Aufbau* column:

> "I am one of the untold many who had a previous life dissolved in a painful fog: my homeland, my house, my possessions, my family, my profession, and my name. Then it is important to answer the question "what shall we do?" Yet, I can only try and sketch the elements of that other question: "how shall we make sense of any of this?"[4]

For Werfel and for his generation of emigre intellectuals from Hitler's Germany the latter question was paramount. He and his colleagues were the uprooted legacies of the "Weimar Spirit," which like its national, political, and social personification, the Weimar Republic, had been an "idea in search of its realization."

That the idea had succumbed to the demonic spirit of Adolf Hitler only made the dilemma of refugee German-Jewish intellectuals doubly painful. The failure of the Weimar Spirit meant for them an even greater tragedy: the failure of *Bildung* as a way of supporting a German-Jewish dialogue and as a way of "humanizing" the rampant nationalism of German society.

But back to Werfel's first question: "What shall we do?" For my own family, which had emigrated in 1939, this question of practical survival was paramount. We German-Jewish refugees were fish out of our linguistic, economic, and cultural waters. And while the participants in the (by now clearly) one-sided German-Jewish dialogue tried to make sense out of it all in the pages of *Aufbau*, the majority of German-Jewish refugees sought to rebuild the shattered sense of our Jewishness. And because *Aufbau* was written in German, it made a statement to us that our German roots—cultural, linguistic, and historical—were positive elements of our identity. There was no need to jettison them simply because the brown-shirted criminals claimed those similar roots in an illegal and gruesome manner.

If we can in some way define the German-Jewish legacy I imagine we can do it in terms of describing what the German-Jewish refugees brought with them. I would describe it as a sense of "big-heartedness," of refusing to despair even though they had been through the worst. I would further describe it as a work-and-worship ethic where no sacrifice was too great and where the festiveness of the Jewish home was maintained in its highest and most beautiful religious form.

And no, my father did not quote Goethe and we had in place of our obligatory set of great German classics numerous *siddurim* and *machzorim*. In America, during the war years, my father worked on Shabbat. The reason this *shomer Shabbat* (Sabbath observer) worked on the Sabbath was because he was employed in a defense plant. The salary for the day's work went to charity. To work on the Sabbath to help defeat Hitler was a necessity but not one from which he chose to profit. That was part of his German-Jewish legacy.

Although we lived in Brooklyn, my mother and I would travel to Washington Heights on the weekend and visit family. We would exit the subway at 168th Street and walk to 180th Street and Fort Washington Avenue, where our relatives and friends lived. It would sometimes take hours for my mother and me to walk the relatively few blocks because she would stop along the way every few yards to greet people, have a cup of coffee in a cafe, and discuss in German the events which masked the discontinuity of upheaval in her life and theirs: births, deaths, bar mitzvahs, and marriages.

There was an ethnic world in Washington Heights where, as the saying went, "You could tell a Yankee from a Yekke." On the Sabbath the men strolled in formal dress with hats, canes, and umbrellas.

My mother is still a part of this world at eighty-two years of age, although most of it is gone. She and the survivors of the German-Jewish refugee experience have recreated the consciousness of a kind of German-Jewishness but it has an American flavor to it. She and her friends will discuss their *Kaffee und Kuchen* sessions in German, but will discuss their synagogue service in English, because that is the language of the service.

And it is to American Judaism that, I believe, the German-Jewish legacy has contributed in a most significant way. I can address myself specifically to Reform Judaism, where not long ago the four heads of our movement were all German-Jewish refugees.

In the last analysis I would say that the German-Jews brought a certain style to the Reform movement, a way of looking at the value of something. Because of our experience as refugees, we brought a certain humanizing effect to Reform and American Judaism as well as a distaste for intellectual shabbiness and flashiness, so characteristic of the American style. Perhaps that is an extension of the *Bildung* concept.

Hans Steinitz, the former editor of *Aufbau*, has written that German-Jewish refugees are part of a *Schicksalsgemeinschaft*, "a community of fate." Indeed, that was the designation which united the diverse strands of German-Jewish life during the darkest hour of its existence under National Socialism and replaced the need for *Bildung*.

In the five decades since the end of German-Jewish life and its dependence on the notion of *Bildung* it has become apparent that all Jews are part of this *Schicksalsgemeinschaft* and that we all share in that sense of community and in its fate. That realization may be German Jewry's only lasting contribution and its most important.

## Notes

1. For an excellent discussion of the effort at interfaith dialogue in the Weimar Republic, see Paul R. Mendes-Flohr, "Ambivalent Dialogue: Jewish-Christian Theological Encounter in the Weimar Republic," in Otto Dov Kulka and Paul R. Mendes-Flohr, *Judaism and Christianity under the Impact of National Socialism* (Jerusalem, 1987), pp. 99 – 132.

2. For a description of the Werner legend, see Willehad Paul Eckert, "Der Verhaeltnis von Christen und Juden in Mittelalter und Humanismus," in *Monumenta Judaica. 2000 Jahre Geschichte und Kultur der Juden am Rhein* (Cologne, 1984), pp. 158 – 159.

3. Hugo Mandelbaum, *Jewish Life in the Village Communities of Southern Germany* (New York, 1985), p. 48. For a highly interesting analysis of relations between Catholics and Jews in a southeastern German village, see Alice Goldstein, *Determinants of Change and Response Among Jews and Catholics in a Nineteenth-Century German Village* (New York, 1984).

4. Franz Werfel, "Unser Weg geht weiter," in Will Schaber (ed.), *Aufbau. Dokumente einer Kultur in Exil* (New York, 1972), pp. 265 – 269.

# The Elusive German-Jewish Heritage in America

*W. Gunther Plaut*

When German Jews awoke on the tenth of November 1938 their lives had been radically and irretrievably changed. Their nearly two-thousand-year-long sojourn in Germany had come to an end. From here on theirs was the age-old cry: *Rette sich wer kann!* Jews scrambled for the exits, only to find few countries willing to receive them. But some still managed (or had already managed) to come to the Western Hemisphere and primarily to the United States. I was amongst them.

This article will attempt to discuss two questions: one, is there still a recognizable German-Jewish heritage in America?[1] and two, what are its components?

I

In 1988, fifty years after *Kristallnacht*, the traces of German-Jewish influence on the American continent are no longer as clearly visible as they had been fifty years before that seminal event. In 1888 there were three identifiable Jewish communities: the Sephardim on the East Coast; the Germans spread throughout the country all the way to the West Coast; and the East Europeans now arriving in ever larger numbers and for the time being preponderantly concentrated in the East. There was no question then that the German Jews were dominant; they had already "arrived" and had joined the middle class; and their rabbis were the spokesmen for all of American Jewry. Their local institutions were highly developed, their national organizations firmly in place, and their thought patterns clear transplants from the old country. They were mostly (though not exclusively) Reform Jews; integration into the American pattern was a basic aspect of their striving. The way in which they described themselves provides a key to their goal: while other ethnic groups would put their ethnicity first and their American identity second (German-American, Spanish-American, Irish-American) Jews from Germany called themselves American Hebrews and not Hebrew Americans—a direct mirror of their past. For in the land of the Kaiser too they had been *deutsche Juden* and not *juedische Deutsche.*[2]

Today the role and identity of these Jews have become nearly invisible, and without the events of *Kristallnacht* and the attendant emigration of German Jews to America they would have become an historical footnote only. Yet they are still there, though one needs to look rather closely to detect them. Two contrasting incidents will illustrate this point.

I remember the day when the Beth Ha-Tefutsoth museum was dedicated on the campus of Tel Aviv University and Abba Kovner and Nahum Goldmann cut the ribbon. Goldmann, of course, was the *spiritus rector* of and prime fund-raiser for the institution, and when I had once asked him how he would define his own cultural identity he had answered without hesitation: "German." But it was Kovner, the East European Jew, who was responsible for the content of the Diaspora Museum. It was evident then (though this may have changed since) that in Kovner's view German Jews had played no worthy role in European Jewish history and that in America too the likes of Isaac M. Wise and David Einhorn had paled before the Lubavitcher rebbe. No mention of the fact that the chief religious movements of our time—from Reform to Conservatism to Orthodoxy, all the way to the Agudah—had been invented and shaped by German Jews; and though of course Herzl, Wolffsohn, and Shapira received their due as founders of political Zionism, they appeared disconnected from their own background.

Contrast this with the year 1983 in America. In Los Angeles, at the annual convention of the Central Conference of American Rabbis, a German-born president (Herman Schaalman) was yielding the gavel to another president of like origin (the writer); and at the same time the presidents of the other three Reform institutions were all German-born as well: the Union of American Hebrew Congregations (Alexander Schindler), the Hebrew Union College – Jewish Institute of Religion (Alfred Gottschalk), and the World Union for Progressive Judaism (Gerard Daniel). Since that time the president of the Jewish Theological Seminary (Ismar Schorsch) has also joined this surprising constellation of German-Jewish influence. One might be tempted to apply the well-known words coined in a different context: *anachnu ka'n*, we are still here.[3]

Was this mere coincidence? Possibly, yet the confluence was startling enough to make one wonder. Perhaps there is a heritage which exerted a motivating influence and which in this late moment surfaced long enough to pose the question. But while its traces are still there, its characteristics are like covered tracks which await the discovery of the searcher.

II

The nature of German-Jewish influence has been described in terms of *Bildung*, a view of priorities which gave to education in the broadest sense a place of primacy. To be called *ein gebildeter Mensch* was a greater accolade than being described as rich or successful. A German doctor or lawyer was not just a good specialist in his field; he was expected also to be *gebildet*, and usually was. He would be conversant with Homer and Vergil, and would know the difference between Aristotle, Archimedes, and Aristophanes. He would properly quote the date and significance of the French Revolution. He would have studied Racine and Shakespeare along with Germany's own poets and thinkers. (To be sure, he would also think that Germany was the heart of the world, but that kind of self-perception was paralleled in other nations.) In addition, he would have a sense of order and obligation. In this respect the Jewish heritage with its emphasis on *mitzvah* blended perfectly with its German counterpart, as Moses Mendelssohn had tried to show long ago. Not surprisingly, almost all German rabbis obtained their doctorate in some field before they assumed congregational posts.

One is therefore safe in describing German-Jewish influence abroad by this kind of cultural apprehension. In Israel, the *yekkes*, though they have all but disappeared in person, survive as popular characters who are ridiculed and admired at the same time. While their pedantry gives rise to jokes, their constancy is held up as a worthy goal worthy of imitation.

And in America? Here too the traces are all but gone, but the aforementioned confluence of "presidential" office holders gives rise to a fascinating inquiry: What was it that propelled these men—who after all were but a few brands plucked from the fire—to their positions of leadership in their new environment? The answer is not as easy as it might appear, for several of the men, while born in Germany, were not raised there. Yet they too give evidence of this German-Jewish inheritance.

A hundred years ago the question did not arise, for there was a predominantly German constituency in our congregations. In a few of them, as in Baltimore, the rabbi[4] had to be able to preach some of his sermons in the German language, and his listeners would likely be less patient with bad German than with faulty English. Their culture was still German-based, and in a number of communities such fraternal orders as B'nai B'rith and the Free Sons of Israel conducted their meetings in German. Isaac M. Wise, Bohemian born and German speaking, had come to America in the late 1840s, and when in Cincinnati he began to plan a national journal he decided on a German version (*Die Deborah*) and an English one (*The American Israelite*). Both publications were replete with *Bildung*—literary references and academic discussions and a pervasive belief that knowledge and moral education would bring about not only a higher level of Jewish commitment but also a readier integration with and acceptance by the gentiles, for they would see the Jews in their true role: as a light unto the nations. In many ways David Einhorn and his two sons-in-law, Emil G. Hirsch and Kaufmann Kohler,[5] put their stamp on what has become known as "classical Reform," with its emphasis on the spirit rather than the form of Jewish existence.

But in the 1930s, when the first five refugees from Nazi Germany arrived at Hebrew Union College, the constituencies of their future congregations had already changed drastically. Men of East European background were now in the majority and the control of the old German founders and their offspring had already disappeared or waned drastically. Yet what these five men brought with them still had relevance in America and would afford them and those who followed them from Germany in the next few years a disproportionate influence on American Reform and the larger environment.

What then precisely did they bring with them? The answer I propose is two-pronged: those who had gone to school in the old country had been shaped by their high school education; and they, as well as those who had never attended a German educational institution, had been raised with a set of identifiable expectations.

I mention the German high school and not the university, for the latter (as I can testify from my own experience) served as a trade-and-technical training institution rather than one which would create and foster a broad appreciation of the liberal arts. These were taught in high school, which began at an age when in America students would go into grade five of their elementary schools and lasted for nine years of a six-day school week. High school ended with comprehensive written and oral examinations in all subjects and proffered the so-called *Abitur*, or "going away" diploma. Possession of the *Abitur* meant readiness to go into law school or medical school or whatever further training one chose to pursue. On the average, we were nineteen years old when we graduated and had been exposed to a wide spectrum of knowledge. Its details depended on which of the three major types of institutions one had attended: the old-type *Gymnasium*, which specialized in the classical humanities and taught its students a thorough knowledge of Latin, Greek, and ancient history; the *Realgymnasium*, which combined the classics with some natural sciences; and the *Oberrealshule*, which stressed the sciences as well as a knowledge of French and English. All three school systems had extensive courses in literature and history, and in my time they still insisted that memorization was a worthwhile part of education, for it would allow a person to cite many literary passages from memory and lace one's speech with them. That practice extended also to the biblical text. In the rabbinical seminary over which Rabbi Leo Baeck presided,[6] we had to learn fifty Hebrew psalms by heart, as part of our first-level requirements.

Teaching followed a rigorous schedule with lots of demanding homework. All subjects save athletics were academic, and once one had chosen the type of high school to which to go (a choice usually made by parents for their children) all courses were compulsory. Failure in any two of them meant that the whole year had to be repeated. The school day lasted from eight until two, and on Saturdays until one o'clock, with a twenty-minute break at ten o'clock to consume the "second breakfast" one had brought along.[7]

I mention these details because my education outside the home was fashioned in high school.[8] All five of us carried this background to the United States. It meant, *inter alia*, a respect for ideas and the conviction that education had salvational aspects.[9] To be sure, the Nazis had shown that this was not enough, for they had turned the "land of poets and thinkers" (as the Germans liked to call themselves) into an obscene caricature of the ideal. Education could be perverted, they proved, unless it had its moral component. For us this was provided by our own Jewish tradition.[10]

But what of those leaders who had been born in Germany but had not gone to school there? They shared with us a home background in which there were certain standards and expectations. They might not have been to a German school but they were taught by parents who brought up their children in an atmosphere where *Bildung* had a primary place. Add to this the "immigrant factor"—the added incentive to make it in the new world—and you have the ingredients which may help to explain the role which German Jews played in their new environment. Quite aside from rabbis who achieved positions of leadership there were scores of German-born academics who contributed significantly to American thought and the national polity, from the likes of Kurt Lewin, Hans Jonas, and Hannah Arendt to Bruno Bettelheim and Henry Kissinger.

In this way the final destruction of German Jewry which was set in motion on *Kristallnacht* made its unplanned contribution to the New World. Hopefully history will judge it to have been worthy of the opportunity. As for me, my own fate was inextricably intertwined with the event. For during that very day when in Berlin my father was hiding from the enemy, my bride and I—not knowing of the events in Germany—were married in Cincinnati.

## Notes

1. The article will use the terms "America" and "American" as a shortcut, to stand for "North America" and "North American."

2. In part this may also be a reflection of the fact that Jews saw themselves not so much as an ethnic but as a religious group and compared themselves to American Protestants and American Catholics. This self-perception tended to reinforce the integrationist thrust of their cultural and religious life.

3. I might cite another example. In 1961/1962 in Toronto—a city where only a handful of German Jews were to be found—the rabbis of the leading Orthodox and Reform congregations were German-born, and so were the rabbinical heads of two of the four major Conservative synagogues.

4. He was David Philipson, member of the first graduating class at Hebrew Union College.

5. Einhorn began his American rabbinate in Baltimore, in the 1850s, and his German-language prayer book *Olath Tamid* became the model for the *Union Prayer Book*. Hirsch was rabbi at Temple Sinai in Chicago, a bold social reformer as well as a brilliant and erudite preacher. Kohler became president of Hebrew Union College and the author of the widely read *Jewish Theology*.

6. Originally called Hochschule fuer die Wissenschaft des Judentums, it was later (at the behest of the Nazis) renamed more modestly Lehranstalt.

7. One of the four Jewish students who graduated with me was Orthodox, and he was excused from writing on Shabbat and could take his examinations at another time. This, of course, was the era of the Weimar Republic (we graduated in 1930); shortly after the Nazis came to power all Jewish students were shifted to Jewish schools.

8. In law school I learned very little and like most other students attended only those courses which either were seminars or had outstanding teachers. I was prepared for my examinations by a professional *Repetitor* who drilled his charges with subject matters tailored to the questions that would be asked. Law school was, for me, a chance to do what I wanted; the basics of *Bildung* were provided by high school and home.

9. This idea had strong antecedents in Jewish tradition, best exemplified by the rabbi who, upon visiting a schoolhouse, declared its teachers and children to be the true guardians of the city.

10. Readers may wish to read more about this whole subject in George Mosse's *German Jews Beyond Judaism* (1985).

# A Precious Legacy

*Joseph B. Maier*

*Besitz* and *Bildung* defined the spirit of modern German Jewry. With some important modifications, to be sure, they may be said to define the legacy of German Jews here and now. Scion of a long line of rabbinical families, I believe as firmly as I did in September 1933, when I escaped from Nazi Germany, in the synthesis of Western Judaism, the proposition that Western civilization owes as much to its Jewish heritage as the emancipation of the Jews owes to the blessings of Western civilization.

Illustrative of the dominant mood among the great majority of German Jews from the time of Enlightenment and emancipation to the eve of their destruction are the words of Abraham Geiger (1810 – 1874), pioneer of the Reform movement: "Jerusalem is an honorable memory from the past, the cradle of the religion; it is no hope for the future, not the place from which new life will be developed. . . . honor to Jerusalem and its memory, as to all the great dead; but let us not disturb its rest!" The same mood, the same faith in the spirit of classical German literature and philosophy, found expression in the words of Geiger's great opponent, Samson Raphael Hirsch (1808 – 1888), leader of Neo-Orthodoxy, spoken in commemoration of the centennial of Schiller's birth, November 10, 1759:

> It was man, the most human in man and the most divine in man, that found its proper expression in Schiller. . . . The fact that universal homage is here being paid to the spirit, in particular to the morally ennobling spirit of Schiller, that fact, my friends, would have been greeted by our Sages as the dawn of the day when all men will arise and let the blindfolds fall from their eyes.

The intimate passion that the relation to things German assumed for the Jews is, as Gershom Scholem has pointed out, connected with the specific historical hour in which it was born. The timing was fortunate. When the Jews turned from their medieval state to the new era, the overwhelming majority of them lived in Germany, Austria-Hungary, and Eastern Europe. Due to prevailing geographic, political, and linguistic conditions, therefore, it was German culture the Jews first encountered on their road to the West. Moreover, says Scholem,

> the encounter occurred precisely at the moment when that culture had reached one of its most fruitful turning points. It was the zenith of Germany's bourgeois era. One can say that it was a happy hour when the newly awakened creativity of the Jews, which was to assume such impressive forms after 1780, impinged precisely on the zenith of a great creative period of the German people, a period producing an image of things German that, up to 1940, and among very broad classes of people, was to remain unshaken, even by many bitter and later most bitter experiences. For the Jews this amalgamation of a great historical hour was defined and symbolized by the names of Lessing and Schiller, and in its intensity and scope it has no parallel in the encounters of the Jews with other European peoples. Due to this encounter, the first on the Jews' way to the West, because of this new image, a high luster fell on all things German. Even today, after so much blood and so many tears, we cannot say that it was *only* a deceptive luster. It was more: it contained elements of great fruitfulness and the stimulus to significant developments.

It may be hard to calculate precisely the importance of the German classics in the formation of Jewish attitudes to Germany. I was brought up to look upon "our poets and thinkers" as the spokesmen for pure humanity, the bearers of the highest ideals of mankind. Indeed, my encounter with them, it would seem to me in retrospect, was more real than my encounter with actual Germans, including my classmates in the *Gymnasium*. To people like my father, an Orthodox rabbi, who saw in the tenets of Western humanism points of contact with Jewish monotheism and the social ideas of Jewish law and lore, Lessing, Schiller, Kant, and Goethe provided welcome confirmation of the rightness and truth of Judaism. To put it in Hermann Cohen's words: "German classicism had this sense of world citizenship in common with Prophetic Judaism; its historical root lies in the Messianic idea of God."

The year 1935 was decisive for me. Columbia University had just awarded me an M.A. for a thesis on "The Social and Political Ideas of Lessing." I joined the German-Jewish Club (later New World Club), publisher of *Aufbau* (which still carries the Midrash column on the portion of the week that I started more than a generation ago, in addition to articles on Jewish philosophy and literature), and was asked to deliver the principal address at the unveiling of the Heinrich Heine monument in front of the courthouse in the Bronx. Paraphrasing Heine's prophetic pronouncements in his essay "On the History of Religion and Philosophy in Germany," I spoke with uninhibited passion about the universal importance of classical German literature and philosophy. Fate, I said, had destined us former German Jews to be the faithful keepers of a precious legacy, a powerful ally in our struggle against Nazism. I don't remember how many friends and/or enemies I made with my speech. It did, however, earn me the attention and respect of two people who have since played major roles in my life: a bright young woman named Alice Heumann, who two years later became my wife, and her boss, Professor Max Horkheimer, founder and head of the Frankfurt School, thenceforth my fatherly friend and teacher, who had just established the Institute of Social Research at Columbia University and gave me my first job—a job in the rarified atmosphere of his intellectual hothouse.

Of all the waves of immigration to the United States, ours was one of the smallest, comprising no more that 140,000, but its impact on American culture was, we may say with due modesty, probably the greatest. These immigrants were mostly Jewish. Others were not, but like Thomas Mann, his brother Heinrich Mann, Paul Tillich, Bert Brecht, to name only a few of the most famous, were close friends of Jews and/or married to Jews. They had hardly arrived, when, in the words of a professional observer writing in *Commentary*,

> They began to exert an influence far disproportionate to their numbers on American science, social thought, the arts, the academy, and intellectual discourse in general. They quickly rose to prominent positions as writers and professors, fashion and news photographers, psychoanalysts, movie directors, orchestra conductors, and eventually presidents of academic associations. Remarkably, in many of the fields they entered they quickly began to produce cultural products that stood out as representative expressions of the American spirit and style.

Yes, indeed, this sums up what happened to one part of the German-Jewish legacy in the American context. It had found a home in this country.

There is no question in my mind that this legacy will continue to be as important to the future of a democratic American society, and the future of American Jewry, as it has been to their defense in the past. My long apprenticeship with the principals of the Frankfurt School during their years on Morningside Heights, with Max Horkheimer,

Friedrich Pollock, Theodor W. Adorno, Herbert Marcuse, Leo Lowenthal, Erich Fromm, Henryk Grossmann, Franz Neumann, Otto
Kirchheimer, while at the same time pursuing graduate studies in philosophy and sociology with the luminaries in these fields at Columbia,
decisively shaped and sharpened my sense of the special role of the
academic professions as practitioners and guardians of free inquiry
and circumspect judgment, vigorous critics and resolute defenders of
democratic institutions and values. When the time came to do their job
in the war against the Nazis, Marcuse, Neumann, and Kirchheimer
joined the OSS, even as Lowenthal served with the Voice of America
and I with the OWI, first in New York, from D-Day until after VJ-Day
in London, and finally in the Office of the U.S. Chief of Counsel at the
Nuremberg trials against the major war criminals.

Of the many scholarly projects the American Jewish Committee
sponsored in the interest of American Jewry, none had made a
stronger impact than the *Studies in Prejudice* series conceived and
directed by Horkheimer. *The Authoritarian Personality* volume was
certainly a special event in American social science, occasioning further research on the psychological and political causes of anti-
Semitism and fascism and providing the stimulus for a veritable ava-
lanche of secondary literature, the like of which was unequaled before
or since. So highly, indeed, did the American Jewish Committee es-
teem Horkheimer's scholarly resourcefulness and political savvy that,
after his return to Germany to reopen and direct once again the famous Institut fuer Sozialforschung in addition to assuming the presi-
dency of the University of Frankfurt, it made him its principal on-the-
spot adviser on a whole number of educational and political initiatives
in the Federal Republic. He continued in that capacity almost until his
death in 1973.

Regarding our group's contribution to the religious life and learning
of Jews in America, we can say that its members are now among the
leaders in all branches of American Judaism, even as their forebears
were the inventors of Reform and Neo-Orthodoxy. Whatever their
ideological differences, the spark of the *Hasidei Ashkenaz*, the Devout
of Germany of the Middle Ages, continues to be discernible in their
peculiar combination of love of God, devotion to learning, and sense
of social service. In colleges and universities as well as rabbinical seminaries throughout the land, they continue to add to German Jewry's

greatest achievement and proudest legacy—the *Wissenschaft des Judentums*, the Science of Judaism, the creative merging of enthusiasm for the timeless message of Judaism with critical scholarly investigation of its changing historical forms. It was this synthesis of Western Judaism that has facilitated the transformation of the traditional into the modern rabbi, university educated in philosophy, history, Semitic philology or classical languages, in addition to his rabbinal training. We might say that the German *Rabbiner Doktor* was the model for the professor at the Jewish theological seminaries, if not the rabbi in all branches of American Judaism.

What is alive and dead in the German-Jewish legacy? Whatever the differences among them, whether liberal or orthodox, Zionist or not, German Jews shared an essentially common ethos. Principal ingredients of that ethos were a firm belief in Western values, a strong sense of shared destiny, and a steadfast refusal to return to the ghetto or to betray the faith of their fathers. They continue to share that ethos. To be sure, they remember the past, but they see their future only in America or Israel. They have become acculturated, not assimilated, in America and in Israel. Kurt Blumenfeld, an early leader and highly articulate spokesman of German Zionism, confirmed to me on more than one occasion that he was *ein Zionist von Goethes Gnaden*, "a Zionist by the grace of Goethe." He candidly described a fact which he felt no need to change or feel ashamed of.

Meanwhile I have lived and been schooled in America over half a century, long enough to recognize that there has always been something brittle and painfully deceptive about the notion of *Bildung* as a refining, moral-character-molding, ennobling and redemptive force. It was, no doubt, an important factor in the Jewish belief in mankind, but at the same time it was the occasion for idealistic self-deceptions and delusions, engendered by the relations of the Jews with the small sector of the *gebildete* German bourgeoisie. It gave rise to a dubious *Bildungsjudentum* whose language began to sound hollow as soon as it had taken off.

For some of us who were brought up in the belief that Latin and Greek, if not Hebrew, were the unique garments of the truth, it may be difficult to appreciate that our classical education was not, as they say in the vernacular, "all it's cracked up to be." It never was, nor will it be, the exclusive guide to a life of universal bliss and peace. I have learned to look at such claims with a jaundiced eye. I observed that less than the whole truth can be revealed as easily in Latin and Greek, even Hebrew, as in German and English. I remember that *Bildung* has often led to a display of *Bildungsduenkel*, contempt for those who are poor and lack *Bildung*. I have come to note that it is so much more becoming and attractive to carry one's learning lightly, and forgo the compulsive invocation of Goethe and Schiller. Especially after a bitter discovery: "We know now that a man can read Goethe and Rilke in the evening, that he can play Bach and Schubert, and go to his day's work at Auschwitz in the morning" (George Steiner).

Of course, I do not mean to suggest that the liberal arts are no good and of no earthly use to a liberal democratic society. The devil, too, may be schooled in the liberal arts, even render the Horst-Wessel-Lied in fine Greek verse, and be quick to quote Scripture. But that's no reason to abandon either Scripture or the humanities. A free society thrives on free inquiry, diversity, and vigorous debate of viewpoints. Important skills and knowledge are generated on the playgrounds of the spirit. The humanities help to strengthen the societal enterprise, even as in turn it will be inclined to strengthen the humanities. Of course, continued institutional changes must be made to strengthen the stake of all groups in our liberal democracy. Yet, with this said and done, I fully share Sidney Hook's conviction:

> In our pluralistic, multi-ethnic, uncoordinated society, no institutional changes of themselves will develop that bond of community we need to sustain our nation in times of crisis without a prologued schooling in the history of our free society, its martyrology, and its national tradition. In the decades of mass immigration in the 19th and 20th centuries that bond was sharply forged by the American public school. What I propose is that our schools, reinforced by our colleges and universities, do the same job today in a more intelligent, critical and sophisticated way.

Ever since the Holocaust and the emergence of the State of Israel, American Jews, including those from Central Europe, have been reaching toward a more explicit and meaningful Jewish identity. For our particular group that has meant shedding some elements of its heritage—its inordinate capacity for self-delusion and its thoughtless equation of the spiritual and cultural with the unpolitical. In foreign policy, we owe it to ourselves, to American Jewry, to America, to ally ourselves with groups opposing groups who are pro – Third World and anti-American, pro-PLO and anti-Israel. In domestic policy, we owe it no less to ourselves to become concerned with small beginnings, such as the tendencies at Stanford and other universities and colleges to banish Western Civilization courses from the core curriculum as racist, sexist compendia of "European-Western and male bias" and institute instead courses with required reading of "works by women, minorities and persons of color." Maybe I'm too sensitive, but it causes me great distress when I see and hear hundreds of students joyfully chant, "Hey hey, ho ho, Western culture's got to go."

But let us take heart. We must not unreflectively think in the categories of friend and foe, view the political and ideological rival or opponent as our mortal enemy. Not in America. The democratic ideal is a composite of many images, including some I may not like. As an American citizen and educator, at any rate, I am committed to foster, by precept and practice, those habits of thought and conduct which assure the perpetuation and survival of this democracy.

# Emancipation and Post-Emancipation Identities: Reflections on On-Going Research

*Herbert A. Strauss*

One cannot reflect on the German-Jewish legacy in America without being conscious of the basic *avelut* of our generation of survivors. The assignment has a positive ring: "legacy," says the Oxford Dictionary, "II, 2: fig., anything handed down by an ancestor or predecessor F(1586)." One cannot celebrate this legacy without "playing marches for conquered and slain persons . . . Battles are lost in the same spirit in which they are won," in Walt Whitman's words.

Fifty years ago, the final night descended on Jewish culture in Germany and Austria. Of institutes of higher Jewish learning, only the Lehranstalt (Hochschule) fuer die Wissenschaft des Judentums, presided over by Rabbi Leo Baeck in Berlin's Artilleriestrasse 14, was allowed to endure until June 1942. It wrote the last chapter of unbowed and unshaken *Wissenschaft des Judentums*; a fact widely unknown and unrecorded to this day.[1] On a moral plane, the books do not balance between culture passed on and humankind destroyed. Still, between 450,000 and 500,000 German-speaking Jews managed to escape from Germany, Austria, and Czechoslovakia before the *Shoah* began. They carried with them one of the most articulate forms of modern Jewish culture. Today, the generation that saved what could be saved has almost passed from the scene. The Jewish émigré culture they created in the major countries of their dispersion is fast disappearing. Buber's injunction that Judaism does not have a history, that it *is* history, lives on in the minds of the survivors. Reconstructing a legacy destroyed asserts the legacy for the future.

## II

To reflect on the legacy of German Jewry (I shall confine myself to Jews from Germany proper)[2] means asking about the significance of Judaism in the late phase of emancipation for post-Holocaust Jewish consciousness in the period of Israel's statehood.

American public attitudes towards ethnic strains in American life have changed considerably since I arrived penniless at a less than memorable pier of the city of Hoboken in 1946. It is easily forgotten today, as verbal patterns of Jewish national identification pace signs of cultural debilitation, that the imperatives of the "Anglo-Saxon superiority" and "melting-pot" theories had been the dominant force behind the "Americanization" paradigms of immigrant and minority life, including the Jewish immigrant minority. The polls right up to the late 1940s suggest that American Jewish perceptions of widespread anti-Jewish stereotypes were not unrealistic. Restrictionism in immigration law and practice reflected not only the attitudes of congressional committees dominated by senior Southern congressmen, but also of public opinion. A bill to admit Jewish refugee children outside the quota (Wagner-Rogers Bill, 1938 – 1939) died in committee, lest its reporting to the floor might decrease the number of quota immigrants admitted. By now, this story has been told and retold.[3] The most comprehensive study of refugee immigration ever undertaken by a broad spectrum of immigrant aid organizations conveys much of the friction under which Jewish immigrants from Germany labored—the urge, ideological as much as tactical, to slough off the edges of foreignness and make them "fit in."[4] The literature and practice of Jewish social work for "refugees"—post-Depression universalism and social radicalism imposed on a Jewish ethnic base—conveyed the message.

German Jews responded at several levels to this situation. Economically, linguistically, in dress, leisure time, reading habits, the liberal loyalties and identities of the Roosevelt period—these lower middle and middle classes reached prior social levels thanks to the war economy and the postwar boom, even if the higher rites of baseball had to be acquired through the children. First-generation refugees responded in middle-class ways. If Jewish immigration is perceived as the immigration of Jews, i.e., persons professing the Jewish religion or persecuted on account of Jewish ancestry, one facet of the legacy is revealed: a Jewish subculture at mature stages of postindustrial re-orientation had anticipated the turn to a service society in the Western world, and had nurtured a professional, university-trained class and world-level artists and intellectuals. Approximately four-fifths of the scholars and artists meeting the high standards for inclusion in the *International*

*Biographical Dictionary of Central European Emigrés 1933 – 1945* were Jewish or had Jewish "backgrounds."[5] Their significance for Jews in America was obvious if hard to quantify: it ranged from the "Einstein-syndrome" in the public relations efforts of numerous Jewish causes, including good will for Israel, to being the first Jewish appointments in colleges and universities that used to be *"judenrein"* as a matter of agreed prejudice. There were numerous such "secondary effects" derived from the primary set of events—having been persecuted as a Jew in Germany. Research in this field, carried on since 1983 at the Zentrum fuer Antisemitismusforschung in Berlin, Germany, will supplement on an international level the pioneering studies produced in this country during the last two decades.[6]

Today, the not infrequently hostile anti-Jewish animus of the actual period of arrival has given way to mellow reappraisals of this Jewish group as "Hitler's gift to the country." Three out of every four prominent artists and scientists included in the selected sample of the *Biographical Dictionary* and persecuted for "Jewish background" by the Third Reich professed the Jewish religion.

German Jewry in emigration did not consist of a *Who's Who* group of professionals. When World War II broke out, whoever could had emigrated, a cross-section of the community, including most of its religious and lay leaders. They transferred their communal structure, to an astonishing extent, to such major countries of settlement as Great Britain, the United States, Latin America, and, to some extent, Palestine. German Jewry had never been monolithic in any aspect of its legal position, culture, religious orientation, politics, population, or any other area. It represented a plural world of differences. About 100,000 of the 500,000 Jews living in Germany in 1933 had been immigrants, primarily from Eastern Europe, not including Jews originating in the formerly Polish, then Prussian and German, eastern border areas. The large majority of Jews in Germany had been concentrated in cities; yet a sizable percentage were removed only by a generation or two from their original rural habitats, and those rural areas, especially in southern, and northwestern Germany or in Hesse, retained a strong Jewish flavor of their own. Culturally and religiously, Jews had shared Germany's double cultural pressures: rural Jews and Jews in Eastern Europe contributed the vitality of a communitarian folk frontier to the urbanizing and cosmopolitan dynamics of the cities. Immigration from abroad, and *Binnenwanderung* (migration within a country) within, paced ever-renewed integration and upward educational and cultural mobility. The tensions so created were certainly not unique to German Jewry alone: they occurred (and occur) wherever peripherally modernized groups are attracted by post-folk civilizations and social subsystems. But Germany was different from France or England because of the intensely nationalistic environment in which these exchanges took place after 1871, and because of the extent and thus centrality of these processes for Jewish identity.

Thus, the more the distorted stereotype of German-Jewish culture dims into history and memory and loses its usefulness as a counter-symbol, to ban what keeps tempting us in ourselves, the more clearly emerges its paradigmatic value for the paradoxes of the present. By the grace of its peculiar polarities, it created viable Jewish identities and embodied them in a structure of public activities filled with the tensions of Jewish life. Their majority self-understanding as German citizens of the Jewish faith reflected not only their never-ending struggle for full civic and political equality; it also demanded that Jews in Germany remove the repressions imposed on them by their mono-nationalistic environment as trustees of Jewish tradition and existence. The facile image of the German Jew barely restrained from jumping into the baptismal font, however much truth there was in it for some, missed the essential quality of this late-emancipation community. When the Third Reich threw Jews in Germany back on their Jewish existence—identity is the present fad word—German Jews had long begun the process of casting themselves as an ethnic community, whatever the words used at the time to describe their communal realities. The implications of this legacy for the changed circumstances of American Jewish culture are well worth contemplating.

### III

The last chapter in the history of German-Jewish culture was written in emigration, and émigré culture, thus the methodological axiom of migration history, embodies an encounter between the old and the new. Research concerning the impact of individuals and groups of Jewish professionals—scholars, artists, scientists, engineers, doctors, architects, writers, etc.—on their countries of settlement, and vice versa, has been given primary attention, for a variety of scholarly and political motives. The social history and, above all, the Jewish communal history of the about 278,000 Jews who managed to leave Germany and escape the *Shoah*, including about 132,000 Jews who arrived here before World War II, is still inadequately known.[7]

On one level, the network of organizations German Jews set up in the United States and other major countries of resettlement belongs in the context of immigration history everywhere and in all epochs: they express not only the minority consciousness of immigrants in a foreign country, but serve also as launching pads for the acculturation process of successive generations. For the present context, however, it is not the form that is of interest here, but the contents: here, a community had been forced to migrate, and had been able to reproduce the quality of its communal history almost in its entirety. Its ethnicity was not imposed by its immigrant status; it revealed its original ethnic quality.

On the religious level, all directions except extreme *Reformgemeinde* were represented. At one point, over thirty immigrant congregations gave about 40,000 members a religious home in New York City alone. For many congregants, this was sacred ethnicity, proof of the strong communal cohesion and *Lebenswelt* of many rural and regional *minhagim* and *nigunim*. For many rabbis, acculturation meant joining the tradition of high-level teaching of Judaism to new concepts of synagogal social service, interfaith work, and congregational sociability—sisterhoods had been unknown in Europe, although religious instruction for children had been considerably more continuous. Rabbis made significant contributions to Jewish political, denominational, and rabbinical life—many continued publishing as they had been wont to do as *Rabbiner Doktors* in Germany. Major efforts went into social services, in part on a nondenominational basis. German *Wiedergutmachung* (restitution) payments and the Great Society program of the 1960s permitted considerable expansion in developing a model social-service system further. Numerous Jewish social and political groups reproduced the organizational patterns of the homeland, faithfully and at times with tinges of absurdity. The most representative (and at times most literary) émigré weekly appeared in New York, in the German language, promoting American patriotism for the war effort. A social service agency serving concentration camp survivors claiming compensation from the German government employed over 200 lawyers and secretaries at its peak. One international research organization, the Leo Baeck Institute, succeeded in placing German-Jewish history of the pre-Hitler period on the agenda of international scholarship, while another, the Research Foundation for Jewish Immigration, began research on Jewish (and other) emigration and resettlement from German-speaking Central Europe in cooperation with scholarly institutes in other countries. A central coordinating agency of German-Jewish émigré organizations in the United States, affiliated with a world-wide Council of Jews from Germany, proved very effective not only in articulating political and intellectual issues but, for several decades during its peak, in functioning as an international representation and lobby in Bonn, Washington, and other centers of postwar Jewish politics. It continued the Reichsvertretung der Juden in Deutschland in a free political atmosphere, realizing a design of representation that was denied to Jews in Germany to the very end.

Space limits even this entirely inadequate enumeration of a subject now being researched in several ongoing projects.[8] Some of the organizations listed above have gone the way of other immigrant organizations when the founders had faded away. Others have refined their purposes and maintained distinct functions within larger American or American Jewish systems. Still others have merged with parallel groups or attracted new members giving new directions. The legacy it leaves behind will emerge as differentiated as the community that created it.

The process is about to be completed: a mature Jewish culture of the emancipation period found that the systems of meaning it had created, in conformity or protest, faced the supreme test of uprooting and resettlement and demonstrated its existential and intellectual vigor precisely in its displacement. For the long run, some shortcomings also emerge clearly: the last phase of German-Jewish scholarship or theological thought was transmitted also, even though not primarily, with the help of émigré scholars or theologians, not by the émigré congregations: an attempt to establish a Lehrhaus at a German-Jewish congregation foundered on the rock of German-Jewish and American Jewish eclecticism. Outside of Hebrew Union College, American-Jewish theological institutes proved less hospitable to Wissenschaft des Judentums than, say, Hebrew—or, for that matter and at a later stage—Brandeis University. German-Jewish émigré institutions have, on the whole, failed to share the concern with the *Shoah* that has moved our colleagues here and abroad. Living in an organizationally mature Jewish society, we have not sufficiently insisted on better training for Jewish communal functionaries, especially in the field of Jewish learning and international relations, have not bequeathed enough of our experience and training. But we are leaving the insight that even in its supreme hour of need, under persecution and faced with the problems of uprooting and resettlement, the paradox polarities between the new ethnic consciousness and the facts of successful integration need not be resolved by a return to an earlier stage of communal existence and cultural identity.

## Notes

1. The history of the Hochschule for the entire period (1872 – 1942) or for its last phase has never been written, and its graduates have not issued a memorial volume comparable to those issued for other institutions (e.g., Juedisch-Theologisches Seminar, Breṣlau, or Israelitische Lehrerbildungsanstalt, Wuerzburg). Attempts to locate relevant archival materials have failed as recently as 1987 – 1988. At this writing, a doctoral dissertation based on whatever materials are available is being prepared at the Zentrum fuer Antisemitismusforschung, Technische Universitaet, Berlin, in cooperation with the department of Jewish studies at the Free University, Berlin.

2. A comprehensive study of the transfer of Jewish scholarship (Wissenschaft des Judentums) from Germany and Austria is being prepared, at present, by Dr. Christhard Hoffmann, Zentrum fuer Antisemitismusforschung, Berlin, in cooperation with Prof. Daniel Schwartz, department of Jewish studies, Hebrew University. In its early stages, the study was sponsored by the Research Foundation for Jewish Immigration, New York. It is now supported by the Deutsche Forschungsgemeinschaft, Bonn.

3. Cf. Henry L. Feingold, *The Politics of Rescue: The Roosevelt Administration and the Holocaust, 1938 – 1945* (New Brunswick, N.J., 1970). For other studies to 1988 see *Classified, and Annotated Bibliography of Books and Articles on the Immigration and Acculturation of Jews from Central Europe to the USA since 1933*, ed. H. Friedlander et al., vol. 2 of *Jewish Immigrants of the Nazi Period in the USA*, ed. Herbert A. Strauss (New York, Munich, etc., 1981).

4. Maurice R. Davie et al., *Refugees in America: Report of the Committee for the Study of Recent Immigration from Europe* (New York 1947, reprinted 1975).

5. *International Biographical Dictionary of Central European Emigrés 1933 – 1945 / Biographisches Handbuch der deutschsprachigen Emigration nach 1933*, eds. Herbert A. Strauss and Werner Roeder. vol. II (Munich, and New York 1983), Introduction, p. lxxviii – lxxvi.

6. Research on the transfer of scholarship through emigration in the disciplines political science, medicine, physics, and Jewish studies *(Wissenschaft des Judentums)* has been underway since 1985 at the Zentrum fuer Antisemitismusforschung, Berlin and Muenster University in cooperation with the Gesellschaft fuer Wissenschaftsgeschichte. An extension of this area of research is now being supported for other disciplines at other institutions in the Federal Republic of Germany by the Deutsche Forschungsgemeinschaft, Bonn.

7. Cf. the author's "Social and Communal Integration," in *Essays on the History, Persecution and Emigration of German Jews,* vol. 6 of *Jewish Immigrants of the Nazi Period in the USA,* ed. H. A. Strauss, (New York and Munich, 1985), pp. 317 – 336, and Steven M. Lowenstein, "The German-Jewish Community of Washington Heights," in *Year Book of the Leo Baeck Institute,* vol. 30 (1985), pp. 245 – 254. A forthcoming book by this author on this subject was not available to me at the time of writing.

8. American Federation of Jews from Central Europe, History Project, sponsored by Research Foundation for Jewish Immigration and Jewish Philanthropic Fund of 1933, New York, 1987 – date. Research is carried out by Judith Marcus-Tarr and Joseph Maier.

# A Heritage Freighted Across
# the Abyss

*Michael A. Meyer*

On *Kristallnacht* I was too young to be aware of what was happening. My memories are only of tales my parents told me later. Fortunately, we had been warned that all Jewish men would be rounded up and held in concentration camps until the Jews paid a collective fine of a billion marks to compensate insurance companies for the damage Nazis had done to Jewish property. My father fled the house, rode around Berlin on buses and subways, and finally found an office where he could safely sleep. During the day my mother stayed out of our apartment as much as possible. She sat on one of those few benches in the Tiergarten that were reserved for Jews while I played nonchalantly at her feet. In the middle of the night the Gestapo came to our house. My mother told them her husband was out of town, in Hamburg. For hours they waited to make sure. Finally, they left. Some days later she wrote to friends in Palestine in German words disguised as decorative Hebrew script at the edge of a letter: *"Karl wurde gesucht, aber nicht gefunden"* ("They looked for Karl, but they didn't find him").

They did find my grandfather, though. He opened the door himself and proudly showed the Gestapo an Iron Cross with which his commander had decorated him in World War I. They laughed and took him to Sachsenhausen, where he languished until he could get a visa to Chile.

My parents remained in Berlin up until the summer of 1941. By now my father was doing forced labor for the huge Siemens electrical company. My mother was desperately trying to get a visa from the stingy American consulate in Berlin. Bribery finally did the trick. We were fortunate since we had relatives in America who signed an affidavit, and my father had a foreman who, when asked to sign an emigration release for him, supposedly said: "Let Karl Meyer too see better times some day."

Later on, in Los Angeles, my parents did not speak much of *Kristallnacht*. More often they talked about the *anstaendige Leute*, the decent people, among the Germans, who continued to treat us as human beings down to the time of our departure. And they remembered the better days—before Hitler came to power.

My grandmother, who raised me in Southern California, was persuaded that I would never amount to anything if I lacked the capacity to read and appreciate Goethe and Schiller. She spoke German to me and read me stories from the Kasperle books—adventurous, humorous, fantastic tales set in the atmosphere of eighteenth-century German courtly life. Later came piano lessons, not because I had any talent for music, but simply because the bourgeois German-Jewish culture from which she came demanded it. In retrospect, I can see how my grandmother was desperately trying to transplant her own German cultural identity into her American grandchild. She was fighting a battle against my Americanization with the weapon of German *Bildung*. Very little of the heritage she wanted to convey was Jewish. It was German literature and German music that she wanted to implant. In my family, it was the grandparents who were more assimilated than their progeny.

*Bildung* was an important element for my parents too, but less so. They were younger when Hitler came to power and could more easily tilt to the Jewish side of their identities. We became a synagogue-going family in America and made occasional gestures toward *kashrut*. The Reform temple opened the possibilities for new relationships with non-German Jews. But that came only slowly. What my parents appreciated about Temple Israel of Hollywood was its German-born rabbi (who had married them in Berlin) and the familiar music of Sulzer and Lewandowski. What remained strange in synagogue was the pronunciation of Hebrew and some of the Jewish vocabulary. Only at home could my parents sing familiarly "Ki *lau* no-eh" on Pesach and call challah by its proper name of *Barches*.

My parents' closest friends in America remained German Jews who were refugees like themselves. There were organized circles and informal ones. In Los Angeles the "Jewish Club of 1933" long remained a social focus. Even more important for my father was the local circle of survivors from his old German-Jewish fraternity, the KC. They met regularly, ate the same foods and drank the same wine punch that they had enjoyed as students back in the twenties. Before my father died, he asked that his fraternity colors be draped across his chest in death as they had been many years earlier in German student days.

Informal gatherings were just as heavily laden with the pre-Hitler German past. My father's favorite card game remained the German skat. At gatherings of friends he would sing the old lieder, and when the recordings of the famous German baritones became available in America, he was among the first to buy them.

I suppose my parents brought with them to America some of the ancestral prejudices against the *Ostjuden*. In America it was the East European Jews that were in the majority, even in most Reform congregations by the forties. German Jews arriving in America as refugees from Nazism had to adjust to a situation where the tables were turned. They were the penniless immigrants who sought aid from Jewish charitable organizations largely supported by American Jews of East European ancestry. That required some adjustment of viewpoint. In addition, they found they had little in common with the prominent, established German Jews whose grandparents had made the voyage to America seventy-five and more years earlier, and who were wholly Americanized, separated from Jews of East European origin only by prejudice, social class, and family ties.

The German-Jewish refugees' clinging together was largely a matter of shared pleasant and unpleasant memories, a nostalgia that grew with the years. But was there any more to it than that? Did they feel there was something in their legacy as German Jews that was worth passing on? My parents were quite ambivalent about it. They were revolted by the crassness in much of American Jewish practice, especially the gaudy displays at Bar Mitzvah and wedding celebrations. German Jews possessed a modesty and a penchant for understatement that seemed very un-American. And there was that untranslatable quality of *Gemuetlichkeit*, a kind of warm at-homeness which was German to be sure, but also had its Jewish coloring: it reigned where a small company of fellow Jews gathered intimately, unpretentiously among their own, with no need for pretense of any kind. German Jews absorbed some of the formality of German class society, but they managed to bend its stiffness with Jewish humor.

The German-Jewish sense of family was both powerful and exclusive. Birthdays of family elders were invariably commemorated with original verses and songs performed by the children. But along with that veneration went an insistence by parents to control the marriages of their children, to assure that they married into the "proper" families. In America, in most instances, it was only the sense of extended family that remained—the more Jewish and less German-bourgeois element.

Although they participated for many years in a "Great Books" discussion group, neither of my parents considered themselves intellectuals. They would have had difficulty in formulating the German-Jewish legacy in terms other than the personal ones I have already mentioned. From the historian's perspective it is easier to see how much American Jewry has been shaped by ideas that came from Germany. If there is modern scientific study of Jews and Judaism in America today, we owe it to the invention of *Wissenschaft des Judentums* by German Jews in the 1820s. If religious Jews in America are nearly all modern Orthodox, Conservative, or Reform, they are so because the ideas of Samson Raphael Hirsch, Zacharias Frankel, and Abraham Geiger were transported to America from their point of origin in Germany of the 1830s and 1840s. Only anti-modern Orthodoxy and Reconstructionism lack German roots. Yet this, of course, is a heritage from earlier times. We would possess it whether or not a new German-Jewish exodus had occurred with the rise of Hitler.

The more recent immigration brought to America great minds, of whom Einstein is simply the most outstanding. The contributions of Jewish refugee scholars to the sciences and humanities in America are legion. They transmitted new ideas and invigorated the university departments that they joined. Those that worked in Jewish disciplines brought with them the tradition of rigorous scholarship that made the efflorescence of Jewish studies on American campuses in the 1970s more than ethnicism turned academic.

It is fatuous to believe that the manners, customs, and values of German Jews will outlast the generation of the refugees' children. These require personal inculcation from someone steeped in them from childhood. What will remain are those elements mentioned last: the German-Jewish contributions to Jewish religion and to the study of the Jewish heritage. The bridge of personal memory can stretch across the Holocaust abyss only for those who themselves bore German Jewishness from Europe to America. For their children it is mostly memories told them and experiences of customs transplanted. For the third generation it must be the broad, more ambiguous legacy: of a

Jewish community that felt rooted in a land until it spewed them out; but also of pioneers in Jewish modernity, who set a pattern for Jewish religious and intellectual life in America; and of convinced believers that reason, culture, and quiet dignity are keys to a human life worth living.

# Engagement and the German-Jewish Legacy

*Aryeh Neier*

I was an infant when I left Berlin and recall nothing of my life in Germany. My first memory is of the boat that brought me to England in 1939 and the images are so hazy that it seems possible that I have only imagined this recollection of that voyage at an early age. Any claim that I might have to a German-Jewish legacy is further diminished by the fact that my parents were not actually German Jews. They were born around the turn of the century in what is now Poland and went to Berlin in the years following World War I. Accordingly, the family sojourn in Germany spanned less than two decades. Moreover, as the principal language we spoke at home after we got to England was English, I grew up knowing only a smattering of German.

Despite such tenuous links, I tend to think of myself as an American (having migrated to the United States with my parents a couple of years after the end of World War II) with a German-Jewish heritage. It is not possible for me to assert a cause-and-effect relationship between that way of identifying myself and the particular way I have lived my life. I find myself unable to look back and say that I have followed a certain path for a single reason; there have been too many influences to sort out, and chance has played too large a part, for me to be able to attribute the choices I made with such precision.

At the same time, defining myself as of German-Jewish origin has made me unable to imagine a life in which I would not be engaged in dealing with what I think of as vital public issues. Even when I was in high school and college in the 1950s—at a time when American students were commonly known as a "silent generation"—I was deeply engaged in various causes. And, in the thirty years since I left college, there has never been a moment when I was not principally engaged in that way.

In my case, of course, my identification of myself as of German-Jewish origin had a special cast because I began conscious life as a refugee. I spent a year at a hostel for refugee children in England before being reunited with my family in London, and I was always aware that I was an exotic species in the otherwise homogeneous schools I attended in England because I had been born in the country with which England was at war; because I was a Jew and, therefore, exempt from the compulsory prayers with which every school day began; and because I was a refugee. I was also conscious that my distinctive situation in those English schools was attributable to the contradictions in my background. That is, we had fled to England and I had become a refugee because it was no longer possible to be a Jew in Germany. German Jews, and the achievements of German Jewry, were on the way to extinction in Germany. Accordingly, thinking of myself as a German Jew meant thinking of myself as different from all my school fellows and believing that existence itself could be imperiled. That I have never been able to picture myself except in the middle of a struggle over vital issues has seemed to me, therefore, an inevitable consequence of my background and of the circumstances of my childhood.

The matter of my background has become a public issue from time to time, especially on the occasions during my fifteen-year tenure on the staff of the American Civil Liberties Union when I was called upon to defend freedom of speech for Nazis. It happened fairly frequently. I joined the staff of the ACLU in 1963, not long after the organization had successfully challenged New York City's denial of a permit to George Lincoln Rockwell to hold a demonstration in Union Square Park. Several hundred members of the ACLU had resigned in protest over the Rockwell case—the first of many in which the ACLU defended his free speech rights before he was assassinated by one of his Nazi followers in 1967. On one occasion in 1966, I had accompanied Rockwell and a rival who had formed an even smaller Nazi party to a hearing at which several New York State legislators were attempting to promote their own political careers by purporting to investigate Nazi influence. I testified at the hearing about the inappropriateness of such inquiries concerning beliefs, expression, and association and found myself reviled in some quarters because I, a Jew and a refugee from Nazi Germany, had taken on the defense of the First Amendment rights of American Nazis. I believe it was on this occasion that I first heard the expression "self-hating Jew" which was used with some frequency in subsequent years.

On another occasion, a couple of years later, I traveled to Toronto to take part in a television debate about whether the Canadian Broadcasting Company should broadcast an interview with a Bavarian neo-Nazi leader, Adolph von Thadden. He had been scheduled to go to Toronto for the interview, but the protests were so vehement in that city, which has a large Jewish refugee community, that CBC canceled his visit to Canada. Instead he was interviewed at his home in Germany and the film of that interview was shown on Canadian television after I debated the president of the Canadian Jewish Congress over whether it was permissible to show it. When I arrived at the CBC studios, I encountered a large picket line outside denouncing me, again as a Jew and as a refugee from Nazi Germany, for taking on myself the defense of free speech for von Thadden.

Of all such controversies in which I got involved, none was more virulent than the battle in 1977 and 1978 involving a tiny neo-Nazi group's effort to demonstrate in Skokie, Illinois. Although this took place more than a decade ago, the story is still well known.

A self-styled Nazi leader, Frank Collin—who turned out to be the son of a Max Cohn who had himself been interned in Buchenwald and changed his name to Collin after migrating to the United States—sent letters to several suburban communities around Chicago expressing an intent to hold demonstrations. Most of the communities ignored the letters, but Skokie, with a large Jewish population that included hundreds of concentration camp survivors and their families, responded by saying it prohibited such a demonstration. Collin sought the help of the American Civil Liberties Union in taking the matter to court.

Much of the public abuse for defending this group of Nazis focused on the Chicago staff lawyer for the ACLU who represented Collin, David Goldberger. But as I was the national executive director of the ACLU, I frequently spoke out on the matter, and my own background as a refugee from Nazi Germany became an issue. Rabbi Meir Kahane—still a resident of the United States—and his colleagues in the Jewish Defense League conducted disruptive demonstrations inside our offices. JDL members also followed me home to learn where I lived and used the occasion of Hitler's birthday to present the receptionist in our office with an obscene gift for me. I was not much more pleased by the actions of some of those who supported the stand we took. On one occasion, a prominent television producer wrote and paid for full-page advertisements to appear in newspapers across the country that described my background, noted my role in the ACLU and the ACLU's defense of free speech for the Nazis, and concluded with the line "That's what America means to me" and his signature. Fortunately, he decided to telephone me just before the advertisements were published to let me know they would appear and I was able to persuade him at the last moment to withdraw them.

Looking back on the Skokie battle, I am more persuaded than ever that it was the right thing to do. Though no great legal precedent was established, the case seems to me to have had a lasting symbolic significance. Though the Skokie matter was highly controversial at the time, and no doubt many still would argue that those identifying themselves with the views of Nazis do not deserve free speech and that their rights should not be defended by Jews (much less Jews who are themselves refugees from the Nazis), the actions of the ACLU in that case have also secured a high degree of public acceptance. In the process, the public conception of freedom of speech has been expanded; the understanding has grown that defense of civil liberties means defending those you don't agree with and, indeed, defending even those whose views may be anathema to their defenders; and the realization has spread that liberty can only be protected through adherence to principle.

Since engagement is what I consider the main legacy of my background as a Jew born in Germany and forced to begin life as a refugee, it never occurred to me to try to avoid battles such as the one over Skokie, or any of the hundreds of others that I have taken on in a career as a professional advocate for civil liberties and human rights. My understanding of my own legacy is that its tragic aspects derive to a certain extent from the reluctance or failure of many persons in many quarters to engage in struggles over matters of principle. Since I have the advantage of hindsight, I have no excuses for not engaging. It was a twist of fate that placed me in a spot where I was engaged at one stage in my life as the defender of civil liberties for Nazis. But I do not believe that I was deceiving myself when I asserted then, as I would assert today, that the defense of rights for all, even Nazis, is just what is needed to ensure that Nazism never again prevails.

# The German-Jewish Heritage: A View from 1988

*Hans Juergensen*

## I

On January 30, 1933, at 5 p.m., all of Germany was informed that Adolf Hitler had been appointed Chancellor of the Reich.

I still vividly recall the bitter shock I felt at the announcement.

I was just thirteen years old.

Despite the warning signals sent out by the Nazis over the years, with the slogan *"Die Juden sind unser Unglueck"* ("The Jews are our misfortune"), far too many of the approximately 600,000 German Jews refused to believe that, in Rabbi Leo Baeck's words, "The end of German Jewry had arrived." Hitler could not last, they argued. The German people were too sensible, *too cultured* to follow such a leader. Moreover, the Jews had proved their patriotism again and again, especially during the World War, in which 12,000 of their number had sacrificed their lives for the *Vaterland*. And: had they not—since their emancipation in 1812—and even before—contributed their share to that shibboleth of the middle and upper classes, *Bildung*? They proudly reminded their non-Jewish countrymen of the great poets, scientists, statesmen, et al., who had helped make German culture and civilization respected—and envied—across the globe. They were, in the official phrase, Germans of the Mosaic faith, bred on Goethe and Schiller, Kant and Hegel far more profoundly than on Maimonides and Ibn Ezra. And many had remained *Kaisertreu* during the Weimar Republic years. Not all, of course, for the artists and intellectuals yearned for democracy. Yet, it is a curious fact that many of the famous writers—Jakob Wassermann and Alfred Doeblin, to name two—did not address the growing anti-Semitism while profiling the economic and social problems of the working classes.

Theodor Herzl's Zionism was loudly repudiated by the vast majority of German and Austrian Jews.

My personal experiences were totally German. And my religious training was perfectly in tune with conservative Jewish practices. All the Jews I knew were Germans first.

As a boy, I was exposed to some anti-Semitism, but only at the hands and voices of ignorant proletarians. My middle-class friends and schoolmates—all but two non-Jewish—accepted me as "one of theirs." I certainly did not consider myself to be "an alien element." In truth, with few exceptions the Jews in Schwiebus (now Polish) were ardent nationalists. Among the few exceptions, however, were my adoptive parents, Herrmann and Dora Juergensen. As active members of the Social Democratic party they stood out and were looked upon as "dangerous" by the more conservative Jews. My father, originally Danish, had become a naturalized citizen (like Hitler!); he had fought in the German Army from 1914 to 1918, and had converted to Judaism upon being married.

He was a highly cultured man, a fine amateur pianist, and a pacifist. My mother, less cultured, was a courageous fighter for the underprivileged. Thus, I became aware of poverty and social injustices early in life. But the educational environment made me into the young nationalist who belonged with the middle-class friends with whom he went to school in that small provincial town.

In 1924 my parents' dry-goods store was vandalized by Nazi hoodlums, then known as Werwolf. As a result, my family went bankrupt, not once, but three times. Finally, in 1927, my parents and I moved to Berlin. We were desperately poor at a time when Germany was recovering economically. For two years my father was without work; my mother and I became very ill in the Berlin slum where we barely existed in one room.

Our experience of 1924 was blamed on my parents' political activities. No one really thought of anti-Semitism at the time.

During the winter of 1927 – 28 I was taken back to Schwiebus, on the orders of our physician, to live with my mother's sister, Mrs. Ulriecke Riesenfeld. My mother, worn out by illness and poverty, died in 1928, at the age of fifty. I remained with my aunt until I left Germany in 1934.

In 1930, I started *Gymnasium* on a scholarship. The school was coed, since a town as small as Schwiebus could not support segregated high schools. The education I received was typically German, and excellent as well. My teachers turned out to be atypical in that they did not conform to the Prussian rigidity practiced elsewhere. Most of them had been soldiers in the 1914 war; yet they were no martinets. Several members of the faculty were politically liberal. Thus, I and the other four Jewish students felt completely at ease and fully integrated into all school activities.

My favorite subjects were German, history, and art. I thrived on literature and read beyond the level of my class. The teachers encouraged me. And since I discovered that I was physically agile, I became an athlete who won prizes in the annual games, particularly in track.

German *Kultur* governed my boyhood. Even then, everybody prophesied an academic career for me—that is, until January of 1933. After that date life became increasingly difficult for Jews in the provinces. We were isolated and frequently demeaned by the Aryan citizens.

In my case, the teachers and schoolmates remained loyal; but early in 1934 I was forced to leave school because my scholarship had been terminated. For the last months of that school year, my fourth, the faculty paid my tuition; this was a most unusual action by a German school. And I remember my teachers' generosity with gratitude.

Already in 1933 I knew that Jews had to emigrate and voiced this knowledge publicly, to the dismany of my elders.

I was fortunate to be selected as one of fourteen boys to constitute the first children's transport to America. I landed in New York on November 9, 1934.

II

The German heritage still remains strong in my life as well as in the life of my wife, who is a refugee from Frankfurt am Main. Steeped in the arts of Germany, we refer to them constantly. The best works, both classical and modern, influence us. This is natural since I am a professor of humanities who has taught German history, literature, and philosophy as well as English, ranging from freshman composition to graduate courses in British and American literature. However, I have also become profoundly involved in Judaic studies ever since I arrived in the United States. And my participation in the U.S. Holocaust Memorial Council as special consultant has certainly deepened my awareness of the Jewish experience.

Being a product of three cultures—German, Jewish, and American—I can attest to the lasting influence of German thought. Goethe and Kant are as important to me as Maimonides and Buber. The development of democratic philosophy and practices, starting with John Locke and reinforced by Spinoza, governs my personal beliefs and actions. Add such names as Duerer and Beethoven, and the reader will recognize the importance of German greatness that may be termed universal. Add further my long American experience, including my frontline years in the U.S. Army against the Nazi forces, and the sum comes to a very rich and often dangerous personal drama.

I am, therefore, the result of a symbiosis. It has been my personal privilege and professional duty to select the highest values from three cultural entities and to communicate them to Americans for forty years.

German-Jewish liberalism, imported into America nearly 150 years ago, gave rise to the Reform movement, which left its mark on American democracy. But I hasten to add that the immigrants from Central Europe contributed materially to advances in American social betterment. They, more than the German Jews, worked toward the betterment of the working class. For it is a fact that the German-Jewish immigrants, even those from Hitler, considered themselves an elite.

There is no doubt that the German-Jewish legacy remains active and has its effect on succeeding generations. My daughter's attitude is ambivalent, especially after her visit to Germany in 1980. She admires German art, particularly the theater, but is still disturbed by her experience in Dachau.

My older grandson has been informed about the Holocaust and elected to write a term paper on the subject two years ago when he was eleven.

Certainly, the Jewish experience in Europe over the past hundred years has strongly affected American attitudes, culture and, very importantly, its politics and economics.

One result of the horrors initiated by the Germans during the Hitler era is the opening of the gates to newer victims than myself.

Undoubtedly, the most significant legacy left us of the German-Jewish experience is the need for constant vigilance concerning the constitutional rights of all Americans and the active amelioration of the fate of the oppressed all over the world.

## DACHAU: LEST WE FORGET

The grief will not be assuaged!

—even though these infernal gates
spewed out the surviving shadows
in 1945;
and the mounds of bone-wreckage
were summarily bulldozed—
by retching liberators—
into the reeking loam

upon which ruthless hyenas
—some *yet* among the breathing—had coldly, viciously executed
satanic orders on human flesh.

(What words are sufficiently cruel
to itemize total depravity?)

       \*   \*   \*   \*

When I saw the country again
after more than forty years
of my deliverance,
it *did* stir flashes of nostalgia,
for there was once a boyhood
worth recalling.

But the wrathful pity for my dead
blazed doubly high—
and will keep burning
as long as I live.

1980

# Le Déraciné:
# Finding New Roots in Exile

*Henry R. Huttenbach*

It was in my senior year in college, in the midst of the Korean "conflict," that I encountered the concept that explained the essence of my past experiences, pinpointing the origin of my chronic restlessness, and setting the tone of my perspective on the future. After six initial years in a Germany that was convulsed out of the unstable Weimar Republic into the early upheavals of the Third Reich; after another three prewar years in Mussolini's Italy; and then, after eight more years in wartime and postwar England, began the encounter with the United States. By the time I entered college—quadro-lingual and on my fourth national anthem—rebellion set in: what a later generation would dub an identity crisis struck with a vengeance. The Jewish outcast from Hitlerian Germany, the German refugee in Italy, the enemy alien in England, and now the immigrant from Europe looked around for permanence and stability and found neither, certainly not in a small far-western town where the solaces of urban civilization were studiously avoided by the post-pioneer generation. And then came the instant revelation, a sudden enlightenment embodied in one word—*le déraciné,* the uprooted one.

Life—history—had torn me from the familiar and counseled me to adjust, chameleon like, to each new country, to its society and its cultural variant. "Adapt," it whispered. So I put on and discarded the conformist's mantle as circumstances dictated. By the time I reached these shores, I had learned and unlearned with equal enthusiasm to speak street Milanese, London cockney, the rural brogue of Somersetshire, the clipped tone and mannerisms of the British public school, all superimposed on my hometown dialect of the central Rhine region, plus a smattering of the *Hochdeutsch* that had permeated the conversations of the bourgeois/bohemian German refugee circles that formed nuclei of *émigré-kultur* away from "home." For, it must be made clear, the presumed temporary status of our condition, the assumption that there would be a return as soon as "the crisis had passed," was never questioned until the first glimpses of the death camps had their traumatic effect. Only then did the brutal fact of not going back begin to work its way into a psyche so long oriented towards a resumption of familiar ways in a post-Hitlerian Germany.

Until coming to the United States in 1947, every alignment had been a temporary tactic, a provisional device to survive in the unfamiliar among strangers. Now, established in the land of immigrants, I had to convert "in depth" as a strategy; becoming an American was the only future. Not only had a German mode of life to be readjusted; not only had a grating British accent to be jettisoned and all the finesses of the American language to be mastered; not only had Italian-acquired hand-histrionics to be tamed; but a new lifestyle embraced and loved. In the late 1940s in a "suburbia-town" in the state of Washington, this meant becoming "white," with all the prejudices and idiosyncrasies associated with it. The attempt could only lead to abysmal failure, much sophomoric soul-searching, superficial guilt, and considerable overt and covert anger, until that moment of self-discovery, of recognition in the magic of one word, *déraciné*.

Instantaneously, what had transpired over the course of three and a half years of college life in the midst of an America barely touched by World War II made eminent sense. Befriending a Japanese-American—one of the "niggers" of the Northwest; starting a fencing squad on a football/boxing-obsessed campus; joining a debate team to assert language "supremacy"; founding a French club and newspaper with which to coalesce the foreign students into a lobby of the "dis- and malcontents"; pursuing three majors and not one; playing baroque chamber music on period instruments: these were all symptomatic of a determined refusal to shed one's skin again and don yet another. My system had reached a point of assimilation-indigestion, and any imposition on this will to self-immunization against further identity-tampering simply led to more violent forms of rejection. There simply was no formulaic way of "becoming" an American by following the traditional edict to "do in Rome as the Romans do." My Appian Way was to lead elsewhere; the way of *le déraciné* commanded and pointed in another direction, still unclear, except for the unswerving beckoning of New York City, the long-time metropolis of the refugee/immigrant, of the stateless, of those *in* but not quite *of* America.

New York, in 1951 the mecca of millions who spoke with an accent, where everyone was immigrant-related, the city that had become a home to the homeless from World War II, this New York was a separate country, a Europe in the New World. It beckoned like a siren. In due course, during my first graduate years (1951–53), I became a New Yorker, though I did not grasp it fully until several years later; these included years as a reluctant draftee in the army, "occupying" West Germany and keeping back the "Iron Curtain"; a year after military duty exploring the utopian lure of remaining in Europe and forging a brave new condominium of national states along with other young idealists who were entranced with Schumann's vision of a "new" post-war continental order; five years spent acquiring a Ph.D. in history—the only discipline to satisfy and fulfill after numerous misadventures with architecture, mathematics, the classics, and comparative Romance literature; and then years teaching in the trans-Hudson "wasteland": in Washington State, in Nebraska, in Texas, in Louisiana, until fortune smiled and the Holy Grail of a position in New York made possible the return of a fully converted and naturalized New Yorker.

The Prodigal Son had come home to his "roots" after several abortive efforts to defy and circumvent what was truly his locus. A liberal illusion that Germany in ruins would "welcome back" one of the genuine loyal adherents of the "decent" past was shattered in Heidelberg in 1955 where my first encounter with murderous anti-Semitism, in the form of a German SS officer turned landlord, sent me literally fleeing the country a second time, this time as a young married adult and father. An offer in 1956 to assume a senior post with the promise of later full control in a leading Left-oriented publishing firm in England foundered on the shoals of ideology: my once, but since abandoned, socialist proclivities had assumed too many characteristics of American pragmatism. A naive gesture to volunteer to settle in Israel after completion of my studies was kindly but realistically rebuffed—Israel in 1959, I was informed, needed tractor drivers and businessmen, not another specialist on the Soviet Union. Attempts to blend into the fabric of U.S. college and university societies west of Manhattan always proved stillborn: my obvious lack of enthusiasm and glances eastward were rewarded with few promotions and no bestowals of tenure. By 1965, after a year "academically exchanged" in the Soviet Union, the unambiguous fact of being a New Yorker had sunk in. Peace at last in what had become the urban war-zone of the second half of the 1960s!

"Peace" in New York City meant having come to terms. The city, not accidentally, was situated mid-point, so to speak, between the new and the old, between the future and the past, between the fluid post-frontier west and the rigid but well-defined ways of the "east"—Europe. Here was an amalgam of the best and worst of both, of the tensions that once had forged Athens, Florence, and Paris and, ever so briefly, war time London. I had intellectually "teethed" in World War II London, whose refugee population contained the highest concentration of German-speaking, Central European Jews. Between 1939 and 1945, a flood of Jews from Germany, Austria, and Czechoslovakia momentarily inundated the capital of England, transforming it for the duration of the war into an international metropolis, a highly volatile intellectual and cultural cross road. Highly educated and experienced minds, nurtured by all the streams of thought and experimentation that characterized European culture in the decades straddling World War I, congregated in London, a haven from the barbarism that had engulfed the continent. Torn from their native environs, robbed of language, podium, lectern, stage, publishing outlets, they vented their creative energies while in exile in extraordinarily verbal social sessions, twenty-four-hour rounds of endless talk, fertilizing and cross-fertilizing one another, thrown together pitilessly, forced to find satisfaction from one another in a pressure-cooker London in which they were freely caged. For a young man living in a home in Hampstead, the epicenter of the refugee world, a home whose doors stood open to a constant stream of refugee visitors' comings and goings, in which the kitchen never ceased to manufacture gallons of coffee and whose walls never stopped reverberating from the sounds of heated talk, always in German, about Kafka and Kierkegaard, Mahler and Monteverdi, Fallada and Franz Werfel, about Epstein and Einstein, about Thomas and Heinrich Mann, about baroque music and the 12-tone system, about the latest manuscript find in the British Museum, a concert in Wigmore Hall, a lecture in Keats House, and on and on. The grave of Karl Marx was visited; Heine was recited, Schubert lieder sung from memory. Chamber music never ceased: everyone could play an instrument; all were passionate amateurs. Conversation never stopped, always focused, always engaged. Once it was about Kokoschka; then about Kaminski; then about Landowska; or, when his daughter was present—she never failed to sit cross-legged on the floor smoking a cigarillo—the subject was Kurt Eisner and the Bavarian Communist uprising. For a young man in his teens, this exposure to the frenetic world of the Jewish refugees was nothing short of exhilarating, disconcerting, and discomforting.

Outside the home was the bland and constrained British society: boarding school and its frozen rituals, aloof imperial London, the gentle countryside were in stark contradiction to the whirlpool activity that took place behind the doors of home. Home was exciting, stimulating, disturbing, irritating, always interesting. Within the walls of home, no one committed the sin of boredom. Life there consisted of urgent issues, imminent problems, questions that had to be answered. Everyone seemed driven, in a hurry, eager to make a statement, to argue, to contradict, to disagree, never to be "polite" (the restraining and dampening hallmark of disquisition in the company of the British). Whenever they visited and participated, they seemed remote, *dégagé,* disinterested, emotionally removed from the fray, and, of course, polite. They seemed to crave a certain neatness of thought, reflected in their well-groomed attire, quietly offended by the aggressive, untiringly combative manner of their German-Jewish hosts. Their discomfort was apparent; and yet they were fascinated, even mesmerized, by the frantic activity of the *déracinés* refugee minds, who, had they been returned to their former state, would have happily redonned the veneer of bourgeois respectability that had once characterized their former lives in Berlin or Vienna or Prague. But time was too precious; the crisis dictated a new agenda and hence a commensurate behavioral pattern. Denied being journalists, editors, authors, playwrights, critics, poets, sculptors, academicians, and lawyers— only musicians escaped spiritual unemployment, and that is why music supplied the ultimate consolation to so many—they concentrated all their creative powers into endless talk, and thus, unwittingly, supplied the young man in their midst with a total education.

Immersed in their talk, unknowingly, I inherited the last of Habsburg *fin-de-siècle* Vienna, pre – World War I Prague, and, of course, the spirit of post – World War I Weimar Berlin. Through total immersion, I became fluent in Central European *Kultur:* the names of its personalities rested on the tip of the tongue, become second-nature, common reference points like comic strips or baseball scores in the America I entered a few years later, except for New York, where in

1967 so many still spoke the same "language." I did not know then that I had been the beneficiary of a crash-course in an era that had been wiped off the map by two world wars and genocide. I had not been aware that I had inherited an almost extinct mentality from the remnants of a once-thriving intellectual community, survivors who had managed, by force of circumstances, to keep alive in London, for a few more years, a way of life whose environment and practitioners—the majority Jews—Hitler had irrevocably stamped out. The products of *Gymnasia,* the assimilated German Jews, were briefly compressed into the hot house that was London at war. By 1947 they were dispersing; the "Weimar Ghetto" quickly broke up, and its "graduates," such as myself, were left to fend for themselves, condemned to speak a foreign language wherever they stopped to speak, to be only partially understood and all too often to be misunderstood, strangers in a modern world, cursed with a modernity that outstripped that of their neighbors. The graduates such as myself who immigrated to the United States found tiny oases of kindred souls in Seattle, in New Orleans, in San Francisco, even in Boston; but the largest nucleus, much dissipated by the immensity of the city, clustered in New York. The grandchild of Weimar reared in London found accommodation, at long last, in New York, but only imperfectly, in the mid-sixties.

A large but fast-aging number of German Jews, ensconced in Washington Heights or its equivalent, continued the process of assimilation that had been so rudely and inhumanely interrupted by the Nazis. Whereas they had been forced to recognize that the century-old flirtation with a symbiosis with German *Kultur* had been a false dream, and emancipation a cul-de-sac, their disenchantment with Western liberalism had not been sufficient not to begin the process anew in the United States, this time proudly patriotic in the land of quotas, whose democracy had cruelly and tightly closed its doors to tens of thousands of their co-victims seeking to save their lives from the fury of a murderous racist anti-Semitism. Blinkered by their typical German bourgeois a-politicism, they myopically gave thanks to the new *Vaterland,* were the last to lend open support to Israel, and congregated around their homemade Parthenon, the Leo Baeck Institute. (Rabbi Leo Baeck, it should be recalled, upon his release from Theresienstadt, during his first visit to the United States, expressed his unqualified gratitude to the United States before the assembled members of Congress, including those who had supported the turning back of the *St. Louis*.) With these *gemuetlichen* souls, this recent arrival to New York, originally "baptized" in London by the yeast that had for so long quickened life in Europe, had little mental patience with their quest for Americanization.

By the time he reached New York in the mid-sixties, the last of those kindred souls he so craved was dying. The New School's corridors no longer echoed with their provocations. Symbolically, the scholar he had been hired to replace at CCNY, the venerable Hans Kohn, had died abruptly, prevented from serving as a mentor to his young successor for a few more precious years. To this day I reread his books to touch base with his encyclopedic grasp, his wide-ranging interests, his multilingual readings. Only one man remained, the controversial but brilliant Karl-August Wittfogel, who, ten years earlier, while visiting the University of Washington from Columbia University, had taken me in tow and generously introduced me to the intricacies and convolutions of Marxism, the traps of Leninism, the egregious mendacities of Stalinism, and the inhumanitarian potentials of Maoism (this before the unleashing of the Red Guards and the sonderkommandoism of Pol Pot). He opened up the dialectical world of discourse as practiced by a growing segment of the world's intelligentsia, anticipating and, therefore, preparing me for the leftish fulminations of the 1960s which invaded every campus and whose anti-intellectualism sought to extirpate all that I saw as essential to a civilized life of the mind. Once, while we had been discussing his theories of bureaucracy—learning the lethal connection between the bureaucratic state and genocide policies—Karl-August warned me of the mindlessness of the left, especially its integral anti-Semitism, potentially even worse, he warned, than the anti-Semitism of the right, which had reached new heights during the Holocaust. But his was a fading voice, the last of the last men of letters, securely at home in universal knowledge, a European who had mastered Asia, for whom the pentatonic was as harmonious as the dodecanonic scale, who read classical Greek with the same ease as the Chinese of Confucius. The past was dying out before my eyes as this octogenarian giant, who had led Communist rallies in Leipzig in the early 1920s, had less and less strength to talk to me.

Third-generation New York Jewry from Eastern Europe provided some limited soul touching: but too many prejudices surfaced—the

*Yekke* versus the *Ostjude*, the Teutonic versus the Slavic. Its teeming masses had retreated to suburbia, and its vital elite, that of the *Partisan Review*, had aged and become peripheral, its humanitarian socialism preempted by the post – New Deal affluence. The Manhattan of old had also come to an end, having room only for ghosts, for sentimental reveries of what once was, almost making a neo-Proustian out of me as I searched the present for the past. I had arrived just in time to witness the burial of the few citizens of a world dead before I was born but whose dying whispers had made me a *post facto* fellow member, slated to live recollecting what might have been had those *temps perdus* endured.

Karl Loewith, the historian, had sat out the war in London and then soon thereafter returned to Heidelberg, "to be understood," as he explained to me in 1955 in the cluttered library of his home. In England, he smiled, everyone had agreed with him in Cambridge because they had not understood him; at least here in Germany, his colleagues and students would disagree with his thoughts because they grasped his meaning. "I need the land of my enemies; they appreciate my adventures of the mind carried on the sublime wings of the German language," he confessed, fully aware of the bitter irony of his circumstances during the last years of his life. "I want to die in the shadow of a German university. That is my true home." Those were his last words on my final visit. His advice to me had been not to try and make my home in Germany, despite the temptations. "Take what you have elsewhere, " he counseled, "even though you will never be content." He failed, however, to fill in the blank that followed his rubric "elsewhere." He left me a man without a country, a *déraciné;* a man who thinks German but speaks American with a British accent; a man more at home with Dostoyevsky and Bartok than with Bellow and Gershwin; one who looks back to days visiting the Pinakotek and reading *Simplicissimus* more fondly than looking forward to stopping by the Guggenheim or leafing through the *New Yorker*; a professor who tries to show his students beyond the parameters of required information, a historian poignantly aware that his past will fade but never enough to make the future welcome.

# Fifty Years After Crystal Night and Forty in America

*Werner Weinberg*

In writing down my thoughts on this topic I cannot suppress the disturbing feeling that each contributor to this volume of my age group and background will of necessity come up with practically the same story. But this is really something for the editor to worry about, and I may even be wrong.

I agree with Professor Mosse's idea about German Jews and *Bildung* with the following modification: If one wants to express one essential trend of the spirit of middle- and upper-class pre-Hitler German Jews, this would be *Bildung*. Moreover, pride in our *Bildung* was, among liberal Jews, one of the strongest pillars of pride in our Jewishness, simply because percentagewise more Jews possessed it than German non-Jews. Another such pillar was being proud of Jews of high achievement in the sciences, in literature, music, the theater, and also in commerce and industry and politics—especially, of course, of the Nobel Prize winners among them, again for the same reason: percentagewise we had a leading edge.

This pride, incidentally, was always tempered by some uneasiness; doubtlessly a number of vestiges from the pre-Emancipation time (which was not all that far remote) dwelled still in us. It was good to keep somewhat in the background. "*Keinen Risches machen*"—Don't bring on anti-Semitism! was still a valid slogan, don't rub their noses in our achievement of almost equal opportunity.

(Regarding our Jewishness it must be added that it certainly did not rest on the pillars of *Bildung* and pride alone. A good deal of *Yiddishkeit* [may my co-German-Jewish brethren forgive me the word] came from within also with *Westjuden*.)

I do not go along with the notion that we believed our *Bildung* "could be used as a means to support a German-Jewish dialogue." First, because we did not acquire *Bildung* for any other purpose than (*lehavdil*) *lishmah*, rather than as a "spade wherewith to dig." And second, because I do not remember a "German-Jewish dialogue" in any organized form or shape. There was nothing to dialogue about. Jews were Jews and Christians were Christians. I am just as uninformed about, say, a Catholic-Protestant dialogue. One took each other for granted. There was no missionizing to speak of, and our much-decried assimilation stopped at the door of most Jewish homes and at the portals of the synagogue. Sure, there was anti-Semitism; but then, many Jews did not exactly love Christians either, nor did Catholics Protestants and vise versa.

Another suggested potential effect of our *Bildung*, namely that we should have considered it as a means to tame the National Socialist beast, is pure fantasy. On the contrary, in times and places of crisis we Jews rather hid our *Bildung* before them, because it made them furious. This self-denial was different in the case of German groups and individuals who were themselves *gebildet*. They often accepted *gibildete* Jews as their equals and even socialized with them.

When I played down the "*bekovete rishes*," as we called "the good old pre-Hitler anti-Semitism," and likewise did not acknowledge *Bildung* as an instrument of dialogue with German Christians and of causing Nazis to change their idea about Jews being subhumans, there was one phenomenon that possessed a good deal of realism, and that is the likewise often cited Jewish-German symbiosis. "Living together"—with now and then a genuine friendship or a bad case of mutual contempt thrown in—but at any rate coexisting in a live-and-let-live atmosphere and absence of xenophobia can form a solid platform for a social order. Even the most Orthodox Jews took part in this quite comfortable symbiosis under the motto *Torah im derech eretz* and with the reservation of *chukat goyim*. The Zionists extended the phase of symbiosis even beyond 1933 because of their declared goal to emigrate; which agreed with the Nazi goal for us during the first half of the twelve-year period history had assigned to them.

So what did we bring with us to these shores after leaving Germany? Above I called German *Bildung* only "one essential trend" of German Jews. Some of the others are well-known; we brought them along to America as we did to Israel, but also to Uruguay and Shanghai, and to every place that offered an emigration loophole. I am referring to those other "essential trends" that may be summed up as the "*Yekke* syndrome." As everyone knows, among its symptoms are: a sense of duty, responsibility, and dependability, of punctuality, exactitude, orderliness, obedience to authority, neatness of attire, politeness, pedantry and, perhaps, especially, of dignity.

We were not proud or even cognizant of these trends, it was simply the way we were brought up. This *Yekke* syndrome gave rise to much teasing and joking, especially in Israel but also in America; but I do not think that it made us a laughingstock. Rather did we have many occasions to sense that some admiration and perhaps even a little envy were hidden behind the *Yekke* jokes and cartoons. One ancillary feature of the syndrome, though, was sure to stir up resentment in the countries of immigration: the inclination of some of our group to boast about the country which, it is true, had thrown us out, but also had been conducive to our *Yekkut* to develop. (Hebrew has no difficulty in forming an abstract noun from a word whose etymology is still escaping us.) Possibly, because this happened mainly in France, or because the French term for *bei uns* (i.e., in Germany), *chez nous*, lent itself to grammatical inflection, we, the refugees, did oppose the *"chez-nousen,"* as we had opposed the *"rishesmacher"* among us.

I do not think that the second wave of German Jews, those catapulted here by the Crystal Night, was essentially different from the first, of between 1933 and 1938. They were still traumatized and often could not quite believe that they had gotten out of Germany before what many thought would be the closing of the gates, and to a choice emigration land such as the United States, at that. But this was soon overcome by the necessity to catch up with those who had arrived between 1933 and the Crystal Night. Those Johnnies-come-early helped them in many ways, even though the relationship was occasionally strained by some gloating that they had seen it coming and had not lingered because of a foolish hope or belief that Hitler would go away. After a few years, when the war had started and the third wave, the survivors of concentration camps, was still to arrive, the two groups had pretty well merged, and like the Russian Jews before them, or for that matter, like the Irish, Italians, and all other immigrant groups, strove for cohesion and preserving certain features of their way of life within the melting pot.

While Washington Heights in New York City became the prototype settlement of the pre – and post – Crystal Night Jews—they formed their own congregations, and social institutions, and opened their delicatessen, wherever there was a sizable group of them in the country.

They socialized mainly among themselves.

Again, like most or all immigrant groups, these German Jews were eager to find work, to seek advancement, to obtain their American citizenship, and to become integrated as soon as they could in the existing Jewish-American welfare and community organizations, ambitious to pay back what had been expended on them. But—once more, like the other immigrant groups—their real Americanization, at least that of the first generation, remained on the surface. Most of them switched to the English language also for home use within their first decade. They sent their children to public school in addition to Hebrew school or a yeshiva, and did all in their power to give them a college education. Possibly the percentage of individuals who became outstanding in the professions, in commerce, even in politics, was higher than the average of other immigrant groups. But for all this, most held on to their German *Bildung* plus *Yekkut*; they did not assimilate to Americanism wholeheartedly and without reservation, much as their assimilation to the former German surroundings had never been "all the way" (with some exceptions, of course, in either situation).

Fifty years after the immigration to the United States, elderly German Jews may still speak of "real Americans" or even only of "the Americans," not necessarily critically but at any rate as different from themselves, from a way of living with which they differed in a dozen respects, beginning perhaps with white bread and soft rolls.

Therefore, if the question of a German-Jewish legacy is being raised, as well as that of a possible influence of this legacy on American Jewry and on America altogether, this writer can only observe—again, and for the last time—that like other immigrant groups, the first generations of German pre – and post – Crystal Night Jews (and now we may add the "third wave," post-1945 escapees) hold onto and live out this legacy. They pass on a very small portion of it to their children (eager not to put anything in the way of *their* Americanization), and for their fully Americanized grandchildren, they are what they are in every immigration country: the grandparents who came from the old country—nothing less, but also nothing more.

Speaking about legacy-influence on America as a whole: some individuals from any of the three German-Jewish Holocaust immigration waves may have left or may still leave an impression or make an important contribution here and there, but this has to do with those individuals—not so much with any legacy.

Is not the process the same in the State of Israel? From the time when the first *olim* were unfairly asked, "Do you come out of conviction or out of Germany?" through a few decades of their considerable influence on the political, economical, cultural, and educational scene, any possible German-Jewish legacy has been integrated in the total fabric of Israeli life, of which the individual threads are now difficult to tell apart.

For the United States, with its exclusive history of most divergent immigration waves, this process is still more outspoken. In the all-American quilt there may be stitches of German-Jewish *Bildung* and *Yekkut*—but except for a few monuments, such as the Leo Baeck Institute, the New School of Social Research, the Rabbi Breuer complex in Washington Heights, there is no distinctive legacy. The hard-to-define spirit of "real Americans" has swallowed it up, and like Pharaoh's lean cows, did not become appreciably fatter for it.

# Thoughts About the German-Jewish Legacy in the United States by a Man from *Aufbau*

*Hans J. Steinitz*

"The end of German Jewry has arrived," said the great and wise Rabbi Leo Baeck, president and spokesman of the National Federation of Jews in Germany, in 1938, in the face of the unbelievable tragedy of the Nazi *Kristallnacht*, followed by anti-Jewish government decrees, one always more brutal than the previous one.

But was the great rabbi really right? Had the end of German Jewry really arrived? Today, fifty years later, with the benefit of today's hindsight, and in recognition of the awesome Jewish will to survive, we might well have our doubts.

Yes, German Jewry did survive: in spite of unprecedented persecution and in spite of many, all too many victims who could not escape. It did survive in the United States, in Israel, in smaller groups in other countries such as Britain, France, and Canada—and even in Germany, where new Jewish communities, albeit very small ones, arose shortly after the end of World War II, and are today flourishing in a modest way.

* * *

But, of course, the massive immigration of Jews from Germany and Austria in the 1930s and 1940s, the result of Hitler's pressure and persecution, was not the first German-Jewish impact on American Jewry (which had been quite insignificant before the German-Jewish immigration in the first decades of the last century). Earlier, a hundred years before the arrival of the Hitler refugees, Jews from Germany had contributed enormously, maybe decisively, to create the impressive structure that is today's American Judaism: its congregations, its theology (especially its Reform wing), its charitable and cultural institutions, its lodges, and its whole institutional superstructure.

The impact of the second German-Jewish immigration, the one which is the topic of our discussion here, was not quite as overwhelming, and its legacy, though also quite remarkable, is not as predominant. It should not be underrated, either; but it requires a somewhat more careful look to define clearly its values and its achievements.

Speaking of achievements: in this context here we do not mean individual achievements of outstanding personalities among those refugees whose fame and glory are a matter of general knowledge; but it is an undeniable fact that the general level of education and cultural background—what they might have called their *Bildung*—was even on the average superior to that of other waves of immigrants who have reached these shores, either before the Hitler-fugitives or after them. It is, of course, a huge overstatement to say, as has been said partly in jest, that it was an immigration of Nobel Prize laureates: but the sentence was not completely unfounded.

It is absolutely amazing what these people, counting generously and including their second generation, not more than half a million souls, have created and achieved in this country. Many have reached commanding positions of influence in all fields: in arts and letters, in business and public service, in the sciences and the media, in academic life and even in sports. Very often, fame and success crowned their lifetime's work. Incidentally: among those refugees who settled in Israel, in Great Britain, and elsewhere, the balance sheet was not much different.

However, one big question arises: have those individual achievements been exclusively due to individual qualities of strength, brainpower, and intelligence, or have they been propelled by the German-Jewish "legacy," the remnants of specific German-Jewish traditions which may have, as it were, traveled with them across the Atlantic?

* * *

Of course, these German-Jewish immigrants of the 1930s and 1940s did not live entirely by themselves. There was a strong collective conscience of mutual responsibility alive among them from the beginning: they created their own congregations, their own charitable and scholarly institutions, and their own newspaper, which they called—*nomen est omen*—*Aufbau*, i.e., "Build-up" or "Reconstruction"; as President Kennedy once said, a little later: "they rebuilt their shattered lives, smashed elsewhere, successfully here in our country."

Even though in the beginning they mostly clustered in specific neighborhoods in the big cities (in Manhattan, people spoke of "The Fourth Reich" and "Frankfurt-on-the-Hudson"), the general trend pointed in the direction of rapid integration with the larger American Jewish community surrounding them. The older people largely stuck to themselves, especially in the beginning; the language barrier and the preoccupation with their own fate, plus the usual "greenhorn's problems" prevented, except in rare cases, any closer social contact with English-speaking neighbors.

It was quite different with the second generation, which was born in this country or at least grew up here. There the language problem was of no (or only minor) significance, and there occurred, beginning already in the 1950s but increasingly so in later years, an inner-Jewish "melting pot," bringing scions of German-Jewish immigrants in harmonious contact with youngsters from an American Jewish background.

One by-product of that development was what I might call a "negative legacy." German Jews had had, in their old country, the hideous habit of looking down on the less educated, less assimilated, less established, and frequently less wealthy *Ostjuden* from Eastern Europe. This ugly habit disappeared gradually under the completely changed conditions of their country of asylum: certainly a highly welcome trend.

On the positive side, German-Jewish tradition still reveals itself in many instances of synagogue music, in tunes originally composed by some celebrated cantors in Germany and Austria, as well as in some forms and shapes of celebrating Jewish festivities, such as the formal Seder meal at Passover and the Simchas Torah services. And then there is the Leo Baeck Institute in New York (with branches in London and Tel Aviv), which is collecting and preserving a beautiful collection of books, documents, and art works on German-Jewish history—a very rich source for American students of history, both Jewish and gentile. And I would certainly be remiss in my duty if I did not point out once more the German-language newspaper *Aufbau*, published for more than fifty years in New York—a pillar of strength of its community even beyond the borders of this country, and still today respected and admired by many for the tenacity of its mission. In quite a few instances its influence has extended even to the second generation, the children of the original immigrants from Germany or Austria.

\* \* \*

This writer can testify that in his parents' home, when he was a child in Germany, we had every winter in the living room a Christmas tree as well as Chanukkah candles, often simultaneously; and the older generation has very often continued this apparently illogical tradition after coming over to this country. The younger generation, however, seems to have radically broken with that habit.

Also in my childhood, I had of course some superficial contacts, so to speak onlooker-contacts, with the world of the *Ostjuden* residing in my hometown, mostly in their own quarters of town, like the notorious "Scheunenviertel" in Berlin—but those were exceptions without lasting consequences. It was only in the United States that I learned more about the Yiddish language and its literature, and it was only here that I became acquainted with American Jewish specialties like latkes and gefilte fish previously unknown to German Jewry.

To conclude, I would say that the greatest impact of the German-Jewish legacy consists of the harmonious melting pot of the Hitler emigrés, and especially their children and grandchildren, with the bulk of American Jewry. This merger, mostly in the form of inner-Jewish "mixed" marriages, is a very big and a very important event. That it could occur and continues to occur is a great achievement and holds the promise that Judaism in this country will, enriched and invigorated by the German-Jewish influx, be able to look forward to a bright and secure future.

# Thoughts About My German-Jewish Legacy

*Tom L. Freudenheim*

In a certain sense, I only found out I was a German Jew after I left home and went away to college. The awareness of being Jewishly "different" gradually came into focus at that time, accompanied by my learning the word *yekke* (from college roommates)—not previously a part of my family's vocabulary. I also found that other Jews, presumably non-German Jews, had a real hang-up about what they assumed to be my sense of superiority over them and their backgrounds.

Looking back on this now, over thirty years later, I am reminded again of the irony. My father had taught us that, after Hitler, there really were no more German Jews or Polish Jews, Litvaks or Galizianers. Hitler (I don't recall that we ever used the term "Holocaust" in my post – World War II youth) had created a new kind of obsolescence, different from what the Nazis may have intended for us: we had all become simply "Jews" without additional hyphenations. When I was a child, young boys (not girls!) still dreamed of growing up to be President of the United States. But I knew that, being foreign born, I was clearly excluded from such a goal, even if I saw it as an annoying technicality: I was a mere nine months old when I arrived in this country. I knew I had a different background from other people, because our home was filled with foreign things, and we ate differently. I knew I was different from other kids in my neighborhood, because my parents had accents and theirs generally did not, or because most of them were not Jewish and I was. It would be naive to say that I didn't know we were German Jews, and yet the notion that this involved a more subtle subethnicity was not a part of my consciousness, even when I was quite aware of my family history.

My parents did not generally associate with other immigrants, except in those situations where they were helping people to resettle (e.g., the singular and now-notable group of refugees who entered through official U.S. auspices in Oswego, New York, not all that far from Buffalo, where some of the Jewish social service activities took place). In part, this standoffishness may well have been one aspect of their German-Jewishness. Yet I believe it was also because my mother and father sought their primary associations in relation to the deep Zionist commitments which occupied them so heavily in the forties and fifties. They were also committed to being Americans, and integrating themselves into the fabric of their new community. Socializing with other German Jews—being part of a *kaffee klatsch* circuit— would have been in conflict with this goal. I don't recall ever having a conversation about the meaning of being a German Jew; but I recall many about being Jewish. And no father could more eloquently assist his children in writing the standard Americanism school essays that were the required fare of my youth.

We were intensely patriotic. We flew the American flag on every possible occasion; the party my parents gave in honor of their becoming American citizens was the single most important event of my young childhood. The parties in our home to celebrate the partition of Palestine, in November 1947, and the declaration of the State of Israel, in May 1948, were the two other major celebratory events of my youth, eclipsing even my brother's and my own Bar Mitzvah celebrations. And yet, thinking back on it now, I recognize in the American national patriotism something akin to what we know about German Jews in an earlier Germany.

Into these values, others were also mixed. Among them I would include standing up publicly and visibly for beliefs strongly held. This could involve making certain that the entire family was sitting up front in the synagogue at a service when Zionism-related issues were sermon topics, and then marching the whole family out in the middle of a sermon in which the rabbi would not take a strong pro-Zionist stance. Or it could mean picketing the local British consulate to protest Palestine policies. Or it might involve taking strong and public liberal stands during the McCarthy era. These attitudes do not especially conform to the conventional "good citizen" German Jew image—and I'm proud of that. Indeed, it was to some extent the oddly selective family value system, different from much that surrounded us, that gave us a sense of difference on which we prided ourselves. Perhaps this has analogues in the assumed arrogance of the German Jew. But we certainly never had a family ethos of pride in the mere fact of being German Jews!

If language can be seen as a unifying factor in conveying tradition, then my family's relationship to German was again complex. I was brought up in a home where only English was spoken. My father had learned English in his youth, and spoke it with the vague atavistic British accent of the educated European. My mother learned English by using it in her daily life. They were in their mid- thirties when they arrived in the States, so it would have been natural for them to converse primarily in German. But my father said that he did not want his children to speak the language of murderers!

That we should be expected to absorb the language of Goethe, Schiller, and Heine, somehow seemed a separate issue. It was as though simple genetic factors would enable me to recite "Kennst Du das Land" or "Im wunderschoenen Monat Mai." Obviously there were still subliminal messages that selected pieces of our inherited culture were legitimate. Could we permit the murderers to rob us of this as well? I don't know that this question was ever adequately answered in my family. But determinism has its ways. I wrote one of my very first college papers on a comparison of how Heine and Hauptmann handled the revolt of the Silesian weavers; stumbling through the German, I relied mostly on English translations.

If I have to look at other such matters from which there seemed no escape, I would have to include my father's interest in art—which he had learned from Hermann Struck, having lived in the same house in Berlin. Did this lead me into art history? Since my father also learned his Zionism under Struck's tutelage, did his sense of the unity of the Jewish people derive from Struck's depiction of *Ostjuden*? My parents' dining room was covered by Struck etchings of those bearded Jews, who didn't look anything like family photos of *my* ancestors. In the late twenties, when my father was in the *Juedisches Altkunst* business in Berlin, it certainly also must have taught him, even before Hitler could, that there was more to unify Jews than there was keeping them apart. Was it coincidence that I was handling some of those very same pieces of Judaica over thirty years later in my museum work? My father's diary from his first trip to Palestine, in 1928, discusses the concept of a Jewish state with a full array of the good and bad people that every country has. This vision could not have admitted the social separations among "kinds of Jews"—such as are now helping to undermine the Zionist ideal.

Ours was definitely not the traditional world of *Bildung*, with its sure sense of higher levels of being. *Our* family culture was elsewhere. When we stood around the piano singing songs together, they were never Brahms or Schubert lieder, but rather the *z'mirot* we imagined *chalutzim* to be singing in Palestine at the same moment. My mother's favorites, George Gershwin and Cole Porter, were then (and remain now) carried over from when she had first learned to love them—in Germany. Can I trace my own interest in this music, now updated via Sondheim, to these roots?

*Bildung* smacks to me too strongly as part of the world of the privileged, who are born into their status. (Was it a construct to vie with the Renaissance notion of *virtù*, suggesting that we, too, might become Medicis?) Indeed, as I have learned in my travels, many Europeans believe they don't really have to know culture. They are considered cultivated, by themselves and by many Americans, simply because they are European. I reject that. Culture and education come from immersion and work and commitment, not from some geographic or genetic superiority. If genetics is an unacceptable determinant for those who almost succeeded in exterminating us, why should we buy into it? I don't know that the Frankfurt Jew can necessarily be considered any more *gebildet* than his Warsaw cousin. Even as a code word for "the right degree of assimilation" it would still pose problems; on whose judgment will we rely to figure out how far that assimilation ought to go?

My skepticism about these issues must be viewed alongside an extensive family archive, mostly from my father's side, including not only the usual funky photos, documenting the appropriate *bürgerlich* nature of the family, but also papers and diaries, and a detailed family history which my father wrote over the past sixty years. I don't know that any of it testifies to the primacy of *Bildung* as a significant issue. My grandfather writes about his business supplying veneers for the new Reichstag a century ago; about being in a restaurant with Johann Strauss, who played the piano while people danced. And he uses that strange German-Jewish mix of words that assures us he did not speak Yiddish (God forbid!). Our loyalties were not toward the concept of *Bildung* or any specific set of German-Jewish values, but rather toward the immediate family and *k'lal Yisrael*.

In enumerating those overriding values which guided my parents in this country, and continue to guide me, I am struck by their being

Jewish, rather than specifically German-Jewish. Perhaps that is only a reflection on my parents, who were probably conflicted about these matters, even when they could articulate opinions about them with great clarity. A list might include:

- A concern for history and the past, not to play at nostalgia, but out of a genuine conviction that this is an essential part of self-knowledge (my father often quoted the Delphic oracle's *gnauthi seauthon*—"know thyself").
- A commitment to working with the Jewish people. For my parents' generation this meant primarily the establishment of a Jewish state, and concern for its continued viability. For me it involves reasserting the intellectual and cultural potential of the Jewish diaspora, which has been weakened by an exclusive concern with Israel.
- Involvement with the community at large. My parents gave of themselves to all kinds of community organizations, from the old Community Chest to hospital work to the Urban League. Sharing of yourself, not only financially, but also giving of your person, was always a central family value.
- Maintaining a commitment to the validity of the American liberal political tradition—both for its own value, and as heir to the most essential ethos of the Jewish tradition.

I don't know that any of these values can be especially claimed by the German-Jewish legacy to which I am heir, even while they may conform to the concept of *Bildung*. Yet I care deeply about conveying them to my children, who are now emerging as adults. Pride in who I am and in my personal/family history has to be without a sense of superiority to other Jewish traditions. Which is why I remain interested in my German-Jewish roots, while also concerned that they be viewed in a larger context.

Three of my grandparents (and all of their ancestors) are buried in Europe. The exception is my paternal grandmother; arriving in the States at the age of sixty, she also learned English and spoke it most of the time; she is buried in San Francisco. Her husband, who died long before the Hitler time, is buried in a peaceful grave in the Weissensee cemetery in Berlin (along with lots of other relatives). Despite their current Berlin venue, most of these ancestors came from East Prussia, from a town near Posen. Now it's Poznan! My mother's parents both predeceased extermination possibilities, and are buried in the Jewish cemetery in the city where they lived, Beuthen (O/S). Now it's Bytom!

I've been to Weissensee several times; the last time (November 1983), I was there with my then-twelve-year-old son. I also visited Dachau with him. I've been to Beuthen a couple of times; the last time

(March 1988), I was with my then-eighty-one-year-old mother. I also visited Auschwitz with her. Does it really matter whether East Prussia and Upper Silesia are German or Polish? I know that it matters to the Germans and Poles. But need I care?

One of Gauguin's great Tahitian paintings is called, "Where do we come from? What are we? Where are we going?" It's a good summary for the sense of values transmitted to me by my parents. Accompanied by my wife, I expect to continue conveying similar values to my children. But I don't know whether they are German-Jewish or Jewish, American or Western, humanistic or human. And I'm not certain that I care. That probably sounds like a kind of ignorance of which one ought not to be proud. Yet I'm quite convinced that Goethe would have approved. And I know my father would have. Which is why this essay is dedicated to his memory.

# The German-Jewish Legacy: An Overstated Ideal

*Theodore Wiener*

The principal contribution of modern Judaism in Germany to world Jewry was made long before the arrival of the refugees during and after the Nazi period. That was the reshaping of Judaism from its pre-Emancipation understanding, impervious to outside influences, to a way of life fully compatible with modern culture and civilization; in the catchword of Samson Raphael Hirsch, *Torah im derech eretz*— Torah, however, defined by each thinker in his own way, covering the whole spectrum of views represented by such diverse figures as Samuel Holdheim, Abraham Geiger, Zacharias Frankel, and others. This all happened over a century ago.

I grew up in a home which in many ways was typical of those described by Professor Mosse in his work. Born in Stettin, Germany (now Szczecin, Poland), in 1918, the son of Max Wiener (1882 – 1950, cf. *Encyclopaedia Judaica*), a leading German liberal rabbi, I belonged to the fourth generation of a family with a secular education. My great-grandfather, Meyer Landsberg (1810 – 1870), was a rabbi with university training, officiating in Hildesheim, Germany (cf. *Jewish Encyclopedia*); my grandfather, Meyer Hamburger (1838 – 1903), a mathematician, taught at the Technische Hochschule (Engineering College) in Berlin (cf. *Neue Deutsche Biographie* and *World Who's Who in Science*). Other members of my extended family were public high school teachers, something relatively rare for German Jews; still others were in the more usual Jewish professions, such as physicians and lawyers, although most were business people with varying degrees of success. They represented all shades of Jewish ideologies, Zionist, anti-Zionist, Orthodox, and even the extreme German Reform in Berlin, one uncle belonging to the congregation originally served by Samuel Holdheim.

Culturally they all had this in common, their formal secular education predominated over their religious training, although there was always an emotional attachment to their Jewishness, yet some had little Jewish background, in many cases less than those in this country who had attended the late afternoon Hebrew school. The relative imbalance between German and Jewish education was brought home to me in an address delivered by Rabbi Leo Baeck before the German Club of the University of Cincinnati around 1952. There he paid special tribute to the German *Gymnasium*, the high school, in his education. I do not believe it was simply politeness to his hosts on this occasion, when he reflected on conditions in the 1880s. The rigorous systematic course of study in such a school, which took up a large part of a boy's time, would naturally overshadow the home training in Jewish tradition, even that received in a rabbinic home from which he came.

In singling out at the beginning the major contribution of German Judaism, I was in part guided by the focus of my father's major work, *Juedische Religion im Zeitalter der Emanzipation* (1933). This work, very much praised, has been called the best book on the subject (cf. *Encyclopaedia Britannica: Macropaedia,* vol. 10, p. 329). Among the many fine insights displayed there is the time frame upon which he concentrated, as explained in the preface. After stating that the German branch of Judaism exercised leadership of religious life in the nineteenth century, he then considered the time span of this creative period. He started with Moses Mendelssohn and ended with the sixties and seventies of that century, because by that time all the significant ideas had found their expression.

These ideas had found their way to this country with the so-called German wave of immigration in the middle of the past century. They were reinforced by the influx of rabbis and teachers from the German-speaking areas infused with the new spirit. Among them was the son of Meyer Landsberg, Max Landsberg (1845 – 1927), pioneer Reform rabbi in Rochester, New York, one of the most radical representatives of that movement, who came to this country in 1871 and was the first vice-president of the Central Conference of American Rabbis at its establishment in 1889 (cf. *Jewish Encyclopedia,* with incorrect death date, and *Who Was Who in America,* vol. 1.).

It is my contention that his generation of immigrants was far more influential on American Jewry than our group, because by the time we arrived American Jewry was not all that much different from the German-Jewish community as I remember it. Increasing acculturation and assimilation to the American environment was accompanied by relatively ineffective Jewish education, so that the secular training for most people outweighed that in the Jewish sphere. Now, this pattern repeats itself with each successive immigrant group, and the first American-born generation looks for rapid assimilation to the dominant culture, with a modest corner preserved for the Jewish heritage. This has been true throughout the modern period in every country of the diaspora where Jews were not completely rebuffed, as they were in Eastern Europe before the Russian Revolution.

Therefore, I fail to see whether we can speak of a unique legacy of German Jewry in its last decades that was brought over by the new immigrants. One distinction might be considered, however. In general there was a much higher level of education—at least in the upper classes—of Germany as compared to the United States. That also was reflected in the Jewish community of Germany, which like its counterpart here had even a higher degree of education than the average of the general community. (A popular Jewish saying was: *"Doktor ist der juedische Vorname,"* of course a gross overstatement.) Also in Germany academic education had much greater prestige than it used to have here. Titles like *Doktor* and *Professor* commanded enormous respect. Professor Mosse's preoccupation with the word *Bildung* reminds me also of another German-Yiddish saying: Wenn du wirst sein *ausge*bildet, wirst sein *ein*gebildet ("Once you are trained for a specific vocation, you will be conceited"). Here we see the downside of this striving for *Bildung* with its accompanying boastfulness and snobbishness.

Thus there was a disproportionate number of academics or academically inclined people among the "newcomers," as the Jewish community in Cincinnati liked to call them, which brought it about that a relatively large number tried to reenter their professions and raised their children with this bias toward these occupations. The large number of prominent figures in American Jewish religious leadership of German birth comes to mind, like the current presidents of the Hebrew Union College and the Jewish Theological Seminary, two recent presidents of the Central Conference of American Rabbis, a past international director of the Hillel Foundations, and many others. A recent issue of the *Hebrew Union College Annual* listed among the twelve members of its board of editors four that were born in

Germany. My impression is that this is not limited to the field of Jewish religious leadership, but that this group is also represented to a greater extent than their number in the whole spectrum of academic and professional endeavor. A more in-depth study can be made now regarding this phenomenon, since a biographical dictionary of the German emigration during the Nazi period has been published (*Biographisches Handbuch der deutschsprachigen Emigration nach 1933—International Biographical Dictionary of Central European Emigrés, 1933 – 1945*). This should be compared with the various *Who's Who* and professional directory publications that seem to proliferate.

I happen to belong to the less prominent group, yet am still represented in the former dictionary as well as in *Who's Who in American Jewry* and *Who's Who in World Jewry*. I came to these shores in 1934 to stay with relatives in Syracuse, New York, finished high school there, and then attended the University of Cincinnati (B.A., 1940) and the Hebrew Union College (rabbi, 1943). After a few years in the rabbinate I went into Jewish library work, first at HUC under the guidance of the head cataloger, Moses Marx, (1885 – 1973) a self-taught bibliophile from Germany, with special interest in the Hebrew book, a brother of the better-known Alexander Marx. I succeeded him for a while before becoming associated with the Library of Congress, now serving as senior cataloger of Judaica in the Subject Cataloging Division.

With regard to my personal involvement in the transfer of Jewish lore from Germany, I have a few modest contributions to record. As a student at Hebrew Union College, I wrote the articles "Theism," "Theophany," and "Theocracy" for the *Universal Jewish Encyclopedia*, under the guidance of Professor Samuel Cohon. Originally they were to be translated from the *Jüdische Lexikon* (1927 – 30), whose American rights the publishers of the *UJE* had acquired. Of course I used German sources to carry out this work. My two other works in this area are "The Writings of Leo Baeck, a Bibliography," in *Studies in Bibliography and Booklore* (1954) and "Jewish Refugees at the Library of Congress," in the festschrift for Leon Nemoy, *Studies in Judaica, Karaitica, and Islamica* (1982). In addition my articles in the *Encyclopaedia Judaica*, "Biographical Lexicons," "Festschriften," and "Encylopedias," also utilized German sources, especially the last article, which built on the same entry in the earlier incomplete German

*EJ*. My principal other "literary" activity over the years has been the feature "Jewish Literary Anniversaries" in the *Jewish Book Annual* since 1959. I confess that in selecting many of the entries I may have been biased toward the German-Jewish scholarly fraternity with whose names I am most familiar.

My father, who came to this country in 1939, also helped on a much more scholarly and enduring scale to transmit the German-Jewish heritage to this country. His most important work was the posthumously published *Abraham Geiger and Liberal Judaism* (JPS, 1962; reprinted by HUC Press, 1981). This is an anthology of Geiger's writings in English translation with an extensive biographical introduction. In 1944 there appeared his "Aufriss einer juedischen Theologie" in the *HUC Annual*, his personal understanding of Judaism. Just before his death he wrote "Judah Halevi's Concept of Religion and a Modern Counterpart" (*HUC Annual*, vol. 23, part 1, 1950–51). There he compared the *Kuzari* with the work of the German Orthodox leader, Isaac Breuer (*Der neue Kusari: Ein Weg zum Judentum* [Frankfurt, 1934]).

In spite of our personal efforts in attempting to enrich the American Jewish community with our insights from Germany, I cannot pinpoint the exact Jewish component that was brought to this country, but I rather think that the relatively large number of Jewish professionals (rabbis, teachers, organization executives, etc.) was in part the result of the higher educational level referred to above and also was induced by the impact of persecution, which forced many people to look back to their Jewish roots, however tenuous they may have been before Hitler.

I believe that the German-Jewish spirit was tied to the German soil with the cultural values of Germany. It was an integral part of the German environment and could not be transferred to this country. The immigrants came here and tried to find their niche as best they could in a community that was fundamentally not so much different from their original home. Jewish learning in recent years has taken an upswing. But I believe that it has occurred because of the impact of the Holocaust, the establishment of Israel, and the new emphasis on ethnic studies. Thus, many different influences flow together to propel American Jewry into the next century. No element in that largest of Jewries can claim particular credit for the success or failure of its endeavors.

# A German Past,
# an American Future

*William W. Hallo*

I was eight years old when I left my native Kassel, and eleven when I departed Germany for good in March 1939. By then I had enjoyed five years of education, at the elementary and *Gymnasium* levels, under Jewish auspices, including three at the prestigious Philanthropin in Frankfurt. Together with private tutoring in Hebrew and an active religious life at home, this provided a solid basis for my personal and professional interest in Judaism ever after.

Another formative influence that I took with me at emigration was the profound sense of stability—in retrospect readily described as bourgeois—which I encountered in the homes and offices of my grandparents and older aunts and uncles. This stability left a far more powerful impression on me than did their obvious vulnerability to the sporadic outbursts of disorder and violence that characterized the emergence and consolidation of the Nazi regime.

A third component in my pre-American phase was my one and a half year stopover in England. Coming as it did at an impressionable preteen age, it had an impact on my personal and intellectual development out of all proportion to its brief duration. Comparable experiences could probably be registered by those who stopped in French-, Spanish-, or Russian-speaking countries, however briefly, en route to their eventual destination.

Once arrived (in New York in 1940) I adjusted with relative ease to a new environment. Among major influences here, I would count Rabbi David de Sola Pool of Congregation Shearith Israel, as well as a number of my teachers, both at Boys High School in Brooklyn and at the Seminary College and Teachers Institute of the Jewish Theological Seminary. At Harvard (1946 – 1950), I spent much time with Professor Harry A. Wolfson, but majored in Roman history and wrote a bachelor's thesis, of dubious distinction, on Antioch in the Hellenistic period. A Fulbright grant allowed me to return to Europe, and I chose to begin my study of Assyriology in what I took to be a hospitable climate for so arcane a field—Leiden University in the Netherlands. I avoided Germany, but included in my grand tour a visit to Switzerland and the first of several reunions with my great-uncle Otto Rubensohn, retired archaeologist and excavator, among other things, of the papyri from Assuan (Elephantine) in Egypt, published by him in 1907 and by Ed. Sachau in 1908 – 11. Meantime my newly forged ties to Holland and to the remnants of its Jewish community were permanently strengthened when I met the young woman, then studying at Amsterdam, who was to become my wife. And the year was rounded off with the first of many visits to Israel.

Returning to Chicago and its famed Oriental Institute, I found it dedicated to the "conceptual autonomy" of ancient Mesopotamia preached by Benno Landsberger, dean of the world's Assyriologists. I eventually became his assistant, and for five years (1951 – 56) dutifully subordinated my Jewish and biblical interests to the mysteries of cuneiform. But I became a disciple of I. J. Gelb, and it was from him that I learned a research methodology.

My first teaching position, at Hebrew Union College – Jewish Institute of Religion (Cincinnati, 1956 – 62), was in "Bible and Semitic Languages." It gave me a unique opportunity to use and develop both my Assyriological and my biblical interests. At Yale, where I have taught since 1962, the latter have taken second place, but a new component has entered. Prodded by Maurice Friedman, and aided every step of the way by my mother (deceased 1986), I undertook to translate Franz Rosenzweig's *Star of Redemption* (published 1971). This undertaking eventually led back to Kassel, and to the conference in 1986 which marked the 100th anniversary of Rosenzweig's birth there. For me, a highlight of this first return in fifty years was the prominence given to the memory of my father, whose life had been cut short by illness in 1933 after an astonishingly productive career in the twin fields of Jewish and general art history and archaeology.

Rosenzweig liked to speak of the German-Jewish symbiosis as a *Zweistromland*, a blending of two cultural streams. But the term originally refers to Mesopotamia, the land of the two rivers Tigris and Euphrates. I have tried to blend my interests in that ancient land with my Judaic concerns. For the general public, I have collaborated on *Heritage: Civilization and the Jews* (both the television series and the two-volume study guide and reader accompanying it) and on the Reform movement's Torah Commentary. For the academic scene, I was a founder and incorporator of the Association for Jewish Studies, and am currently president of the American Oriental Society. At Yale, I organized the undergraduate major in Judaic studies, and have long chaired its department of Near Eastern languages and civilizations. Above all, I have been blessed with scores of graduate, postdoctoral and rabbinic students at Yale, Columbia, HUC, and JTS, many of them now occupying influential chairs and pulpits around the country and across the globe, and all of them to some extent committed to my "contextual" approach to biblical and ancient Near Eastern studies.

If I were to draw any general conclusions from my own experience, I would have to assign a sizable place in my personal and professional development to my past. This past, however, includes not only my boyhood in Germany but also my subsequent stays in England, Holland, and Israel, reinforced by sabbaticals in each of these three countries. I owe to these sojourns much of my linguistic equipment, as well as my regard for humanistic scholarship generally, and for the Jewish component in nearly every major segment of it. Perhaps my case belies some of the usual clichés about the German-Jewish experience of the twentieth century. Whatever the extent of assimilation in Germany, there were ample opportunities for religious identification and instruction to those who chose to avail themselves of them; whatever the disabilities under which Jews lived in and left from Germany, they did not outweigh the positive impact of the family traditions that had prevailed; whatever the hardships of adjusting to new environments, they could prove catalytic and constructive given the right age and a hospitable climate. I have incorporated the positive elements of my Old World heritage in my life and work. I'd like to think I have conveyed them to my children as well.

# The German-Jewish Legacy:
# One Man's Dilemma and Solution

*Henry Meyer*

I am a musician, a violinist, born in 1923 in Germany. My early youth was spent in Dresden, a highly cultured city which especially emphasized music and art. My parents, business people, introduced their two sons—my younger brother and me—to this artistic world. Music belonged to our daily life, all members of the family being active players. My father played the violin and viola and so did I, my mother and brother the piano. Many friends joined us to play chamber music, which became part of my general education and led to my life's occupation.

In 1933, when Hitler came to power, all this ceased abruptly, and nothing progressed in normal fashion thereafter. For various reasons my family was unable to leave Germany in time and so we were all deported. Of a rather large family I am the only survivor of the Holocaust, having lost my parents, brother, and others. My life was spared, and after the Liberation I took up music again, first in Paris, where I lived for three years. Later on I went to the United States for further studies. In my new adopted country I was able to fulfill my life's desire: to play chamber music. Only the United States could provide the right opportunities for this to come about. I became a member of a quartet in residence, which means being attached to a university with professorial rank. It permits devoting full time to study and performance of the fabulous literature which exists for the string quartet. Now, why all these explanations?

The world's most appreciative chamber music audiences are, of course, to be found in the countries where all this literature came from: Germany and Austria, both countries with terrible records against humanity during the last war. The compositions involved are by the so-called First Viennese School—Haydn, Mozart, and Beethoven—and the Second Viennese School—Schoenberg, Berg, and Webern. Our quartet has played them all. I have taught them and they are very dear to me. They are my legacy from these countries. But doesn't this very legacy at times become a terrible burden? Would I really want to go back to Germany to play for the people who murdered my ancestors, even members of my family? My own brother, a child prodigy like me, was one of their victims.

Unfortunately, one can scarcely survive as a working chamber music group without playing in Germany. It is our best market. A string quartet has a hard enough time making it: expenses are fourfold and profits have to be quartered. In truth it must be said that I was, despite everything, drawn to return to see where I had lived and to meet certain old friends who had survived, mostly members of mixed marriages: half-Jews. But to perform there and bow to audiences which would surely include people who had done me harm—that was another matter. So how did I manage?

All survivors have found their own ways of dealing with this question. In postwar Germany I myself first played the kind of music which the Nazis called "Degenerate Art," music which had been banned and consequently not heard in Germany. It gave me considerable inner satisfaction to be the one to reintroduce this to the German public. Our quartet entered the German musical scene by playing in modern music festivals. The music heard there was either written by composers condemned by the Germans or by young non-German musicians. There emerged only gradually a group of young Germans who composed music of the sort which also would certainly have been banned as "degenerate" by the Nazis. These were *young* people, younger than myself, and this is the key point.

I hesitated meeting anyone older than I was. Older people *had* to have been members either of the Hitler Youth or of the Nazi party, depending on age. There was hardly any alternative. And very soon, when Germans I encountered realized that I was a deportee who had survived, they didn't even attempt denying a part in the Nazi scene because they knew I wouldn't believe them. The younger generation behaved very well—I'm referring now especially to young people with whom I came in very close contact through musical involvement. But at times it wasn't easy, as I was frequently reminded of the past by lots of things. And there were difficult situations, such as evenings when the flowing beer brought out stories about the Hitler era from people who revealed themselves as Nazis. But with the passage of time this is disappearing. I have had German students in the United States who, knowing what their parents may have been guilty of, must not have had an easy time dealing with me, whom they actually liked.

This makes up my German legacy. I still speak the language very well. I still go to Germany. I have found myself a circle of very wonderful new German friends, partly met in the United States of course, whom I visit in Germany or elsewhere in Europe. I am at ease in Germany when I perform there, when I teach there. But to stay longer than about a month is not possible for me. I somehow become very edgy and have an overwhelming desire to go somewhere else. Naturally, not to Austria, which irritates me even more, but there still are Switzerland and France—the country where I lived after my liberation—and of course, the rest of Europe and the United States. Here in the United States I got my great chance to rescue everything which was denied me and nearly prevented altogether through the Nazi period. I was taken in, helped, and was still able to live a full and very fruitful life. Once again, what I have absorbed from Germany in literature, in music, and in art has ripened by living in another country, and this enables me to enjoy it to the fullest. Perhaps it has even helped me to forget that which it might otherwise recall. This is my story, my solution to the dilemma.

# The German Jew in America: The Last Wave of Immigrants

*Walter Jacob*

The German-Jewish legacy in America was represented a century ago through pioneer immigrant efforts which led to the establishment of many American Jewish institutions; these became the basis of Jewish life in most major communities throughout the United States. They played a dominant role, as the earlier Sephardic Jewish community was very small.

The German-Jewish immigrants of the 1930s added only a small percentage to the total Jewish population and played a less significant role, as institutions and patterns of life had already been well established. Yet they too made major contributions, as this small, very well-educated, elite frequently represented intellectual leadership in the sciences and arts. Scores of individuals in every field made an impact nationally and in some instances revolutionized their field. Men and women like Einstein, Franck, Steinberg, Lewin, Fromme, Ludwig, Zweig, Walter, Arendt, Schonberg, Weill, Kreisler, Schnabel, Mendelsohn, Reinhardt, changed the scientific, musical, literary, and artistic life of their adopted land.

In the next generation many of the descendants of these German Jews may be found in leadership positions both in the general intellectual world and in the Jewish world. For these reasons the German-Jewish legacy is significant. German Jews through their century and a half of acculturation created a symbiosis between German culture and Jewish values. This proved, for the first time in the modern world, that it was possible to create such a union without the loss of Jewish identity and that this could enrich Jewish life. This symbiosis was accomplished for liberal Judaism by individuals such as Hermann Cohen, Martin Buber, Franz Rosenzweig, and Leo Baeck; for Orthodox Jews by Samson Raphael Hirsch, David Hoffmann, and Anton Nobel. Each of these individuals in their specific field demonstrated that Jewish thoughts could be interwoven with ideas from the surrounding modern world. In other words, as the world was no longer hostile to

Judaism, one could safely adapt to certain elements from it and in turn also influence the larger world of Jewish thought. The isolation of Jewish studies which had occurred in the nineteenth century, when modern Jewish studies began, was no longer desirable in the twentieth century, nor was there a need to create a dichotomy between one's Jewish identity and one's intellectual identity.

In every area of Jewish learning, efforts to bridge the gap between the general and Jewish world were made. Let us look at two or three examples from widely disparate fields. Martin Buber along with Franz Rosenzweig created a new philosophy whose structure was dependent upon the surrounding world, yet the thoughts expressed are specifically Jewish. Benno Jacob, the great German-Jewish biblical scholar, did not feel it necessary to isolate himself from modern linguistic and scientific approaches to the Bible. Yet he brought to his commentaries a specific Jewish understanding which led him to polemicize vigorously and successfully against the documentary hypothesis and many misunderstandings of the biblical text which had developed due to an ignorance of the Jewish tradition. His commentaries demonstrate a vigorous symbiosis.

Whole fields of Jewish endeavor which had not been explored at all before or only in a meager way were developed by German-Jewish scholars who combined Western techniques and methods with Jewish learning. Gershom Scholem opened the world of mysticism and established an entire school. Earlier Franz Landsberger did the same for Jewish art and its historic sources. Eric Werner has conducted pioneer studies in the realm of Jewish music which have brought an entirely new understanding of our musical heritage and will influence succeeding generations.

The German-Jewish legacy therefore is one of creative symbiosis which leads to new paths and to creative survival. This has become an essential element of American Jewish intellectual life, as demonstrated through the efforts of hundreds of professors of Jewish studies.

The German-Jewish legacy has emphasized intellectual curiosity and illumination of the past. The Eastern European tradition emphasized spirituality, while the Western European tradition stressed abstract investigation and philosophy. Neither, of course, as exclusive. Both of these trends have found fertile ground on the American Jewish scene and have played an influential role in forming contemporary

American Jewish life. It is no accident that the president of the Hebrew Union College, Alfred Gottschalk, and the chancellor of the Jewish Theological Seminary, Ismar Schorsch, are descendants of the last wave of German-Jewish immigrants. They and a whole host of other leaders have helped to change American Jewish life in this generation and will continue to influence it in the years to come.

These efforts of the German Jew have been attractive to the disaffected intellectual American Jews, who have frequently found that the Judaism of the normative community is not sufficiently deep or challenging for their intellectual needs. Although some of these individuals will never affiliate formally with a synagogue or find their way into the organizational structure of the Jewish community, they will nevertheless respond to the efforts at symbiosis which continue to be made.

Like all immigrant traditions the German Jew brought a large number of incidental trappings which have been discarded and are hardly likely to survive beyond the immigrant generation. As German Jews who emigrated to the United States made a real effort to become part of the American Jewish scene, they also acclimatized quickly, and this differentiated them from earlier immigrants.

The legacy of the last wave of German-Jewish immigrants is one of successful symbiosis and thorough intellectual inquiry. It is worth preserving and will continue as a creative portion of American Jewish life.

# The German-Jewish Legacy in America: A Second-Generation Perspective

*Lucy Y. Steinitz*

What remains of the postwar German-Jewish legacy in America has largely become embedded in the classic flow of American immigrant history. This transformation occurred quickly. For example, in the 1950s and 1960s the dinner conversations at my parents' home still dealt with immigrant-related topics like *Wiedergutmachung* (German reparations), the politics of Willy Brandt, and the board meetings of the Leo Baeck Institute in New York. By contrast, just one generation later, my own family's dinner table conversations—at least when they reach above the din of our two-year-old—tend to focus on issues of environmental pollution, U.S. public policy, and problems facing the American Jewish family. Moreover, whereas my parents' conversation included inflexions of German (particularly when they did not want me to understand), our discussions are usually in English, replete with American expressions.

The impact of my parents' German-Jewish legacy has diminished and blurred over the years. Moreover, I cannot easily distinguish between the effects of my parents' Holocaust experience and the influence of their prewar cultural heritage on my life, nor can I separate my own identity as a Jew with a Western European background from most of my Jewish contemporaries whose ancestors stem from Eastern Europe.

At first I thought that perhaps this is because I have become consumed by the day-to-day demands of work, parenting, and community life, and lack sufficient time for introspection and intellectual pursuits. (I am reminded here of Natan Sharansky's point in his recent autobiography, *Fear No Evil*, that it is in the prison cell—where one is bereft of all choices and freedoms—where it is easiest to contemplate the deeper, philosophical questions of life. With the innumerable choices and distractions of Western affluence, one tends to live more superficially, with neither the time nor motivation to pursue these crucial questions.) But I do not think this is the only reason, nor is it simply that my parents tried to raise me as *ein amerikanisches Kind*, without the burdens of their own losses and immigration experiences. Rather, a philosophical shift has occurred from my parents' generation to mine. Despite a lifetime subscription to *Aufbau* (the German-Jewish weekly newspaper my father edited for over thirty years), I have come to view the German-Jewish heritage more as a great contribution to America (with its scientists, philosophical precepts, and communal leaders), than as a personal legacy which will directly guide my own family's values, orientation, or future identity. With a husband and children who do not share my own German-Jewish background (our children are adopted from Guatemala, which heightens the cultural differences), the passage of an in-depth German-Jewish legacy to the next generation would be difficult, if not impossible.

Some personal history will help emphasize my point. I was born in 1952 in New York City. My father comes from Berlin, and spent the war years first in the French army, then in two concentration camps, in hiding, and finally in an internment camp in Switzerland. My mother—technically a refugee and not a Holocaust survivor—left Germany for England in 1939 as a chambermaid and worked her way to the States in 1940. Seven years later, my parents met in New York and married. I am their only child. As we lived in the heavily immigrant section of Washington Heights, with many of my parents' friends also coming from Germany, I felt comfortably surrounded by a subculture of liberal thinking, largely nonobservant German-American Jews. This was New York City shortly after the war, with its distinct and often eclectic immigrant neighborhoods, when the scars of the Holocaust were still fresh and big-city life could tolerate many subdivisions within its large and growing Jewish community.

Thirty years later and living in middle-class suburbia outside of Baltimore make all the difference in the world. Culturally, I still feel very tied to the history, traditions, and future survival of the Jewish people. But the direction of my involvement has changed radically: I have come to focus on the Jewish community as a whole, rather than on any one segment. Equipped with a master's degree in Jewish communal service and a Ph.D. in social work, I now serve as the executive director of Baltimore's Jewish Family Services, which is dedicated to strengthening Jewish family life, and to alleviating the pain and suffering that persist in our community. Daily we confront the effects of domestic violence, chronic depression, disability, and death. As the need arises, we also work with Holocaust survivors and their families as they confront normal life-cycle stresses or more severe problems which have been caused—or augmented—by Nazi terror and devastation. But I have learned that most of the tragedies we face know no boundaries between Jews of Eastern and Western European background, or between former immigrants and the American-born. In my work, these cultural and historical differences have become largely irrelevant. Similarly, in the broader debates within the meeting rooms of Baltimore's Jewish Federation—be it on domestic politics, the Middle East, or a preferred curriculum for Jewish education—there is no separate, distinctive German-Jewish perspective which is considered. In fact, except for the charity funds and occasional gatherings sponsored by the *Landsmannschaften* of German Jews themselves, in most American communities there is little organized activity left to mark the German-Jewish immigrant experience of the 1930s and 1940s.

One cause for the dissolution of a distinctive German-Jewish legacy in American life pertains to the sociology of a minority-within-a-minority. Particularly outside the big urban centers of Jewish life, where there are not many Jews concentrated to begin with, any further subdivision of the Jewish community is often regarded as antithetical to the unity needed for us to survive as a people. Increasingly, the American melting-pot mentality seeks to fuse us together into a single American Jewish community. Other issues in contemporary Jewish life related to the Middle East, the changing Jewish family, or the newest Jewish immigration from the Soviet Union, seem more important and have dominated our attention.

In some ways, this saddens me. As the immigrant generation dies, all of us will lose the texture, insight, and living testimony this group brought to the American experience. Soon there will be no more Holocaust survivors around to speak with young schoolchildren and community groups and "tell what really happened." No more first-hand accounts will be available to vividly portray the complexity and richness of German-Jewish life before the war. The responsibility to "witness" for each other and our society at large will fall to second- and third-generation Jews, to museums, literature, and films, and to formal community commemorations determined to keep the memory of our collective past alive.

This will be a difficult task, despite all good intentions. As a result, whatever efforts we undertake to preserve the legacy of German Jewry will probably focus on the years of Nazi terror and destruction, rather than on the philosophical or cultural mores which preceded the war. The Holocaust still overpowers and numbs us; it overshadows prewar history and binds all Jews together in a single destiny.

In a sense, Hitler successfully destroyed the prewar German-Jewish legacy in America. Like most other German-Jewish children of survivors, I identify much more closely as a child of the Holocaust than as a descendant of Goethe, Schiller, or the German-Jewish *Bildung*. The lessons of the war dominate my thinking and my religious practice much more than the thinking and practices with which my parents were raised. Specifically, it is to the war—not the cultural or philosophical precepts which preceded it—that I look for my rationale for political or social acts of conscience. Thus, my past volunteer work on behalf of Indochinese refugees and the anti-apartheid movement in South Africa stems more from the lessons of my parents' oppression under the Third Reich than from their ideology or political orientation before 1933. My family's Holocaust and post-war experiences have also helped propel my commitment to professional social work and service to the Jewish community as a whole.

What was lost as a specific legacy of German Jewry among its survivors and their families has become a common heritage for world Jewry, for all of us to share. To keep alive our German-Jewish past, local Jewish communities must develop school curricula, public forums, and historical exhibits from which to build our common future. Despite its terrible destruction, the war forged new bonds and a new sense of unity. In the postwar generation we have all become *amerikanische Kinder* whose joint legacy in the Holocaust has created a new spirit and commitment to life. Fifty years after *Kristallnacht* this dedication is just beginning.

# The German-Jewish Legacy Beyond America: A South African Example

*Steven E. Aschheim*

I was born in South Africa, and it was in that shaping context, as a child of German-Jewish refugees who had come to the shores of that country during the 1930s, that I experienced the German-Jewish legacy. Over the years, of course, my understanding of the meaning of that legacy has changed and deepened as it became more conscious (and the task of this essay will be to briefly delineate that evolution). But from a child's emotional point of view, to the extent that one can distinguish the specifically German-Jewish components from the general experience of growing up Jewish, it was initially a rather embarrassing inheritance.

It was, no doubt, my parents' German accent, at once comfortingly familiar yet clearly foreign, which first alerted me to the "alienness" of my background. To the outside world (or so I believed) the fact of *German* foreignness was especially unforgivable in the years following World War II. In the first few weeks of primary school, when asked where my parents came from I murmured "Australia." How could a child, even around 1950, acknowledge German origins, admit that in some way *he* had been the mortal enemy? Of course, already at that age one intuited the difference well enough but it was well-nigh impossible to articulate that, no, one's parents were not the enemy but the victims, and that defining *them* as archetypal Germans was an obscene irony.

There was, in fact, a double-bind in such a predicament. For, if from the child's point of view being Jewish did not exempt one from the stigma of Germanness, very often in the eyes of our conventionally bigoted, lower-middle-class teachers, Germanness was a synonym for Jewishness. This was brought traumatically home to me when a particularly sadistic manual-training teacher descended upon me and scolded me for crude behavior (what exactly I had done remains a mystery to this day). He was fully aware that I was Jewish—in South Africa a finely tuned ethnic radar is indispensable—and it was this animus which informed his question: "Where do your parents come from?" Upon hearing the answer he proclaimed loudly for all to hear: "That accounts for your manners."

At other times, the anti-Semitic intent was less veiled and the anti-German, anti-Jewish thrust explicitly fused. One day, in the middle of a science class, the teacher settled his gaze directly at me and asked why I believed the Second World War had been fought. Without waiting for a reply he himself provided the enlightening answer: "Because of the Jews, Aschheim, because of the Jews."

These kinds of incidents pushed me ever deeper into the Zionist Youth Movement (in South Africa—unlike the United States—a vibrant "counter-institution" expressive of an oppositional Jewish youth culture) and at the same time into an increasingly critical stance towards the overall system of racial injustice in South Africa.

To what extent was this sensitivity influenced by the cultivated liberal-humanism of German-Jewish *Bildung*, that inheritance to which this symposium is dedicated? Only, I think, in subtle, perhaps even subliminal ways. For that legacy (forged over a century-long struggle for emancipation) was largely the product and ongoing activity of the Jewish intelligentsia: like my parents, the overwhelming majority of the approximately 6,000 German Jews who immigrated to South Africa in the 1930s came from the (initially almost destitute) commercial, nonintellectual classes. Presumably the refugee German-Jewish intellectual elite carried out a voluntary selection process, rejecting even the possibility of going to what they probably conceived as the remote *kulturlos* jungles of Africa. The manifestations of German-Jewish *Bildungsideologie* in South Africa accordingly bore little resemblance to the cultural and intellectual productivity, the moral and critical acuity which, according to the recent work of David Sorkin [*The Transformation of German Jewry, 1780-1840* (1987)] and George L. Mosse [*German Jews beyond Judaism* (1985)], marked the tradition at its best.

When *Bildung* did manifest itself in South Africa, it did so usually in other, more familiar, ways: as the cultivating complement to successful commerce, the refining twin of Jewish *Besitz*. This is not meant disparagingly. As they rose up the economic ladder some German Jews did indeed become pioneering patrons and practitioners of music, theater, and the fine arts, contributing to South Africa's cultural development (and here their European background doubtless stood them in good stead). But their numbers were not all that significant and, in any case, these kinds of activities, more often than not, served to tame and aestheticize the vaunted critical and moral edge of the *Bildung* legacy.

But the category of *Bildung*, this symposium's frame of reference notwithstanding, does not properly reflect the historical reality of the German-Jewish relationship to South Africa. For it was, quite simply, *gratitude* which was the most characteristic (and understandable) response of these German-Jewish immigrants to their adopted country. At a time when the gates of the world had been closed to them, South Africa had given them refuge. The warmth of the welcome and the gratitude they felt was reinforced by the professional and financial success many of them rapidly achieved in an expanding and industrializing economy: they too had acquired a vested interest in things as they were. This was a powerful combination limiting, if not entirely eliminating, any inclination to generalize from their own experience of racial injustice in Germany and protest against what was happening in South Africa.

For all that, I believe that this German-Jewish background did play a conditioning role in the larger sensitizing process. In the first place, the imprint, brutality, and mystery of Nazism and the Holocaust have been with me ever since I can remember. These were topics that were never really analytically confronted but they were, nevertheless, somehow omnipresent, palpably transmitted through my parents' revulsion for Germans and things German (my father adamantly refused reparation money), their reminiscences about the move from Germany to South Africa, and an unstated (but quite unambivalent) message about the fragility of the Jewish condition. Unlike my parents I was not beholden to South Africa as a refugee, and I could therefore translate this sense of vulnerability into quite different Jewish and general terms.

In the first place, Zionism seemed almost self-evident, the obvious solution to the Jewish plight of victimization, the basic precondition for the recovery of a constantly threatened dignity. At the same time, it went naturally hand in hand with a postadolescent awakening to the fact that one's own society was based upon an all-encompassing racial victimization of its nonwhite inhabitants. Not all children of German-Jewish immigrants, by any means, saw things this way. But in my own case these sensitivities were, surely, colored by the cadences and emotional texture, if not the overt ideology, of a first-generation German-Jewish home. This too presumably provided some of the affective background for a later awareness of the ironies of victimization implicit in my own chosen Zionist solution, an awareness made conscious in great part by discovering the writings of German Zionists like Robert Weltsch and Martin Buber—*Bildung* intellectuals who brought that critical humanizing tradition to bear on their own Zionism.

With all their distaste for Germany my parents, like other new arrivals, carried Europe with them in a way that the Litvak majority of the South African Jewish community never did. This went beyond any ideological stance and reflected, quite simply, inherited reflexes and childhood habits revelatory of the cultural tastes and preferences of almost all German-Jewish homes. It was transmitted in a variety of ways. My father would, for instance, effortlessly and quite unself-consciously, reel off reams of (to me, rather incomprehensible yet strangely attractive) poetry from the inevitable Goethe and Heine. Our house rang with the songs of Josef Strauss, Richard Tauber, and Marcel Witrich, marvelous tenors whose 78-rpm records we possessed in abundance and which set the foundations, no doubt, for a later, enduring passion for German classical music. (There was a hidden, compounding irony here. I always took my father's "Germanness" for granted. His great warmth and humor seemed, indeed, to point to the fundamental inaccuracy of the "stiff *Yekke*" stereotype. It was only years after his death that I discovered he was born an *Ostjude*, a Galizianer who had come to Kassel as a small boy and, like so many others, elegantly combined these two inheritances! The fact that he had chosen never to reveal those origins was made even more poignant by the fact that I learned all this as I was completing my dissertation on the problematic interdependencies between Eastern and Western Jewish identity!)

My receptivity to German and German-Jewish history and culture springs, then, from these domestic roots. I have never doubted that essentially biographical and existential impulses were behind my later scholarly interests —understanding the nature of the German catastrophe and the complexities of the German-Jewish experience. The impulse to study the German world flowed from the dual desire to comprehend (and in some way perhaps perpetuate) the lost reality from which my parents came and, at the same time, to grasp what had made Nazism and the Holocaust possible. To a young mind, part of the fascination of German culture lay in its compelling, although at that stage still quite incomprehensible, combination of the profound and the demonic (I only discovered Thomas Mann's explanation of the *necessary connection* between the two in his *Dr. Faustus* much later). Not yet able to penetrate the esoteric language in which they wrote, to my uninitiated, adolescent ears, names like Kant, Hegel, and Nietzsche possessed a kind of magic, an alluring and almost evil ring, resonant with the promise of dark and dangerous brilliance. The questions and fascination persist to this day.

But there is still another level, pertinent to this symposium, which must be mentioned. Since student days I had, quite unconsciously, equated what I valued most in German thought with what I later understood to be the legacy of German-Jewish humanism. What was most attractive in German intellectual and moral life turned out, in most cases, to be linked to its German-Jewish component. Even if one had not really read them, the giants of this legacy (Marx, Freud, and Einstein) were heroic precisely because they were universal men, makers of modern secular thought and yet, in their different ways, quintessentially (or at least socio-psychologically) Jewish, embodiments of a humanizing, moral, and rational impulse. In a sense this was to be expected—everyone's formative intellectual experiences surely included these figures. But a similar elective affinity applied also (and still does) to the endless other examples of German (and Central European) Jewish cultural and intellectual creativity, to the bewitching names and works of people as diverse as Gershom Scholem, Ernst Cassirer, Theodor Adorno, Franz Kafka, Georg Simmel, Franz Rosenzweig, and Georg Lukacs (to name but a few from just the present century). These, rather than French or British thinkers, acted as magnetic, natural models. Similarly it was the work of post–Second World War German-Jewish or Central European exile-intellectuals such as Hannah Arendt, Jean Amery (originally Hans Meyer), Paul Massing, George Steiner, Raul Hilberg, Leo Strauss, George Mosse, and others that seemed to be most relevant: in the post-Holocaust era they were as much the incarnation of the German-Jewish spirit as they were chroniclers of its disappearance.

Rationally seeking the roots of irrationalism, clinging onto the humanizing fragments of an always vulnerable culture—this is what the German-Jewish legacy has come to mean. To be sure, the totality of the actual German-Jewish historical experience must not be romanticized as the undiluted expression of this spirit (it incorporated much that was simply human, all too human, and some things which were even mean and small-minded). But now that it has been physically extinguished, it is surely this fragile humanizing sensibility, independent of any particular time or space, whose legacy we should take care to preserve.

# Fragments of a German-Jewish Heritage in Four "Americans"

*Carol Ascher*
*Renate Bridenthal*
*Marion Kaplan*
*Atina Grossmann*

Over the winter and spring of 1987 – 88, Carol Ascher, Renate Bridenthal, Atina Grossmann, and Marion Kaplan spent time talking together and writing separately about their German-Jewish heritage. Trained as an anthropologist, Carol now divides her time between writing fiction and working in the university as a research analyst on minority education. Renate, Atina, and Marion are all historians with academic appointments; all teach German and women's history in the modern era. Renate specializes in the history of women in Germany; Atina in the history of German population policy and sexual politics; and Marion in the history of German Jews—especially German-Jewish women.

For a time, several years ago, the four of us, all Manhattan dwellers, met regularly for what we called a "German-Jewish CR group." Following the model of feminist consciousness-raising, we discovered many commonalities that we had each once thought peculiar to our own families. As we talked, we saw how our families had woven varied patterns on elements that were both German, though historically specific to the period of their youths, and Jewish, though again showing variations, depending on their distance from religious observances. The request from the editor of this volume to discuss our German-Jewish legacy came on the day we were celebrating our annual Chanukah get-together with the usual latkes, reflection, and banter— an atmosphere of *Gemutlichkeit*. And this time, with an intellectual goal, we attempted to clarify the similarities and differences among us. The following, therefore, represents our separate and collective musings, divided into the topics that emerged over the winter and spring of our most recent discussions.

## Our Sense of Loss

*Atina:* I grew up with an enduring sense of loss, of grief for lost loved ones, but also of sharp nostalgia for the possibilities that Weimar Berlin had represented to my parents—an exciting world where one could be a scholar or professional in the morning, a political activist in the afternoon, and a denizen of nightclubs and cabarets at night. My own sense of loss translated into a hankering for the Bohemian (but not too uncomfortable) life, a fascination with the drama of politics, but also a conviction and anxiety that everything—especially anything good and comfortable—was tenuous, at risk. At the same time, this sense of marginality, always feeling a bit strange, out-of-place, but also on the cutting edge of culture and politics, produced both a longing for the elusive "normal" and a certain sense of superiority to the *spiessige buergerlich Welt* ("lowbrow bourgeois world").

As a child, I lived on the Upper West Side of Manhattan, in a hermetically sealed refugee world. The butcher, baker, shoemaker, dentist, pediatrician, rabbi—all were refugees and spoke German. My father regularly read the *Aufbau "um zu sehen ob ich noch lebe"* ("in order to ascertain whether I'm still alive"—a reference to the obituary section of the *Aufbau*) and because one couldn't trust the American media—with the possible exception of Groucho Marx, whom we listened to on the radio, and *I.F. Stone's Weekly*. My father had his *Stammtisch* at the Eclair and his regular Monday afternoon *Kaffee* with Frau B., who had red hair and was an old girlfriend. My parents shunned all attempts at assimilation, thinking (quite rightly, I decided a decade later) that there was little in 1950s America that they wanted to assimilate into. I vaguely remember the shocks of McCarthyism (my aunt and uncle burning letters from Bertold Brecht), the stories of going South and seeing the Jim Crow signs in buses and lavatories—just like *damals* ("in those times," i.e., in Nazi Germany).

The problem, of course, was that there was never enough money to support the leisurely life of the bourgeois intellectual we all aspired to. We lived in an entirely too small apartment—I remember teasing my parents about how they could expect me to have good table manners if we ate in the dinette. This cramped lifestyle was all the more painful because it was clear that many of my parents' friends—whose elegant parties I would get dragged to, pretending to be annoyed, but intensely fascinated—had made it to West End Avenue or Riverside Drive and renewed professional success. But they had gotten here in time, before the war; they hadn't lost everything, spent exotic but debilitating years in Persian exile and British internment in India, hadn't had to study all over again. Even the ivory elephants and Persian carpets in my parents' apartment conveyed a sense of loss: that we really deserved something better, but that Hitler had taken it all way—all except for the sarcastic Berlin *Schnauze* (fresh or sarcastic mouth). *"All das haben wir unserem Fuehrer zu verdanken,"* ("For all this we have our Fuehrer to thank"), as my father would remark.

But then the *Wiedergutmachung* money started arriving—a double boon for my father, since he worked as a restitution lawyer. And in true German-Jewish fashion, the money was used for a proper holiday in the Alps, at the Grand Hotel Zermatterhof with breakfast on the terrace and hikes to the Matterhorn. From then on, we led a curiously split existence, frugality at home and bursts of old-style luxury on the annual trips to Europe—as if some of the old magic could be recaptured, but with the recognition that it was only possible on "holiday."

*Carol:* For me, it is difficult to distinguish my mother's romantic nostalgia for what appears to have been a rather magical childhood as the youngest daughter of a large, prosperous Berlin family—*Baumkuchen* at the best cafe on Sundays, with all seven children dressed properly in matching outfits; vacations on the Baltic; the dazzle of being the first to have an automobile and other gadgets—from her bereavement at losing her country, her language, her home, many relatives, etc. (My mother lived in Berlin until in 1937, when at the age of twenty-two, she fled to England; there, two years later, in a refugee camp for children, where they both were counselors, she met my father, a psychoanalyst ten years her senior.) My father, oddly taciturn about anything personal for someone in his profession, was clearly bitter about his own Viennese childhood. It now seems quite in line with the conservative psychoanalytic thinking of the 1950s that what little he said were complaints about his mother. Nevertheless, both my parents had come from property-owning families: both in Berlin and Vienna, their factories and apartment buildings were taken by the Nazis (for which they later received reparations). My father's initial profession had been as a professor of literature, probably a quite common choice for the son of a bourgeois family; and his change to psychoanalysis, whatever personal needs drove it, was also a creative solution to being banned from the university in Vienna of the early thirties. For us children, living in the midwest in the 1950s, having a father who treated crazy people and messed about with the psyche was still odd enough to leave one uneasy about the impression we would create. (In public school, confessing that I was a Jew and that my father was a psychoanalyst were equally difficult—both made me an absolute outsider.) And, since either the war or his personality gave him a fear of the entrepreneurial risks of private practice, his choice to work in clinics and hospitals meant that our family income could generate nothing like the expansive lifestyle that either he or my mother had been used to in Europe. The war had stripped them of the entitlement and luxuries of the propertied class.

Yet I always felt that lost property as a quiet source of pride and even security. It was part of the background of my family's elaborate ethics of consumerism, that mystified how much we really had available to spend—one didn't eat oatmeal or baked beans, which had their obvious enough European parallels to make them clearly lower-class; but it was vulgar and ostentatious to be constantly buying new clothes, as Americans seemed to do. Though my father had carted several shelves of leather-bound books (Freud, Marx, etc.) all through his serpentine trail to safety, and though as I was growing up his forefinger was invariably holding open his place in a book, he now considered book purchases a silly luxury and taught me to use the library by taking me with him on his weekly trips to replenish his loaded reading table.

As for what they found here, in Kansas in the 1950s, it was clear to me that they saw almost nothing as an improvement over what they had left behind. True, this country had taken them in and was giving us all opportunities of a sort; but they were shocked by the shoddiness (even nonexistence) of intellectual and cultural life and by the instinctive, virulent prejudice against blacks and communists—against any and all who deviated from a very narrow and confining white Protestant norm. I remember being afraid to bring home any school chums because of the disapproval my parents would be keeping in check. Yet, in a paradox they must not have thought out, they also wanted my sisters and me to assimilate—to do well in school and with the very schoolmates for whom they felt contempt. While my solution, like my father's, was to bury myself in books, my second sister ignored all the unspoken elitism of our home and became a cheerleader, class president, most popular, most likely to succeed.

*Marion:* For my family, I think there was a feeling of a lost homeland—something stolen by the Nazis, of lost potential in that homeland, of a lost comfort, of lost family, but not of downward mobility. It was similar to Steve Lowenstein's findings for Washington Heights (*Frankfurt on the Hudson: The German Jews of Washington Heights*) and Anthony Heilbut's descriptions in *Exiled in Paradise*: that is, the experience of a temporary slide, but with the capacity to pick up where they had been before. None of the people I knew/know would have expressed their situation as one of downward mobility; on the contrary, they wholeheartedly bought into "America, the land of opportunity." My parents were the children of cattle and horse dealers—small-town folks. Also, my mother was very young, twenty-one, when she arrived here; she was just beginning her life. Trained as a *Kindergaertnerin* in Noerdlingen (Bavaria), she worked in an orphanage and day care centers here. She actually picked up almost where she had left off. My dad, who came from the town of Rheda in Westphalia, and then worked as a manager in a small department store in Bielefeld, became a small businessman here in Newark, New Jersey. Neither experienced a downward slide, and they managed to send both children to college—more than they had ever done themselves.

*Renate:* I was raised with a strong feeling of loss. It wasn't only material, though that certainly was a big part of it. My father, with my mother's active help, had built a successful fur business, which only improved after 1933 and the end of the Depression. It was one reason he didn't want to leave until the signs were unmistakable—that is, the Gestapo came twice to examine his books. He came from Warsaw and was less shocked at the level of anti-Semitism than my mother, who had grown up in Leipzig and was less inured to it. My brother once told me that shortly before the emigration he saw my mother kneeling before her furniture, stroking it and crying. She had never had a beautiful home before. Indeed, she avoided having one again until her last years; she was afraid to get attached to it. I grew up in a furnished apartment in a poor neighborhood, with the agenda of going back "home" as soon as feasible.

But, as I said, "things" were only part of it: the sense of loss was about having been in a familiar place and then being plunged into someplace strange and frightening. The trip alone did that, fleeing into Czechoslovakia and then, just in time, to France, and then, just in time again, to Panama. Panama was tropical, too hot for the European refugees. Some of the men who worked physically dropped with strokes and heart attacks. My parents subdivided a large apartment with curtains to set up transient lodgings for other refugees. My father brought people from the boat, my mother cooked for them. My father and brother also sold perfumes door to door, getting doors slammed in their faces. After the first day out selling, my brother told our mother, "A whole world died for me today." That's loss.

I lost something, too (though I was only four), and my photos show it. From a cheerful, confident, bouncy toddler, I became a skinny, fearful, sad child. I lost a sense of security as my grownups freaked out. My mother had a nervous breakdown in Panama and disappeared for a few days, which I remember with terror, because she wasn't there to tuck me in at night. Then my father committed suicide just a few months after our arrival in New York City. He simply couldn't adjust here and it drove a wedge between my parents so that in the end he felt totally abandoned.

My mother didn't see this country as a land of opportunity, mainly because after my father's death she went back to being a fur finisher and worked long and hard for the rest of her life. She kept hoping to get back what she had lost. In 1951, right after my high school graduation, we went back to Germany. There she finally saw that "you can't go home again," and I saw that I wasn't as culturally German as I had been raised to believe. Back in the United States again, it was something of an opportunity for me to go to a free urban college, though I had to attend at night while working fulltime. It was only when the Soviet Sputnik went up and the U.S. government decided for a short time to sponsor its local talent that I got fellowships all through graduate school. So I'm less sanguine than Marion about the golden land.

### *Bei Uns Tut Man das Nicht.*
### (*"One Doesn't Do That Among Our Kind"*)

*Carol:* I could make a list of things we did and didn't do *"bei uns,"* though the profusion of rules that made us superior comes more from my Berliner mother than my Viennese father. In fact, the one way in which my mother tried to balance the inequities of power between her and my father was through being a Berliner, who knew instinctively what was aesthetically and morally correct in all spheres. My father's mother, who lived with us for a time, sang little Viennese songs my mother thought unbearably cheap. *Bei uns* there were no comic books, chewing gum, soda pop, or spongy white bread; we did not come to the table in pajamas or with uncombed hair; frilly dresses that wore out in one season and patent leather shoes were beneath us (though longed for by all three of us sisters); leaving the family radio on a rock 'n roll station took a unified political siege by us when we reached our teens. *Bei uns* one got good grades in school, even though my father could not be impressed by seeing them and inevitably upped the ante by insisting that he preferred a good moral character to merely smarts. Perhaps *bei uns* one always upped the ante, even on oneself.

*Bei uns* there was a sense of responsibility to make the world better. Gradually, I came to believe that this was also a way of showing that we were not victims—that we had sufficient resources to watch out for others, worse off than we. In every neighborhood where we lived, a tree in our yard was invariably chopped down by some neighbor enraged at my mother's activities for racial integration. I remember being taunted by neighborhood children for not believing in a Christian heaven and hell. They couldn't accept that, relieved of the fear of hell, I wouldn't be a liar and a thief. My certainty that I lived by a secular morality that was every bit as demanding as any of their religious morality—that was, in fact, not merely driven by the self-interest of going to heaven or not going to hell—gave me a secret pride.

*Atina: Bei uns* anything too *Amerikanisch* was viewed with bemused contempt. Much to my dismay, this included some of the same things Carol mentioned: comic books, chewing gum, cartoons on TV, and shoes with pointy toes. As a result, a whole world of 1950s and early 1960s American popular culture remains foreign to me. It also included McCarthyism and sexual philistinism—which instilled in me an enduring skepticism about the American democratic system.

But by the time I reached my teens, the mid-sixties had (finally!) arrived. There were Godard movies, Friday evening SNCC meetings, intense afternoon study dates at the Donnell Public Library, marches on Washington to protest the war in Vietnam, and good smooth marijuana to smoke. All this seemed entirely in the tradition of Weimar, not all that different from my father's Berlin youth. I was happy: America had finally caught up with me and my upbringing. And this time, our memory of what came after, our determination never to let gross injustice go by, our collective strength in demonstrations and organizations, our willingness to take risks (to sit-in, to be arrested) would assure that this time the magical world would not topple in the horror that had replaced Weimar.

*Marion:* In my family there was a clear middle-class attitude: we weren't to be rowdy "street" children, we were to dress and act properly, to be respectful. That is a German-Jewish *class* legacy. At home, I didn't hear *bei uns* at all—in fact, America was the model, Germany old hat, ugly, poor. Only my grandmother might remark, "*Bei uns*, we stayed for coffee for half an hour; here they visit forever." But we found that amusing. It wasn't a statement of superiority. Small-town Jews may not have been as arrogant as Berliners. In fact, they reached out, had many friends, both refugees and what my mother called "Americans" (mostly American Jews). My mother became very integrated into her community and passed that feeling of "belonging" onto us. *Bei uns* was the *defensive* opposite of belonging.

Since I lived in a non-Jewish area, I had non-Jewish friends. When I went to high school, my friends were Jews and non-Jews and I never thought of whether the Jews had a German background. When I married an *Ostjude,* his parents and mine became close friends, without major cultural differences. By that time, my parents had become as "Americanized" as they could/would be.

*Renate:* Yes, I admit we felt superior. Like many assimilated Jews, my mother thought the German-Jewish combination was dynamite. Too bad Hitler spoiled it, she said. We combined the best of both worlds: hardworking, disciplined, introspective (*innerlich*), thorough, even pedantic, which was not a derogatory word. *Ostjuden* were considered not quite up to snuff. Americans certainly weren't, with their lack of manners, chewing gum "like cows chewing cud." I was warned not to become too Americanized. But then, we were going back "home"...

## Our Continuing Interest in Germany, and
## Our Feeling of "Unfinished Business"

*Carol:* I suppose my interest in Germany and Austria remains almost entirely personal. When I was twenty-eight, I took a six-week summer trip alone to Europe with the express purpose of seeing my mother's and father's houses. They themselves had never gone back, and my father was now dead. My mother's home was easy to find; it still stood as she had described it, the sunny *Musikzimmer* facing the tree-lined Wilmersdorf street. Whether because of my own ambivalence or objective alterations wrought by the war, I spent a week in Vienna without ever discovering either my father's family's factory or the apartment building where they had lived. In both cities, I was filled with confusion and dread; every aging couple eating their *kuchen mit schlag* was a Nazi normalized. I trusted no one, felt isolated in the extreme. The trip seemed a prolonged exercise in enduring an abnormal state of mind.

Ten years later, when my mother was invited to Berlin as part of Willy Brandt's *Wiedergutmachung*, I went along. With her as my guide, I could picture her charming childhood in the interstices of changes brought by the war, modernization, and even Turkish *Gastarbeiters*. I started to sense Berlin as a complicated city with a continuing and difficult history.

I have never again returned to Vienna, although two years ago, entering Austria by train when my husband and I were traveling from Yugoslavia to Germany, I burst into uncontainable tears—for the loss of my father, for his exile from a mountainous country, which he loved, to far less beautiful landscapes.

On this same trip, we spent ten days in West Berlin. This time it was a city of museums, luxury shops, parks, and cafes—though with that surreal wall so often in view. But I was no longer paranoid, and I could feel the western city as lively, often pleasant, a place where, despite the political strains, real people lived much as we do in New York. I even felt that in some odd way I had earned for myself a rightful connection with my mother's city.

*Marion:* My interest in Germany came from the ambivalence, as well as silence, about Germany I experienced from both my parents: my father, who grew up in Wilhemine Germany, thought everything German exhibited quality, and that life had been good *unter den Kaiser*; my mother, who was born in 1914 and had more negative experiences than he, would not purchase anything German. This mixture of ambivalence and silence sparked my interest more than any one-dimensionally negative anti-Germanism would have done. When I was twenty, I decided to spend my junior year in Hamburg. My parents agreed, for my "education," but felt very defensive about my decision vis-à-vis their friends.

I visit Germany often, as part of my research and to see relatives and friends. I'm fascinated by the "negative symbiosis" I find shared by Germans and Jews: for both, Auschwitz is at the kernel of their being, though they often draw very different meanings from this. I've written several book reviews on the topic of Jews in Germany and Germans coming—or not coming—to terms with this past. And, in part, I'm involved in their past. German-Jewish history, as a result of the Nazis, now transcends German territory. The German-Jewish "symbiosis" continues in the form of a dialogue between historians and scholars—often refugees or children of refugees and survivors—and today's Germans. (I was going to say West Germans, but Macmillan will soon be publishing Robin Ostow's book interviewing Jews in East Germany, and then that dialogue will begin too.)

Most important for me is how the German-Jewish relationship reflects upon other minority/majority relationships, especially minorities in the United States; how it illuminates the tension between assimilation and identity in minority cultures. Especially because of the Holocaust, I feel it is traitorous not to identify as a Jew, and I think it's wise to remember, "We are all German Jews." They called it *Schicksalsgemeinschaft*, "community of fate," then. To a large extent, any political, ethnic, or religious minority can find itself in that position.

*Atina:* I will always have unfinished business in Germany. There is the concrete legacy of the six children of my father's younger brother, a Catholic convert, who survived Auschwitz and reestablished a medical practice in Germany. My father's legal business was there. The contact with Germany was never broken; there was never any question of moving back, but neither was there a question of cutting ties. Now my son's grandparents and cousins live there, my research is there. I lived in Berlin for the better part of three years, felt very much at home, fell in love with my husband, and at a certain point was desperate to come home to New York, where I could approach German history with more distance, and where being a Jew wasn't such a constant preoccupation and responsibility. Though my professional interest stops with the collapse of the Third Reich, I think that my fascination with Jews living in Germany today derives from a very real sense that I could have grown up there. I remember that in my early teens, I often told people on our European travels that I was a German, and was pleased to get away with this tale. It represented various aspects of my German-Jewish legacy: the reassurance that I could "pass" for German if need be, at the same time as a delight in being rootless and cosmopolitan, the European traveler. Indeed, the very condition of having international ties, of being skeptical of national identity, of speaking more than one language, of feeling comfortable in more than one metropolis, of seeking adventure in travel, is one I associate with being German-Jewish.

*Renate:* Actually, my interest is mainly historical. My contemporary interest is much weaker. Such as it is, it is directed more to the GDR (German Democratic Republic), for which I have some hope. Also, my visits there make me feel more familiar; it is, as critics have said, more in the past. The people are less Americanized, for better or worse. They are also simpler, less superficially charming, more direct. This may be an effect of their isolation and provincialism, too.

Over the years of several return visits, I have finally "worked out" my attachment to Germany and put it behind me. I have lost the need to go back constantly to hear my "mother tongue." I've separated out enough from that heritage and attained enough detachment that visits there are less impassioned now.

### Political Legacy—"We Are All Refugees"

*Renate:* The experience of being a refugee is a lasting one. I permanently identify with other refugees and with persecuted peoples, which makes me particularly sensitive to racism. My own understanding of fascism and its link to capitalism in crisis contributes to my socialist consciousness, though I really got it originally at my mother's knee. She was radicalized in her teen years by students in "Red Leipzig" during the revolution of 1918 and then had her own worker's experience to fortify it.

The direct personal experience of flight from fascism colors all my political vision, so much so that I must factor it out sometimes. When I read that the FBI has been surveilling groups to which I give regular contributions, like the Southern Poverty Law Center, then I hear the midnight knock at the door. Still, I try to do what seems to me to be "the right thing"—in spite of the past, *because* of the past.

*Carol:* I remember right after the American troops pulled out of Saigon and Vietnamese refugees were pouring into this country, my mother, who now lives in California near Camp Pendleton, became enormously active. "Whoever is a refugee, I have to help," she said, in her still awkward English. But I had fought against the war in Vietnam, and I wanted to distinguish among refugees. Many of those people who were fleeing had collaborated with the Americans. I recall hard words between me and my mother. In fact, given the refugees this country takes in, one is left rather too often in the position of helping the educated and propertied classes fleeing left-wing regimes (while ignoring victims of poverty and right-wing death squads). Still, like Renate, I have a visceral empathy for all stories of the midnight knock on the door and the quick exit with everything squeezed into a single suitcase.

Each year, more of the world is uprooted, reduced to wandering in search of temporary or permanent new homes. In this, our heritage becomes increasingly universal.

*Atina:* At the recent reunion of Columbia '68 strikers, Mark Rudd spoke of how important relatives with tattoos on their arms had been to his political socialization, to his conviction that the most important thing in life was "not to be a good German." It was a conviction that led to some grandiose posturing and some bad politics, but it is a sentiment that I can very much identify with. Indeed, what strikes me most strongly in retrospect is how we saw the Vietnamese and the blacks as the "Jews" and ourselves as the potential "Germans" who would go along and not resist oppression.

And one must, of course, speak of Israel, Palestine, and Zionism. It is, I always thought, precisely the German-Jewish legacy that made me suspicious of Zionism, unenthusiastic about a Jewish state, long before I had any political analysis to defend my arguments or historical knowledge to relativize them. To live in a Jewish nation simply seemed so unlike the urban, cosmopolitan, intellectual, critical stance that I identified with being Jewish. I had, after all, learned that nationalism and a sense of racial superiority had led to the undoing of Jews in Europe. Indeed, I sense in myself once again the stirrings of "not being a good German" when I protest current Israeli government policy.

### Bildung

*Renate:* This may be idiosyncratic. My mother had all of four years of schooling—she had been in the countryside in Slovakia with her grandmother and only got to school in Leipzig at the age of ten, when she compressed the whole eight years of elementary education into four to graduate with her peers. She transmitted to me a mixed message about this, as about so many things! The one was the importance of education, and her wish that I be "better" than she; the other was her working-class fear of snobbishness.

But what won me was the marvel of the escape that books offered. Somewhere along the line in my reading, I adopted the model of the (male) hero in the *Bildungsroman* (novel), whose life is a quest for character formation. This, I may add with an ironic smile, has not yet died in me, though I can recognize its narcissism.

Perhaps *Bildung* was (is) an unconscious quest for assimilation, though it also blends nicely into the scholarly tradition of Judaism. The objective fact is that my dedication to *Bildung* has netted me a secure, well-paid academic job, so it has served a material goal too. And the intellectual life is about as assimilated to the great universal enterprise of knowledge as one can get.

*Marion:* My parents didn't have higher educations, yet they adored classical music, opera. My dad was politically interested and aware, my mom introduced me to all of New York's art museums. I was one of the few teenagers I knew who regularly took the long trip from New Jersey to New York to visit a museum. What they both shared was a respect for education. This was probably a comfortable marriage between the idea of *Bildung* and the American belief that education is the way to "make it." We children did not have to do our chores or help out if we had long homework assignments: homework came first. George Mosse has argued that *Bildung*—combining the English word "education" with character formation and moral education—became central to "Jewishness" for many Jews. I think that here it also showed Americanness, so it was easily adaptable and made our transition easier.

*Carol:* When I think of *Bildung* in my family, its positive qualities of character formation, moral education, and a belief in the potential of humanity are tempered by the fact that my parents had three daughters. For my father, who was a strong believer in *Bildung*, the fact that he had only females to work with tore him apart. I see this particularly in the way he treated me, his eldest daughter. He wanted to give me every intellectual and artistic opportunity, both for my own development and to provide himself with a companion and heir. Yet when I grew sufficiently confident to argue my own points of view, he became afraid that I would alienate men and never find a mate. I was given lessons in painting, piano, violin, and ballet; but as I began to take each in turn seriously, I was warned of the precariousness of an artistic life—and in one case the lessons were withdrawn. I was to be cultivated, but not ambitious for myself; clever, but not passionate about any pursuit or subject—in short, ornamental, a salon woman, perhaps, who could stimulate and bring together men. Unfortunately, as my mother optimistically points out, my father died before this last historical wave of feminism; for she (who herself was encouraged by him to complete both high school and college in the United States, at the same time as regularly humiliated by his sardonic tongue) feels sure that he would have seen the logic of women as equals.

*Atina:* I can't remember being imbued with any exaggerated respect for formal education. I don't recall any pressure for good grades or success in school, but perhaps that was because I was always a good if somewhat erratic and idiosyncratic student (that too seemed appropriately Berlin). In our family, intellectual and political passion, rather than *Bildung*, was important. My father's generation, after all, rebelled against the *gute Elternhaus* (stifling middle-class environment) of the German-Jewish bourgeoisie—seeking contacts with artists and writers, political activists, even as they dutifully became doctors and lawyers. I identified with that dual legacy.

This remains perhaps the paradox of the German-Jewish legacy: the memory both of belonging to a cosmopolitan culture that seemed on the verge of creating a more socially responsible and culturally interesting world, and of ostracism, victimization, total entrapment, senseless death. In my own private version, it has meant an openness to adventure, a commitment to left political activism, and a sense of possibility for myself as a woman who need not be constrained by traditional roles (whence grows my interest in the topic of new women between the wars), but also an insecurity and sense of marginality, of never feeling quite at home in the world and only pretending that everything is OK.

## Religion

*Renate:* I was raised with a minimum of ritual. My mother up to the age of two or three was in foster care with a Catholic woman. The highpoint of her childhood was playing Baby Jesus in a Catholic procession. She was somewhat eclectic in her religious views, but never denied being Jewish. In my early years, I remember some agnosticism, but later on she got increasingly religious, and by the time I was in my teens, she was having an intensely personal relationship with what she called *"mein Gottele."* I must add that she was also increasingly paranoid and really needed to believe in that personal hot-line.

She did inculcate some sense of Jewishness in me: I was enrolled for a few months in a Hebrew school, but she soon quarreled with the congregation and pulled me out. She went to various synagogues at various times, but objected to their charging for seats. We observed the High Holidays, though I'm not sure she fasted on Yom Kippur; I couldn't hold out, still can't.

She also imparted a sense of mission as "the chosen people," which translated into doing good, and she did so by giving to charities out of her earnings, helping poorer people in our immediate vicinity, and educating me to work for a more just society. She disapproved of Israel's founding, mainly on practical grounds that it was "walking into the lion's mouth" and could lead to no good. I continue that anti-Zionism. The Jewish tradition I got was universal and messianic, and translated into socialism. The idea was—and I have lived by it—never to deny my Jewishness, to be proud of its heritage, but also not to stand out in speech, gesture, clothing; that is, to place a value on assimilation. It is probably no accident that my two marriages (both ending in divorce) were to non-Jews.

*Marion:* My parents, with my mother as initiator, went to synagogue regularly, and sent me to Hebrew school and had me Bat Mitzvahed. They observed the holidays, fasting on Yom Kippur. My grandparents, who were very close to us, fasted on other days as well. My grandparents went to a German-Jewish synagogue where they spoke German. My parents, in New Jersey, went to an "American" synagogue—always distinguishing between "other" Germans (meaning Jews) and "Americans." Part of the German-Jewish stereotype among American Jews was that German Jews were clannish. The ones I knew were because they shared experiences, language, and culture, not because— as they were so often accused—they felt superior. Their children (my brother and I) "intermarried" with American Jews, as did most of the German-Jewish offspring.

Our religious legacy, as I see it, is that, like in Germany, religion remained most alive in the family. Whereas in most cases, synagogue attendance fell off (surely the case for my brother and me), celebrations of holidays and lifecycle events occur in the family, and the feeling of being Jewish is often connected with the family (the Jewish mother, the close family, and other cliches already prevalent in Germany).

Yet, for me, the German-Jewish legacy has a strong secular component. It remains alive in my intellectual world as a frame of reference for both non-Jewish and Jewish issues. I read *Tikkun* both for its intellectual and its Jewish concerns. I also subscribe to *Jewish Currents* and *Jewish Book World* for the same reasons. But I worry that this kind of "Jewishness"—*Bildung* as a substitute for synagogue—can't last beyond our generation. The next generation will need something more. As a secular Jew, I want to pass on to my child my feeling of belonging to the history and heritage of the Jewish people. My German-Jewish heritage, which gave so much to the religious currents of Judaism today, doesn't help do this in a secular way. Translated as *Bildung*, it means that my daughter could be educated and cultivated—go to the opera and read Shakespeare—and really not feel very Jewish.

Having "intermarried" with the son of Eastern European Jews, I can send our daughter to a Yiddish school. There, she can learn about the holidays, customs, folktales, music, and history of Jews. We participate in Seders, Chanukah parties, and Purim celebrations. The school is not religious but celebrates Judaism in the secular tradition known as "Yiddishkeit"—a far cry from the German-Jewish tradition, as my mother always reminds me. There my daughter is developing an approach to her background that is cognizant of the Holocaust, but doesn't reach *only* to that issue; that takes seriously the importance of learning and of giving; that supports other minorities as well as her own; and that views her religious/ethnic heritage positively and hopefully, avoiding national chauvinism. And there we have a community of similarly-minded Jews to give us a sense of solidarity and kinship.

*Carol:* Like Renate, my religious education was pretty much limited to not denying my being Jewish, at the same time as being rather ashamed of those who were conspicuously Jews. I'm not sure what my father's household was like in Vienna, though I assume they kept kosher. I know that my mother's family observed all the holidays (they were times when my grandfather could show off his large, prosperous family in synagogue) and that her family had two sets of silverware, much of which is still being passed among the dwindling number of living siblings. I also recall her telling me as a child that, if all Jews had been assimilated like her family (in contrast, I suppose, to the Hasidim), Hitler would have had little to complain about.

Once in the United States, in part as a result of bitterness from the Nazi experience, my father took a staunchly atheistic position; and my mother, who was always his intellectual protege, fell into silent embarrassment about her religious yearnings. I remember a couple of Yom Kippurs when my mother went with me to temple, but we did not have the conviction to fast: and perhaps there was a Chanukah or two in which she lit the lights for us. On the other hand, shortly before he died, I recall my father reading Simone Weil and other modern mystics, at the same time as my mother was becoming comfortable with a naturalist explanation for all questions. In any case, we were only sporadically, and then at one of the children's insistence (why couldn't we be like other children?), taken to the Sunday school of a Reform congregation; and by then our intellectual training was sufficient to make a mockery out of the "fairy tales" we were told there, so that we soon tired of the exercise in belief.

Not surprisingly, both my married sister and I are with non-Jews. My sister and her family celebrate the Christian holidays, although recently, with the aid of my mother, there has been a certain preparation of potato pancakes on Chanukah. On the other hand, my marriage to a non-Jew has somehow heightened my Jewish feelings, and given me the awareness that the responsibility for Judaism in the family is mine. Thus, over the past decade, I have studied a great deal about Judaism. Though I find it hard to worship (the God of any religion), I feel deeply connected to our rich and complicated religious and cultural tradition. With my Jewish friends, I find ways to celebrate most holidays, which at a minimum means celebrating a common heritage.

*Atina:* As elsewhere, I think I have a particular "liberal" German-Jewish relationship to the religious aspects of Judaism. I derive no comfort from any kind of faith in God, but I do derive comfort and some sense of historical meaning and continuity from (very) occasional religious rituals, at home and in the synagogue. I love to host a Passover Seder for my extended family of friends and their children. The fact that I have any religious education at all is a direct result not of my parents' religious conviction, but of their obligation to the dead: their feeling that, whatever it was that their families were put into the gas chambers for, their child should know something about. And I enjoyed Hebrew school, although I drew the line at Bat Mitzvah.

I would also very much like my child to have some sort of Jewish religious education, so that he too can recognize prayers and know the stories of the holidays, and feel himself part of several heritages, only one of which is American. I do not know how I feel about formal ritual for my half-Jewish child: it is hard for me to imagine him having a proper Bar Mitzvah, but I want some sort of ceremony marking a kind of historical continuity. The notion that the Jewish diaspora survives is very important to me.

### Our Work

*Marion:* I see myself as continuing a legacy of hard work, discipline, thoroughness, and even pedanticism. (I'll never forget that my American publisher of *The Jewish Feminist Movement in Germany* wanted me to cut my footnotes in half, while my German publisher wanted every last footnote and more.) One reason why German Jews fit in well in America is that hard work and discipline are American virtues as well. Jews in Germany were also deeply independent, leaning to the free professions, to business and commerce, and to academia. When they came to the United States, most remained independent, and my family, including my brother and I, chose independent careers as well. Although I now have an academic appointment, for the last ten years I thought of myself as an independent historian, who worked on grants or in offices for a living—much like Carol, who supports her writing by working at Teachers College.

*Carol:* I've been surprised by how deeply the stream of my German-Jewish refugee background runs through my writing. It was the need to tap this stream, in fact, that prompted me to give up anthropology for writing. *The Flood* expresses fictionally many of the themes of identity, assimilation, and responsibility in the new land that we've talked about here. Looking for my father's house in Vienna became a short story, while my trip to Berlin with my mother is a long memoir, and I have many short stories and essays that explore the quirks of being a first-generation Jewish woman. Sometimes I think I've said all I have to say about all this and can go on, but then I notice how a new story or a new idea for a novel carries some of the same seeds reworked.

*Atina:* My work on sexual reform and the "New Woman" in Weimar Germany reflects my wish to come to terms with a Weimar legacy that is not specifically Jewish, but in its urban, leftist, modern orientation was certainly very much imbued with a European Jewish spirit. I also carry my understanding of the collapse of that culture, and the ways in which it was both destroyed and transformed by National Socialism, into how I think and act politically today, whether it be in regard to reproductive rights or Israeli government policies.

*Renate:* All my research relates to my unfinished business with Germany. For a long time, it was a kind of search for roots. Probably it is a mark of the assimilationist mentality that I sought roots in German, rather than in Jewish or German-Jewish, history. Both my master's thesis and Ph.D. dissertation at Columbia pertained to German intellectual history. The women's movement inspired me to search for women first in European history and then, more closely, in German history. These projects required me to visit both German states again and again, and each time I worked through another level of my conflicted feelings. Currently, I am writing a book on two housewives' organizations between the two world wars that could be described as proto-fascist, so my work is part of the "how did it happen?" quest. With many of my generation, I feel some urgency about "telling the signs" in order to help prevent a repeat performance.

# My German-Jewish Legacy and Theirs

*Anthony Heilbut*

This German-Jewish legacy, how German is it? and how Jewish? Moreover, what kind of Germans? what sort of Jews? Who inherits this legacy, a Joseph or a Judah? What legacy do our Joseph and Judah select? Surely not the same one. It's typically German, typically Jewish, typically German-Jewish to stress the uniqueness of one's group, attended by an inexorable ambivalence, another specialty of the three groups in question.

A perfectly straightforward issue is posed, and immediately my tone seems captious. I have two explanations: a general one—I'm upset by any form of cultural nationalism—and one more immediate: A few months ago, I spoke with a young German. He was both effusive in his praise of German Jewry and obsequious in his apology for crimes committed years before his birth. (In Germany, wallowing in guilt and self-pity seems as timeless as bad taste.) Finally he revealed his agenda: "Let's face it," he said. "Germans are the best people, and Jews make the best Germans." Aha, I thought, there you go. We're either the best or not good enough.

Much about the German-Jewish legacy eludes facile generalization, starting with the question of Germanness. Consider my family's complicated roots. The son of a Hamburg father and a London mother, my father was born in Amsterdam. Maritime links between his parents' cities helped make the Hamburgers spirited Anglophiles. For Hamburg Jews as well, British connections added a whiff of cosmopolitan style, particularly during the nineteenth century when German—or German-Jewish—identity was newly formed and tentative. My father's English relatives were distinguished Jews. Two of them, the elder of whom had been born in Hannover, served as chief rabbi of the British Empire (a designation which links almost too well the pious and the imperial). Another was Elkan Adler, a scholar of Middle Eastern studies. Adler was very much an English character, as were my father's cousins, the Sharp brothers, "Mr. N. and Mr. C.," as their charwoman referred to them. All of them managed to combine Orthodox worship and English eccentricity, a personal style that greatly impressed their German relatives. An overlooked truth about the famous German Jews is that although they lorded it over the *Ostjuden,* they knew that the classiest Jewish role models resided abroad.

When he was sixteen, my Amsterdam-born father moved to Berlin. His Berlin relatives owned N. Israel, where he would very shortly assume an executive position. (N. Israel, the oldest department store in Berlin, was attacked on *Kristallnacht,* almost one hundred and eight years after its founding.) The Israels' life was golden; they provided the models for the Landauer family in Christopher Isherwood's *Goodbye to Berlin.* It was all very high-style, not at all like the arriviste gaucherie satirized by Heinrich Mann in his mildly anti-Semitic novel *In Schlaraffenland.* The British-born Amy Israel conducted her soirées in English; the landscape architecture of their country residence was exquisitely British. Artists and writers partied with the most cultivated businessman. When Enrico Caruso serenaded Mrs. Israel, he did so incognito in her kitchen. (Old class tends to believe if you've got it, *don't* flaunt it.)

While the Israels were not the arbiters of Berlin society, they were a kind of Jewish royalty, and royalty had its obligations. With his joint British-German citizenship, Amy's son Wilfried was able to secure the safe passage of his Jewish employees (aided in his task by my father). He also sponsored the rescue efforts of Youth Aliyah. His death in a 1943 plane crash was a major loss, one immediately memorialized in the naming of my brother, Wilfred, born later that year. If anyone could exhibit German-Jewish snobbery, this family had a right. I'm glad to say they didn't. In the mid-twenties, they revealed another solidarity when Wilfried and my father played active roles in the rescue of Polish Jews threatened by anti-Semitic pogroms. Likewise in exile, my parents never exemplified any Ostjüdophobia. (They were not typical. After *Exiled in Paradise* appeared, several *Yekke* offspring confessed that their elders held eastern Jews in contempt.)

My mother, twenty years my father's junior—and think how that alone complicates any unified legacy—was born in Berlin. Her mother's people, old Berliners, made up the more refined family branch, while her father had migrated from Upper Silesia. With varying degrees of earthiness, both sides enjoyed that fractious, smart-alecky Berliner *schnauze,* a manner I always assumed unique to my family until I visited Berlin and found the whole town doing it. My Polish-German grandfather was a lawyer, as was his son, as would have been his daughter had Hitler not closed law schools to Jews of either sex. While my father, as a Dutch citizen, always lived well in Berlin, my mother left Germany in 1933. But after finding no work in France she returned to Berlin, where they were married. In the late 1930s, while he was abroad soliciting affidavits for N. Israel employees, she hid some of those employees in their apartment.

They left Germany in 1938, hoping to acquire British citizenship, but were encouraged instead to return to Holland. America became for them, as for so many other refugees, a second choice. How could it be otherwise? To men like my father, England was the citadel of quality, America merely a nation of naive upstarts. (The historian Hans Kohn was similarly enamored of British political traditions, almost without reservation, despite British treatment of Jews during World War II.) While some German Jews were famously more German than the *echt Volk*, others admired Great Britain past reason or good sense.

So which German legacy do I claim? My father's: noble, socially correct, good-humored, Anglophiliac? Or my mother's: street-smart, good-humored, Berlin-based? Their peers didn't regard the backgrounds as similar. In fact the "Jewish community" found my mother, daughter of non-Orthodox parents, insufficiently kosher. My parents were obliged to marry three times, as if each ceremony would further mitigate the heresy. Thanks to the Israels, they enjoyed access to the most *raffiné* precincts of German-Jewish life. Yet when I review their history, I see considerable divisions in class and culture—a range extending from a scholar of Middle Eastern languages to an aspiring Berlin Portia—and at least three national components beside the German.

Having alluded to my parents' experience, let me generalize a bit about my own as the American offspring of German Jews. An uncomfortable truth is that despite the refugees' celebrated disdain for American ways, they frequently knocked themselves out in emulation. I mentioned that my brother and I never experienced any *Ostjude* prejudice while growing up. Quite the contrary. My mother was bemused to find ex-Berliners less concerned about their darlings' *Bildung* than whether they had pledged the proper Greek-letter organizations. At Forest Hills High School, refugee children were basketball stars, cheerleaders, presidents of the student organization. You might say they were rehearsing the shift in Jewish identity from scholar/poet/ *luftmensch* to businessman/hustler/maker-and-shaker, and that emigration had encouraged their most bourgeois tendencies. (Or, at least, their chameleon qualities. Marion Kaplan feels the behavior I describe doesn't match her experiences, which suggests refugee culture as a function of neighborhood.) Yet what a sea change! German-Jewish feminists honor the uncompromising positions of Hedwig Dohm, and are fascinated by Rahel Varnhagen's career. Wouldn't both women shudder at the prospect of their descendants turning out Prom Queens?

On a more serious note, I think the German-Jewish legacy was at least initially a vexed one for children born here. Our parents carried themselves differently from our peers'. Also they were frequently much older, the vintage of our friends' grandparents. The psychic costs of beginning the world again were tremendous, even for the matchlessly resilient German Jews. Precisely because this group was so cultivated, so proud of its legacy, there was an added component of bad faith not evident in groups less given to self-conscious reflection. In the blunt terms of American culture, one was either a winner or a loser, and with their curious accents, unfamiliarity with American habits, and inescapable sense of the Holocaust—nagging fears before 1945; a far worse certainty afterward—the German-Jewish parents simply didn't appear winners. The familiar dilemma for immigrants' children—loyalty to the parents' culture versus the wholesale assumption of American mannerisms—was that much more complicated for our bunch, particularly during the monolithically conformist era of postwar America. Not that some German-Jewish children didn't hate their American lives, and retreat to the consolations of their parents' culture. I've met a few like that, but while they attend all the Self-Help concerts and maintain a family subscription to *Aufbau,* I don't know how much their succor is some hallowed German-Jewish legacy, and how much the familiar traits of one's own "soul people."

\* \* \*

The myth of Jewish exceptionality is a notable theme of German literature. It's found in Goethe and Nietzsche, and more recently in Thomas Mann, who saw himself as the custodian of their proper legacy, including their qualified philosemitism. But if you detect xenophobia lurking beneath any form of chauvinism, is a legacy more acceptable because such men endorsed it? Or do you echo Heinrich Heine's remark that he came from an even older tradition, three thousand years of schlemils?

I'm American enough to want my legacy put to practical use. The chief rabbi's descendant won't join a German-Jewish synagogue. But surely there are other ways of honoring one's ancestors. Let's say I look for political role models. I find that the story of German-Jewish politics is more mishmash than midrash. In preparing a critical biography of Thomas Mann, I learned that Mann remains unforgiven by certain radicals for his silence during the early years of exile. The fact is that Mann had noisily denounced the Nazis as early as 1921, and would do so up to 1932. However, for the next few years, he had the not unreasonable idea that he could propagate his humanist principles by continuing to publish in Germany. The author of this scheme was his Jewish publisher Bermann-Fischer. (Likewise his American Jewish publisher Knopf would advise him not to attack Hitler in 1940 or Senator McCarthy in 1950.) German Jews have often been overly cautious, particularly the establishment figures: this left them open to attacks from gentile radicals like Brecht, which were in turn either disingenuous or insensitive to the Jewish plight.

In emigration, the political range of German Jews extends from Albert Einstein to Immanuel Jakobovits, the Berlin-born chief rabbi of the British Empire. As I wrote in *Exiled in Paradise,* Einstein played an heroic part in defense of American radicals, counseling them to risk jail in defense of their principles. The chief rabbi's politics can be gauged by his role as Margaret Thatcher's favorite theologian (think of it—a German Jew outdoing the archbishop of Canterbury). Meanwhile currently important descendants of German Jewry in American politics include the ineffable Henry Kissinger, Senator Rudy Boschwitz, a Republican loyalist (his Rudy a German-Jewish reply to the American Bobs and Jimmys), and Max Frankel, editor of the establishment's house organ. After *Exile* appeared, several German Jews complained that I had misrepresented their group as a bunch of Marxist malcontents, when instead they were exemplary American citizens. Like those Christian converts who call themselves "completed Jews," they'd say that their legacy culminated in American patriotism.

Yet can't German Jews claim Karl Marx, even as they do Freud? Marx may betray an anti-Semitic bias, but his very method instructs us to disentangle the wheat from the tares. Forget the rather disingenuous claim that Marx's ethical concerns are positively Old Testament – like in their reach. He's German-Jewish enough without seeking to make him kosher. The world knows it, friend and foe alike, but to admit him into a German-Jewish pantheon is to considerably, attractively expand its borders. Combine Marx's alertness to the economic underpinnings of every social action with Heine's irreverence—now there's a legacy. Add to that the more contemporary efforts of émigré film directors like Max Ophuls or Fritz Lang, and I become almost chauvinistic myself.

I also like that a few, admittedly fringe figures anticipated the major sexual conflicts of our time. The feminist/gay slant has reformed our views of matters as basic as the family: those who live outside the institution have hastened its reimagining. Hedwig Dohm, the nineteenth-century journalist, lamented that when they stuck a cooking spoon in her hand, they killed a human soul; she never forgave her grandson-in-law Thomas Mann for ending his wife's academic career or expressing a desire for sons. She lived until 1918, despairing over the conventional lives of her daughters. Even more than Rahel Varnhagen, she seems the ancestor of modern women intellectuals. Although she too ran a Berlin salon of artists and radicals, she would side with those who feel no need to be the hostess (Varnhagen) when they can be the guest (Goethe).

An overwhelming sadness of our times is the AIDS epidemic. While comparisons with the Holocaust and genocide seem to me ill-considered, there is an ironic parallel in the gratuitously horrible destruction that befell two pariah groups—Jews and gays—exactly when they seemed to have liberated themselves, socially and politically. Meanwhile the reality is grim enough, particularly as it illumines medical politics and the transparent bigotry toward drug addicts and gay people. In seeking out the origins of that bigotry, some of the best guides are German Jews. Magnus Hirschfeld was the foremost sexual libertarian of the 1920s; disallowing his own flights of cultural nationalist rhetoric (e.g., "the third sex"), he was strikingly prophetic in his analysis of the pathology we call homophobia. Hedwig Dohm's half-Jewish great-grandchildren, Erika and Klaus Mann, idolized Hirschfeld.

While their father would irrepressibly deconstruct traditions German and Jewish, his children hoped to abandon the exhausted strictures of religion and nationalism. They learned that this wasn't done so easily. But isn't their attempt, sixty years afterward, still admirable? And doesn't it constitute a legacy too, a kind of lodestar during the era of AIDS?

I remain confused. What I value, what I need seems so tangential to any record of German-Jewish culture. (As one woman assured me after a lecture, the achievement of émigré film directors wasn't truly "serious"). Yet I'm convinced the good German-Jewish allergy to *Quatsch* (nonsense) steered those ancestors I would claim. The allergy made them recoil viscerally from whimsy and sentiment, and made them very hard to fool. It may seem a poor legacy, this *Fingerspit-zengefuehl*, but it's undeniably German-Jewish.

# Bildung: An Agenda of the Soul

### Uri D. Herscher

Is there a German-Jewish legacy here in the United States? If there is, its avatar was my father, born in Cologne early in the century to parents who had come there from Austrian Poland. My mother, too, is German-born, but the intellectual interests which preoccupied so many German Jews have never meant a great deal to her. Younger than my father, she was scarcely more than a teenager when she left Germany—shortly after the Nazis came to power—for *hachsharah* (agricultural training) in Czechoslovakia and settlement in "Eretz" (British Mandatory Palestine). Neither my father nor my mother had much formal education, but *Abba* and *Ima*—that is how Eli, my younger brother, and I have always spoken to and of them—were most at home in German; whether in Tel Aviv or, later, in San Jose, California, they gravitated to German-speaking Jews, and German was my language, too, until I went to kindergarten in Tel Aviv.

I think German was an outlook as well as a language for my father. For much of his life, and especially during the years he spent in Tel Aviv, he was an avid reader. The street on which he maintained his carpentry shop—Yona Hanavi—also housed a German lending library, and *Abba* was a regular user of the library. He would never miss an opportunity to read—even at the dinner table, which was not altogether agreeable to his family. Now I can understand that books, the German books he loved, Goethe, Schiller, et al., offered him escape from the memory of an unhappy, poverty-stricken childhood in the Rhineland and from the knowledge, when it came in 1944, of what had befallen his parents and other relatives in Nazi-occupied Europe and from the unromantic reality of the embattled Yishuv (the Jewish community in the land of Israel). Even as a child, he had loved and lived in books, which offered him a way to satisfy his eager curiosity about the world. I am told he read by candlelight after his mother had turned off the overhead light, and often enough he would be the last to leave the nearby public library.

It was serious literature which attracted him; I have the impression that he did not turn to these books for entertainment, he turned to them for spiritual survival. He knew Hebrew, too, and Yiddish, his parental language and the language of many of his customers in Tel Aviv, but German was and remained the language of his soul. Not that his relationship with German was uncomplicated. On the one hand, it was through German that he shaped his understanding of humankind and, indeed, his own inwardness. On the other hand, German was the language in which the Nazis condemned his family to death; it was the language in which Hitler polluted all of Europe. *Abba* loved German and was terribly wounded by German.

German was also the language into which he translated his mother's Yiddish letters. From Tel Aviv, he corresponded with my grandmother Sarah, back in Cologne and then in her Belgian exile. None of his letters to her have survived, but a number of her letters have been preserved—in German translation, as I said: he wanted Eli and me to be able to read them; that is why he put them into German. In one of them, written shortly before her flight to Antwerp, she consoled him for her unavoidable absence from his wedding: ". . . my dearest Joseph, everything does not turn out the way one wants or wishes it. But everything passes. After one has had a good cry one goes on." As *Abba* and *Ima* would have to do even after they learned that Grandmother Sarah had been deported to Auschwitz and that Grandmother Hannah, my maternal grandmother, fleeing from Mannheim, had been done to death in the South of France.

When, in the early 1950's, the *tsena*, the economic insufficiency which gripped the new Israeli republic, rendered it quite difficult for my parents to earn a living, they decided reluctantly to join relatives in San Jose, California. There, too, years of economic struggle awaited them, but there was a sense of opportunity in San Jose, and they could hope there to realize the middle-class aspirations which they had brought with them from Germany and found so difficult to maintain in Tel Aviv of the Second World War, the postwar contest with the British and the Arabs, and the *tsena* of the early 1950s. In San Jose, *Abba* and *Ima* both worked; *Abba* was no longer self-employed as he had been in Tel Aviv, and *Ima* worked long, hard hours as a laundress—but San Jose ultimately meant a home of their own with a lovely, lovingly cultivated garden, and it meant educational opportunity for Eli and me—both of us graduated high school there and went on to study at Berkeley and, in time, at the Hebrew Union College in

Los Angeles and Cincinnati. And San Jose meant immersion in English. My parents always sought friends among German-speaking Jews—how well I recall their conversations both in Tel Aviv and in San Jose, their talk of whom and what they had lost in Nazi Germany—and the New York *Aufbau* was often seen in our home, but increasingly English became our language, the language in which Eli and I spoke with each other and with *Abba* and *Ima*.

*Abba*, as I say, was not self-employed in San Jose; he worked as a cabinet maker in union shops, and his time was not his own. He read less—he was forty-eight on his arrival in San Jose, and the long hours he worked there left him too exhausted to carry on the reading regimen he had created for himself in Tel Aviv. Still, *Bildung*—education as a way of life and thought—certainly meant no less in San Jose than it had in Cologne or Mannheim or Tel Aviv. It was simply taken for granted in our home that Eli and I would finish high school and go on to university degrees.

Neither *Abba* nor *Ima* had ever paid much attention to religion; *Abba* had attended High Holy Day synagogue services in Cologne, but neither had done so in Tel Aviv; *Ima*'s father had been indifferent to religion: he had never sought to dejudaize his household and had looked forward to the Jewish holidays, but not for their religious significance—rather for the culinary opportunities they offered! This grandfather, unimpressed by his wife's pious family, had in fact chaired a cremation society: what could more emphatically have bespoken his distance from Jewish tradition? And *Ima*'s brothers, though each had become Bar Mitzvah in Manneheim, joined staunchly anticlerical left-wing kibbutzim in Palestine. In San Jose, however, *Abba* and *Ima* decided to affiliate with the Reform congregation, Temple Emanu-El, and for Eli and me this would be a significant connection.

Both of us, I speculate, chose to study for the Reform rabbinate because we somehow saw in the rabbinate an answer to our quest for *Bildung* and a way to repair the ruptured Jewish life we had inherited. In the Reform rabbinate, we could combine Jewish values with modern culture, we could wed emotion and reason, and we could empower ourselves to resist the painful discontinuities of contemporary Jewish history. None of this was ever a spoken agenda; it was an agenda of the soul, planted there by our parents.

# Reflections on the German-Jewish Legacy: North American Style

*Frances Henry*

In mid-November of this year, the small town of "Sonderburg" in the Nahe Valley of Germany is commemorating the fiftieth anniversary of *Kristallnacht*.[1] A group of civic and historic minded citizens, aided by the town council is sponsoring this important event. To mark the occasion, the town has bought the old Jewish synagogue from the furniture dealer who had acquired it after the war. He had been using it to store furniture and other household goods. Only a small plaque tells the visitor, who must look closely at this old warehouse filled with sofas, lamps, and chairs, that it was once a house of God. Now, the synagogue is to be made into a Holocaust and Judaica museum. The committee has been busy collecting old photographs and other memorabilia about its former Jewish population. But since most of that group of about 150 persons died during the Holocaust, that has not been easy. Some Jews managed to migrate in time and these survivors have been asked to donate materials about their families.

The dedication of the museum will take place during an ecumenical service to be held in the synagogue. A number of people have been invited to participate in the event, including the granddaughter of one of the town's former Jewish families. She has been asked to read from her book which describes the relationships of Jews and their gentile neighbors in Sonderburg before and after the thirties. The events marking *Kristallnacht* from the perspective of the Jewish victims and their watching but passive neighbors are dramatically described in the book.

I was moved to receive this invitation from the citizens of Sonderburg. I consider it an honor that I was asked to attend this important and historic occasion. I could, of course, be cynical about it and suggest that who better to ask than a Jew whose origins are in the community and who has lived to write about the tragic events which took place there and in the rest of the country?

This occasion has another, even more personal meaning for me, because my grandfather spearheaded the move to make the small town of Sonderburg into a Jewish *Gemeinde*. He was also instrumental in getting the synagogue built in 1924 and now, fifty years later, his granddaughter returns for its rededication. What began for me in Germany so long ago, now many years later, takes me back to participate in its rededication. The country that chased me out because of my Jewishness now invites me back to publicly celebrate that Jewishness! Indeed, for me the circle has closed.

What have the intervening fifty years brought in terms of the "spirit of the German Jewish legacy"? If I were to attempt to apply Mosse's concept of *Bildung* to my own personal and professional life, I would have to admit that my values as a former American—and now for many years a Canadian—and a Jew have been profoundly affected.

In Sonderburg, I discovered a few good neighbors, those who supplied remaining Jews with food, who helped some of them get away and, in general, performed what I called "small acts of kindness." Had more people performed such acts, had more people behaved well— had they been what Germans call *anstaendige Leute*—perhaps some of the tragedy of the period might have been averted. It is quite easy to say that people should have acted well, that they should have been more altruistic. How many of us in similar circumstances would risk our lives to help endangered neighbors? I often discussed with the remaining older Germans in Sonderburg the question of why more help was not given to the Jews. The main reason they offered was that they felt powerless—"What could we do? We were only poor powerless people" was a refrain I heard over and over again. This compelling argument came particularly from working-class people in low-paying jobs who lived far away from the centers of political power. Many of them were women with small children. They feared for the lives of their husbands and the economic security of their children. They could not afford to take risks to offer help or protection to the Jews. People also noted that they did not know what to do even if they wanted to help. How could they have intervened in a process that was so effectively doing away with their Jewish neighbors?

These arguments can easily be translated into the events of today. For example, how many persons, Jews in North America or gentiles for that matter, go out of their way to help the disadvantaged in their society? Are Jews in the forefront of altruistic activity? It is probably true that North American Jews have done more to aid in the development of Israel than any other group, but aside from philanthropy to their own kind, formerly victimized Jews have not been eager altruists. While many Jews were in the forefront of the civil rights movement in the United States, it can hardly be said that they have been overly concerned about the plight of Black or Hispanic Americans. In recent times, in fact, relations between Jews and Blacks have deteriorated to the point where the two groups have little to do with one another.

For me, the spirit of the German-Jewish legacy revolves around the need to be generous and helpful towards people who are victimized and jeopardized by the society in which they live. This need stems from the recognition that the concept of equality is, or perhaps more accurately, should be, the central theme in the organization of human society. The essence of being a modern Jew is, for me, the simple and cliched notion that all persons are equal and should share equally in the benefits and resources of society. As a former victim, I have become inordinately sensitive to the plight of other victims and my experiences in growing up in the United States and even my later years in Canada convince me that the simple value of equality and equality of access is still denied to so many citizens in these rich and endowed countries. Fighting for the rights of others, especially minorities, has become central to my professional and personal life. To understand the culture, history, and values of former slaves in the New World has been dominant in my research as a social scientist. More recently, advocacy and applied research designed to overcome the plague of racism and denial of equal access to the resources of society has occupied my attention. I do what I can with my specialized form of expertise. Doing advocacy research, consulting with governments and with other institutions in society in an attempt to make life better for victims of racism occupies much of my time.

At the moment, the world is again standing by, just as many Germans did in Nazi times, as a cruel, racist, and oppressive regime in South Africa tortures people for the sin of being black. Unfortunately it does not appear as if the Jews in that country are leading the struggle for equality. Quite the contrary, they are either participants or bystanders or just in a hurry to get out before the economic and political climate in that country becomes worse. It would appear that the experience of victimization does not always lead to a concern with the less fortunate in society. Selfishness and self-interest and, in the case of the Jews, the need to retain their cultural ethnicity and religion often prevail over the need to help others.

If I have learned anything as a result of my earlier experiences in Germany, it is not to be overly judgmental about the values and behaviors of others. I sometimes criticize the passivity of North American Jews in the continuing battle to safeguard the rights and privileges of all citizens, because they, more than any other group, know the results of prejudice and discrimination. But perhaps, they can do no better. I believe, however, that if the Jews are indeed a chosen people, what then have they been chosen for if not to try to make the world a better place for all people regardless of religion, race, and other cultural differences? That, for me, sums up the "spirit of the German-Jewish legacy" and hopefully that spirit will prevail during the *Kristallnacht* commemoration in Sonderburg's old Jewish synagogue.

## Notes

1. "Sonderburg" is a fictitious name used in the book *Victims and Neighbors: A Small Town in Nazi Germany Remembered.*

# The German-Jewish Legacy in America: A Process of Continuity and Completion

*Robert Liberles*

My connection to the German-Jewish experience in America would seem to be somewhat tenuous in two ways. First, I was not raised in a German-Jewish environment such as Washington Heights or smaller enclaves located elsewhere. Secondly, some thirteen years ago—at the age of thirty-one—I emigrated to Israel and confronted the in-gathering not so much as a German Jew, but primarily as an American of somewhat removed German extraction. As a child in Lynn, Massachusetts, I was not particularly conscious of a German-Jewish identification. English was the exclusive language of my childhood, and German was only a vague echo spoken by my parents on rare occasions with the few other German speakers—mostly Austrian—that lived in Lynn. My self-identification in this predominantly Christian environment was as a Jew, and more specific subidentifications would have been superfluous. This was the case until I came into closer contact with a broader and more exclusive Jewish world. As a teenager, I became active in the Zionist youth movement Young Judea. It was there, at the age of fourteen, that I first confronted certain generalities about the assimilationism that presumably had characterized the German-Jewish experience. I opposed those generalizations then and have done so since in both my writing and teaching. The deep immersion in Jewish values and life-style that I encountered in my movement activities influenced the major life choices that I made subsequently. But in another sense, the historical inaccuracy of that stereotyped view of German Jewry has also remained with me, and in ways I will describe below has greatly informed my message in teaching Jewish history in Israel. Such descriptions, it seems to me, make life rather easy for their authors. German Jewry is described as if it were all urban—which it distinctly was not; as late as 1925, the seven largest communities accounted for only 50 percent of German Jewry; as if it were all Prussian, which it was not; as if it were all Reform, which it certainly was not; and of course, as if they were all naive fools sleeping through the better part of their history, including the better part of the 1930s.

My move to Israel has made me more aware of the American aspect of my identity and that there was in fact a problem in distinguishing between German and American influences. For example, the religious environment of my home was compatible with the religious ambiance of the Conservative synagogue that we belonged to. Decorum, order, propriety became deeply embedded values in my religious outlook. My impression is that other than a few leaders who found elite roles within Israeli society, German Jews integrated far better into American society than did their cousins who emigrated to Israel, raising literally a question of *Rezeptionsgeschichte*. Apparently, American society reinforced certain characteristics deriving from German influences, which Israeli society did not. Thus, it seems to me that my Germanic heritage helped make me a good American—but simultaneously perhaps a marginal Israeli. This requires some explanation. The nature of Jewish life in America represents a continuation, perhaps, even a completion, of the historical processes that began in Germany. While German Jewry sought an emancipation, which eluded them until the end, American Jewry achieved the closest proximity to equality that we have attained to date in our history in diaspora. German Jewry also produced a diversity in Jewish life, especially religious life, that resulted from its confrontation with modernity and its pursuit of emancipation, and American Jewry expanded upon and enriched that diversity. Because of the closeness of those cultural traditions, I now find it difficult to distinguish between their influences on my outlook, but taken together their collective cultural legacy has a significant contribution to make to contemporary Jewish developments.

Recent trends in Israeli religious life indicate an active attempt to eradicate the rich diversity that has emerged, leaving essentially the rather limited choice between old-style Orthodoxy on the one hand and secularism on the other. Even modern Orthodoxy is in danger of sinking into oblivion in Israel. Ironically, Zionism once represented precisely the kind of individuality it now seems to discourage. When Zionism first emerged in Germany toward the end of the ninteenth century and the opening years of the twentieth, it attracted Jews who sought to rebel against what they saw as the program of conformity of the established Jewish community. Thus, Zionism offered a platform which contrasted with the program that characterized the Reform movement. The Zionists emphasized Jewish messianism, Hebrew language, and Jewish peoplehood—values which had come under attack in the meetings and writings of classical German Reform. Obviously, there are complex reasons for these developments. My purpose here is not to explain them, but to contrast the emerging status quo with the German-American legacy. Israeli society has never learned to appreciate that Judaism and the Jewish people are capable of surviving in a free society. Just to cite one example, one of the world's leading scholars of Holocaust research wrote in the introduction to his textbook in that field that the new Jewish community that emerged in the nineteenth century was no longer compulsory, but *merely* a voluntary community. The fact that virtually all of German Jewry had retained their membership voluntarily did not leave an impression that such communal ties were strong and healthy. Nor has the creative impulse found in American Jewish religious life changed the Israeli conviction that American Judaism is doomed because of its environment of freedom and voluntarism. While the Israeli critique may provide some healthy sobriety, the failure to appreciate the opportunities of freedom and diversity is really a loss for Israeli society itself. Zionist thinking concerning Israeli-diaspora relations has been rather reduced to postulating the inevitability of an explosion of anti-Semitism in America. Again the free-associating connection between the German and American experiences supports such an assumption. But Zionist ideology would be far more positive if it could—to borrow an expression from Salo Baron—transcend beyond the *lachrymose conception of Jewish history*. And Israeli religious life would certainly be richer if it could allow for the spectrum of options that emerged within the German-American milieu. A number of years ago, shortly after I came to Israel on aliyah, I was on my way to synagogue on *erev Shavuot* when I found a family waiting at a bus stop, totally unaware that a holiday was about to begin and that the buses weren't running. I think the incident reveals some of the shortcomings of a system that fails to appreciate voluntarism and is oblivious to the educational limits of religious coercion. It is certainly possible to prohibit buses from running on holy days, but quite another thing to prevent people from waiting at bus stops.

Any participant in this symposium will tend to project his personal background onto the general subject matter. If our responses are varied, I would be vindicated in my position that what marked the German-Jewish historical experience was not conformity, but individuality, and that what characterized Jewish communal bonds was voluntarism and not coercion. It is not merely ironic that these traits emerged, even flourished, within the two such different Jewish historical experiences of Germany and America. While American opportunities encouraged the cause of Jewish religious liberalism, the German resistance to Jewish integration split the Jewish community over questions of tactics and accommodation. Religious coercion had no permanent place on the American scene, but in Germany the path to religious multiplicity required a restructuring of traditional communal concepts and essentially emerged as a result of the very difficulties German Jewry was encountering in its confrontations with modernity. I would like to conclude with a striking anecdote related by the German Zionist leader Kurt Blumenfeld to illustrate a number of these points. When his history class in school was studying the wars between Rome and Carthage, his teacher turned to Blumenfeld and asked him with which side he identified. Blumenfeld responded that he sided with Hannibal. The teacher was somewhat taken aback at this affront to the original Roman Empire and asked if Blumenfeld was always on the side of the underdog. After some reflection, Blumenfeld answered that Hannibal was Jewish. Blumenfeld was giving expression in this anecdote to his conviction that Jews must be prepared to respond in the negative to the tremendous pressures of accommodation that were being placed upon them by the successor to the Holy Roman Empire, the Second Reich. Making almost the same point, Richard Lichtheim declared that affirming one's Jewishness had become at that time a matter of personal dignity. There was much in common between the German-Jewish legacy and the atmosphere that the refugees of fifty years ago found on American soil, as America offered them the opportunities they had sought and fought for so hard, but had failed to find on the other side. The long struggle finally reaped its rewards, as the new immigrants were all the more cognizant of what they had been denied and what America now offered them.

# The Last Generation Of German Jewishness

*Steven Lowenstein*

My contribution to this symposium on the German-Jewish legacy will differ from most others because the type of German-Jewish culture to which I have been exposed since childhood is very different from the usual stereotype of German-Jewish life. In fact one of the main motivations for me to devote my main research interests to the study of German Jewry has been the dichotomy between the German-Jewish immigrant community in which I grew up and the German-Jewish community to which I have been exposed in the literature.

The usual picture of the German-Jewish community as highly acculturated, indeed assimilated, with elite economic, social, and educational features, did not fit the immigrant community in the Washington Heights section of Manhattan in which I was raised. The community of my childhood was first and foremost a "typical" immigrant society, with its language, customs, and style of personal interaction heavily influenced by the Old Country. Although German in language and style, the members of the Washington Heights community of my childhood identified primarily as Jews, not as Germans. Jewish religious life was strong and expressed itself in synagogue attendance, celebration of the Sabbath and holidays, and in a high level of religious observance. Most of the people with whom my family socialized were "plain people," many of them blue-collar workers or small businesspeople. Many had not completed high school. This was certainly not "Our Crowd." Rather, it was a traditional Jewish community with a German ethnic twist.

The section of German Jewry from which my community derived is probably the least known of all German-Jewish groups—the *Landjuden* (small-town Jews) of South Germany. They were neither highly acculturated and religiously indifferent like the bulk of big-city Jews in Germany, nor militantly Orthodox and anti-Zionist like the "Breuer Community" of Frankfurt am Main. For them, Judaism was primarily tradition passed down through the family and community without great learning or analysis, but with respect for its hallowed age and sanctity. In some ways it was the German version of the *shtetl*.

Because of my background, I have always thought of German Jewishness not as a specific ideology or set of values, but as a tradition or an atmosphere. Therefore, I do not see the German-Jewish heritage as a "spirit" or ideal which should be exported to other groups or influence them. Certainly there are elements of the traditional German-Jewish way of life which might provide useful models for others, but the German-Jewish heritage as a whole cannot be carried over intact into future generations.

For me the German-Jewish heritage is like a family heirloom which I was brought up to cherish. Therefore I regret what I believe is the inevitable disappearance of a separate German-Jewish community and culture within a generation. This is especially true because German Jewry is the most ancient part of Ashkenazic Jewry and preserves some practices of the early Ashkenazim which have disappeared elsewhere. Nevertheless, I believe that the appearance and disappearance of Jewish subtraditions is an inevitable result of the historical process. The German-Jewish community in America (and most other countries of emigration) is far along in the process of merger into the general Jewish community. Overall, I feel this is a healthy phenomenon, however much I might regret the loss of some distinctive practices.

Having admitted that mine may be the last generation to feel a sense of connection with the German-Jewish tradition, I still feel that my connection with that tradition has given me personally certain valuable perspectives which might have a broader application.

First of all, having been raised in a "subethnic" variety of Judaism, I have been made aware that Jewish tradition is not homogeneous. The Eastern European tradition is an important element of Judaism, but it is not the only one. I regret that this single strand within Judaism has pushed aside the other traditions to such an extent that Sephardic rabbis in Israel feel impelled to dress in Hasidic dress to appear authentic. I believe that interest in, and preservation (at least for the historical record) of all Jewish ethnic traditions is a positive value. Although German Jewry may soon go out of existence, the awareness of Jewish geographic variety will enrich Judaism greatly. In this case it is not the specifics of German Jewry but the general value of folk tradition and geographic variation which is worthy of preservation.

German Jewry has also produced other things of value. Perhaps most important is the ability to remain Jews without denying the value of the culture and peoples among whom we live. This is an especially important contribution of the German trends within Orthodox Jewry and is one which, unfortunately, Orthodox Judaism is in danger of losing. Less vital, though I think still of some value, is a certain type of an aesthetic sense as expressed in the liturgy, folk customs, and way of interaction. Certainly there is much that is stiff and overly formal in the German-Jewish style. Yet, the devotion to structure, to rules, and to a certain style of formal dignity might perhaps benefit a Jewish community which has gone too far in the direction of the informal, the unstructured, and the unadorned. Of course, there are negative values in the German-Jewish approach as well. Clearest among them is a sense of snobbishness and superiority to other Jewish groups. This has been a long-standing criticism of German Jews by others. Although the accusations were sometimes exaggerated, they certainly included more than a grain of truth. Judaism will not miss the disappearance of such attitudes.

The views expressed here are very much personal ones arising out of my own upbringing. I see a certain danger in trying to characterize a German-Jewish "national character" or type. German Jewry, like all groups, was complex and variegated. One important lesson we can learn is to recognize the variation within all groups and not to construct ethnic stereotypes (even relatively benign ones like that of the *yekke*). What one person sees as characteristic of a population group may not be the same as that seen by another. German Jewry, like Jewry as a whole, was not uniform. Perhaps the greatest legacy we can learn from it is that we can preserve Judaism without imposing upon it a uniformity and homogeneity which is not inherent in it.

# A Non-Jewish German Looks at the German-Jewish Legacy

*Gert Niers*

Postwar Germany, a geopolitical entity tarnished by a recent, infamous past and, at the same time, a state of mind laid into a vacuum, void of any recognizable trace of Jewish life: this was the country where I grew up.

What did not exist anymore was easy to forget, and those who did not want to forget, those who actually wanted to learn, had to ask questions, to read, until the facts finally trickled down. Yet it wasn't until twenty-five years after the end of the war that I met Jews for the first time—at a Bar Mitzvah in Lakewood, New Jersey, to which my wife, the German teacher of that student, and I had been invited. A non-Jewish newcomer from Germany, I felt somewhat apprehensive about the way in which I would be approached at this uniquely Jewish festivity. Would I be avoided, would I be lectured about, if not accused of, the German past? Would other guests feel insulted about my presence? Much to my surprise, I was welcomed like an old friend of the family—no stiff faces, sharp looks, scrutinizing questions. When it became known that I was from Germany, an old lady, a German-Jewish refugee from Frankfurt, insisted that I be introduced to her and welcomed the opportunity to converse in her native tongue; she told me of her early days in New York, the stroke of homesickness in alien surroundings.

My next encounter with a Jewish person also occurred in Lakewood, New Jersey, in a bookstore whose clerk was a young man of my age; his parents had come from Poland after the war. He shared with me the interest in the written word, and even our political views were similar (at that time, the Vietnam War was raging).

It seemed as if, in my first Lakewood year (1971), all the Jews I did not meet in Germany had been waiting for me on this side of the Atlantic. Suddenly, I came in contact with Jews in all walks of life: teachers (colleagues of my wife), doctors, lawyers, repairmen, bakers, stationery salespeople, etc. Most of them, as far as their denomination was concerned, were Reform; however, I also met members of the Conservative and Orthodox branches.

Since my immigration papers were still being processed, I had spare time during which I tutored German free of charge to students of my wife. With an advanced group, I also took excursions into the German past, thus being here probably one of the early teachers of the history of the Holocaust.

In the mid-seventies, I made—due to my editorial work at the German-American *New Yorker Staats-Zeitung*—my first regular contacts with German-Jewish emigrants, mainly authors whose readings in New York City I attended, whose books I reviewed, and whose poems I published. (Three of those exile writers eventually became the subject of my Ph.D. thesis.) It was those authors who brought my attention to another German-language newspaper: *Aufbau*, to this day—as the subtitle states—*America's Only German-Jewish Publication* and indeed the only exile publication still in existence. After five years with the *New Yorker Staats-Zeitung*, I joined the *Aufbau* in 1978, and became its first non-Jewish editor-in-chief in 1985.

*Aufbau*, established in 1934, on the occasion of the tenth anniversary of the German-Jewish Club of New York (called New World Club since 1939), has been, and still is, the most prominent and most widely read newspaper representing the cause and satisfying the needs of the German-Jewish emigrants of the thirties and forties.

*Aufbau* became a tool of survival by providing the refugees with information about employment and housing, with legal advice and English courses. After the war, it helped to reunite relatives, friends, and other "displaced persons" (too often, though, the obituary page brought the irrevocable news). A special page regularly reported about West German restitution efforts and new compensation laws (*Wiedergutmachung*). Since the paper adhered to the native language of the refugees, it helped them to maintain their cultural roots. Moreover, *Aufbau* became a highly intellectual and literary magazine by continuously publishing contributions of the most prominent writers in exile. Thus, *Aufbau*, last but not least, preserved the German-Jewish concept of *Bildung* for the new conditions of life in America.

Much has been published about the history and the achievements of this journalistic institution. Instead of repeating it, I would like to insert a short bibliography of the most recent "secondary literature."

On the occasion of *Aufbau*'s fiftieth anniversary in 1984, several newspapers ran articles about this event and its background: the *Daily News Bulletin* of the Jewish Telegraphic Agency (August 3, 1984), the *New York Times* (November 16, 1984), the *Frankfurter Allgemeine Zeitung* (November 24, 1984), *Die Zeit* (November 30, 1984), *Der Spiegel* (February 18, 1985). More recently, the *Frankfurter Rundschau* addressed the subject on November 12, 1988. In addition, an anniversary exhibition was organized and went on display both in the United States and in Europe. In connection with this year's commemoration of the November pogrom, the German television station Suedwestfunk (SWF) has dedicated a feature film to the German-Jewish newspaper and its readers in New York.

An assessment of the German-Jewish heritage in America would probably be incomplete without a look at *Aufbau* today. The newspaper that once could draw its articles from a galaxy of German-Jewish émigrés is today largely produced by non-Jews. While on one hand the children and grandchildren of the German-Jewish refugees have been successfully integrated into the American mainstream, these same generations, on the other hand, are no longer readers of *Aufbau* because they (at least most of them) do not read, write, or speak German and because they simply do not depend on news in German like their parents or grandparents when they first came to this country.

Therefore, the newspaper must turn to other tasks and challenges. As far as Jewish matters are concerned, *Aufbau* has recently dedicated more print space and editorial effort to foster the Jewish-Christian dialogue with the German postwar generation(s). While its original readership is dwindling in the United States, circulation has increased in Germany. By ironic twist or by historic justice, *Aufbau* is returning to that very country from which its original readers and supporters were forced to leave under most inhuman circumstances—indeed a most remarkable form of Jewish survival.

# Fifty Years After *Kristallnacht:* Another Second-Generation Perspective

*Diane R. Spielmann and Lee A. Spielmann*

Because of the imprecision and fallibility of memory, society, in order to facilitate collective remembrance of the past, commemorates specific events. *Kristallnacht*, the destruction of over two hundred synagogues throughout German-speaking Europe, accompanied by the plundering of countless Jewish businesses and residences, on November 9 – 10, 1938, is such an event. A prelude to a far darker chapter in human history, one which ordinary reason seeks to reject, it would become, in the aftermath of events to follow, symbolic of the shattered lives and the destroyed Jewish heritage that had been rooted in European soil for centuries. In retrospect, the significance of *Kristallnacht*, an event whose denouement found expression in mass murder, encompasses more than German Jewry, against whom it was specifically aimed, but extends to all of European Jewry. Remembrance of *Kristallnacht* cannot be separated from remembrance of the Holocaust.

What occurred on November 9 – 10, 1938 has come to be seen as the dividing point; it was the beginning of the end of Jewish life in Europe. Within three months after that night of depredation and senseless violence, Hitler, in his January 30, 1939 address to the Reichstag, threatened to extirpate all of Jewry, a program the official implementation of which was undertaken at the Wannsee Conference less than three years later. Only few of Europe's Jews were to survive.

The passage of fifty years since the occurrence of the brutality of November 1938 represents a watershed period in the efforts to solidify a collective remembrance. It has given the survivors, those most affected by the events that began with *Kristallnacht*, as well as society in general, time to reflect and to attempt to absorb and digest an understanding of the Holocaust and its significance in history. A half century has also facilitated the fading and blurring of memories. This was all too painfully demonstrated by the witnesses describing their ordeal at the Treblinka extermination camp during the recent trial of John Demjanjuk in Israel, and it has also given society the time consciously to forget the meaning of the Holocaust, as was witnessed when an American president honored the rebirth of German democracy by paying homage at a German military cemetery in Bitburg containing the graves of SS members. The present period will undoubtedly assume an increasingly critical role as the transition between those who knew and those who must learn of this most sanguinary period in a far-too-bloodied century.

The survivors, already having been exhausted by their unprecedented life experiences, are now elderly, and their ranks inevitably grow thinner each year. However much time has passed, the experience they endured has left indelible marks, and no amount of time can ever erase the anguish or remove the scars inflicted by the Nazi years. Perhaps more than anything else, the notion that time has healed the wounds left by the Holocaust mirrors the extent of the widespread lack of understanding of the cataclysm that befell European Jewry. Primo Levi, himself an Auschwitz survivor, stated in *The Drowned and the Saved,* and ultimately confirmed by his subsequent suicide, that "the injury cannot be healed: it extends throughout time."[1] Upon liberation, these survivors, distraught and alone, channeled their energies for that which was, most understandably, of prime concern—rebuilding their shattered and uprooted lives. From this rebuilding has emerged the generation imprinted with the legacy of their parents' experiences, the offspring born to the remnants of European Jewry. The coming of age of the Second Generation has reaffirmed its unique position as the bridge between the survivors, those who experienced directly the Nazi horrors, and all succeeding generations who will have never known the survivors or heard first-hand of their experiences.

We, the children of Holocaust survivors, approach this fiftieth commemoration of *Kristallnacht* with a mixture of uncertainty and challenge, sobered by the reality of the inevitable toll extracted by the passage of time. We face the task of confronting a future built upon a past so full of devastation and despair, combined with the challenge to ensure that in a world where no more eyewitnesses will remain their experiences in the Holocaust will not be forgotten. We must do so while recognizing the profound impacts these events have had in making us who, and what, we are.

Any discussion of the effects of the Holocaust on the Second Generation must be prefaced with the caveat that the effects are as myriad and diverse as the people to whom they refer. None can be quantified or otherwise measured with certainty, yet their existence remains beyond doubt. Only now as adults reflecting upon the consequences of our parents' experiences on our lives can we discern trends that have emerged and will mark many of us for the rest of our lives. To varying degrees, these effects are ubiquitous, touching matters of general concern—personalities, attitudes, perceptions, and lifestyles—and those of specific facets of our lives—choice of careers, spouses, and friends.

Common to many of the Second Generation is the acute awareness of time within its historical framework, a phenomenon which becomes ever more apparent with the harsh reality of growing older. Fifty years, which once seemed a lifetime, now becomes far more familiar as we look back as well as ahead. The differences separating us from our peers are underscored through this dual perspective. Whereas most who contemplate the time phenomenon through the kaleidoscope of past and future do so within the confines of their own immediate lifetimes, we, the children of Holocaust survivors, do so with a far more expansive perspective. Ours encompasses not only our individual upbringing under unconventional circumstances, but also the lives of our parents which had been so violently disrupted.

For us, the Second Generation, it has meant not having the luxury of an insouciant childhood, a time in which we merely sensed differences that we are only now beginning to understand. We have carried the pains of having limited families, of being deprived of grandparents and extended families, matters that will continue to remain with us. We remember discussing people whom, but for the Nazi savagery, we could have seen and heard, people who for us will always remain no more than a concept.

Unlike our American peers, we cannot seek solace in the past, for the ties to our collective ancestral community have been severed. We find ourselves in the dilemma of being far more sensitive and aware of the significance of a past that cannot offer the continuity upon which we could anchor ourselves. It is indeed ironic that the more we learn about our collective history, the less we become able to fathom its incomprehensibility or turn to it for direction or guidance. Our predicament in confronting the tenebrous events of the past is akin to the dilemma expressed by Saul Friedlander in describing the "historian's paralysis" in confronting the history of Nazi Germany: "We know the details of what occurred, we are aware of the sequence of events and their probable interaction, but the profound dynamics of the phenomenon evade us."[2]

We nonetheless remain aware that it is incumbent upon us to insist that none be permitted to forget a past whose meaning eludes us. In this regard, the task of the Second Generation becomes more difficult than that of our parents. In projecting ahead we must perpetuate a "memory" of events we never experienced, but only learned of through them and their tales. Obligated to think beyond our own lifetime so that those events will neither become trivialized nor become a footnote to history, we thus have thrust upon us the unique responsibility to make what will soon amount to a lesson in history remain a potent and driving force in shaping a collective conscience.

If, as the Second Generation, our awareness of time and history separates us from our peers, so too does our spatial orientation. As Americans, our horizon of concerns reaches beyond one's immediate environment to circumstances affecting our nation and the world. These interests embrace a greater cognizance of the relationship between the individual and the society of which he is a part, a recognition of the importance of the protection afforded the individual by the state against majoritarian prejudices. Stemming from a knowledge of the experiences of our parents, this perspicacity manifests itself not only with a trenchant interest in the events of our society but with a specific concern for the institutional safeguards that have been erected in order to guard against majoritarian zeal and excesses.

Sensitivity to intolerance and to the precarious position of an individual perceived by the mainstream of society to be an outsider, undoubtedly in part arising from our personal identification with the victims of the Holocaust, has acted as an unquantifiable influence upon the lives of many in Second Generation. This bond among us not only reinforces our intellectual understanding of the Holocaust and its significance, but also alerts us to the meaning and import of the Torah's admonition that "there came unto Egypt a new king who knew not Joseph." Sensitivity to the fate of the individual was clearly expressed by Justice Felix Frankfurter, himself an immigrant Jew who "escaped" the Holocaust through the fortuity of his parents having emigrated some fifty years before. In a decision involving the rights of Jehovah's Witnesses to resist the homogenizing power of the secular state, Justice Frankfurter stated what perhaps has become a major influence on the thoughts and motivations of many of the Second Generation, an expression given far greater urgency because it was written during the Holocaust: "One who belongs to the most vilified and persecuted minority in history is not likely to be insensible to the freedoms guaranteed by our Constitution."[3]

As the Holocaust has been the "central moral question of our time," so too it remains the pivotal event in our collective development, around which we, a generation after, have built our lives, and around which our *Weltanschauung* has evolved. It continues to be a focal point of our existence, influencing, consciously or otherwise, many of our decisions and actions. It is this collective consciousness of the Holocaust that is the raison d'etre of those children of Holocaust survivors who have chosen to associate with the goals of Second Generation.

Abba Eban has very succinctly described this impact on the post-Holocaust generations of Jews, and what he has written applies with even greater force to Second Generation, the people upon whom its meaning has been personally and individually imprinted through the sufferings of our parents and their tormented postwar lives, into which each of us, standing as a surrogate for some unknown ancestor, was born.

> Jewish history and consciousness will be dominated for many generations by the traumatic memories of the Holocaust. No people in history has undergone an experience of such violence and depth. The sharp Jewish reaction to movements of discrimination and prejudice; an intoxicated awareness of life, not as something to be taken for granted but as a treasure to be fostered and nourished with eager vitality, a residual distrust of what lies beyond the Jewish wall, a mystic belief in the undying forces of Jewish history, which ensure survival when all appears lost, all these together with the intimacy of more personal pains and agonies, are the legacy which the Holocaust transmits to the generation of Jews grown up under its shadow.[4]

With the fiftieth commemoration of *Kristallnacht* upon us, it is indeed appropriate, while recalling the suffering of the survivors and honoring their courage and resiliency in triumphing over the Nazi evil, to reflect upon the ramifications and consequences for the generation after.

## Notes

1. Primo Levi, *The Drowned and the Saved*, trans. Raymond Rosenthal (New York: Summit Books, Simon & Schuster, 1988), p. 24.

2. Saul Friedlander, "From Anti-Semitism to Extermination: A Historiographical Study of Nazi Policies Toward the Jews and an Essay in Interpretation" *Yad Vashem Studies* 16 (1984): 50.

3. *West Virginia State Board of Education v. Barnette*, 319 U.S. 624, 646 (1943) (Frankfurter, J., dissenting).

4. Abba Eban, *My People: The Story of the Jews* (New York: Random House, 1968), pp. 416 – 17.

# The German-Jewish Experience: Toward a Usable Past

*Jack Wertheimer*

I am the son and the grandson of refugees from Nazi Germany, but was born in New York and regard myself as an American Jew. In my youth, I attended a synagogue whose leadership was primarily Central European, but whose rabbis were all American-born Jews of East European extraction. I was socialized into the Jewish religion by parents who themselves were raised in two distinctive types of German Judaism—secessionist Orthodoxy and an observant Liberal Judaism—and yet I was taught about Judaism in Jewish day schools whose teachers were primarily the products of East European *yeshivot.* I grew up in an environment where at times only German was spoken, and yet at other times East European survivors of the Holocaust, immigrants from the Shah's Iran, and American-born Jews mingled fairly easily, conversing in English. Perhaps because my own formative years were spent in a culturally diversified environment, I have no sympathy for discussions about a unique and pristine German-Jewish legacy. From my own experience as a member of the second generation, I seriously doubt that many German Jews had much interest, let alone faith, in a unique "German-Jewish spirit." On the contrary: the German Jews I encountered while growing up in the fifties and sixties did not find their heritage a matter of unalloyed pride.

In part this resulted from the shock of having their lives disrupted by their German compatriots—and of knowing that the uprooted were lucky compared with those who did not emigrate. Most German Jews of my acquaintance responded to their encounter with Nazism by regarding their former existence with a measure of skepticism. This, coupled with the practical necessity of adapting to the American environment, dampened their pride in their own history. In some extreme instances, German Jews severed all ties to their former lives once they arrived in America. I recall meeting the parents of three brothers I had befriended who informed me matter-of-factly that the moment they arrived on American shores they resolved never to speak the German language again. Today, their sons are all Orthodox religious functionaries, whose demeanor and outlook are shaped entirely by the Lithuanian-type yeshivas they attended in New York.

More characteristically, families continued to display some attachment to things German, but encouraged their children to integrate. In my own family, this manifested itself in eclectic practices and modes of thinking: I spoke German with my grandparents, but English with my parents; I was raised on German children's stories such as "*Max und Moritz*," but also was exposed to the icons of American children in the fifties, such as Pinky Lee and the Three Stooges. In the religious sphere, we sang Shabbat zemirot set to both German and American— i.e., East European and Israeli—melodies; and I was duly impressed with the homilies of Hasidic rebbes, as well as Samson Raphael Hirsch. Most important, my social circle consisted of Jewish children from a broad range of cultures. In truth, I felt a strong affinity for children of survivors, perhaps because the experience of their East European parents most approximated my parents' immigrant lives. And when we eventually chose spouses, it was exceedingly rare for children of refugees from Nazi Germany to marry each other. The process of social integration was so complete that, as far as I know, the children of German-Jewish immigrants have not founded an organization analogous to the "Generation After," an international body of children of Holocaust survivors (a classification that, as best as I can tell, does not apply to German Jews who escaped Europe prior to 1940). None of this is meant to suggest that the integration of German-Jewish families into the American Jewish community occurred without strains. Undoubtedly, my own encounter with such tensions prompted my scholarly interest in the historical relationship between East European and German Jews. But the underlying assumption of everyone, whether parents, teachers, or peers, was that we all would meld into the American Jewish community. Given the high level of integration into the American Jewish community that characterizes children of refugees from Germany and their failure to establish any distinctive institutions, one wonders who will be the bearers of the German-Jewish spirit that is of concern to this symposium?

There was also another factor that prompted German Jews and their children to distance themselves from their past: within American Jewish society, it is not a badge of pride to be of German-Jewish descent. In contrast to the proud assumptions undergirding the questions posed by this symposium, the legacy of German Jewry as perceived by American Jews is either negative or irrelevant.

For the preponderant majority of American Jews who give the matter any thought at all, the history of German Jewry serves as a powerful cautionary tale. Some time before the Holocaust, according to this folk-wisdom, there lived in Germany a Jewish population that was more assimilated than any other in the world. The Jews of Germany distorted or hid their Jewishness in a desperate effort to win the acceptance of their gentile neighbors. They stifled all feelings of *ahavat yisrael*, a love of fellow Jews, and instead treated their coreligionists, particularly East European Jews, with contempt and ridicule. And in their bearing, dress, and cultural outlook, they were "more German than the Germans." For a while, German Jews assimilated in an unprecedented manner. And then they were punished brutally. Whether it was divine vengeance or the vagaries of history is not clear, but German Jews were taught a lesson by the Nazis that all Jews must remember: assimilation cannot work; the only protection Jews have is to concern themselves with the fate of their coreligionists. The experience of German Jews teaches us all that escape from Jewishness is impossible.

It does not give me any satisfaction to relate this cautionary tale, for I view the German-Jewish experience in a markedly different manner. As the offspring of religiously observant, Jewishly active and affiliated refugees from Nazi Germany, I hardly regard German Jewry as the assimilated Jewry *par excellence*. And as one who has studied and taught the history of German Jewry in a professional capacity, I know of a far more complex history. But on the basis of dozens of experiences in college classrooms and adult education forums, I believe that the distorted, cartoonlike depiction of German Jewry that I have described is deeply embedded in the American Jewish (as well as Israeli) consciousness.

Why is this the case? Why do German Jews serve in the contemporary American Jewish community as object lessons for how *not* to behave as Jews? To an important extent, the answer has less to do with Germans Jews than with an ingrained Jewish outlook that blames Jewish victims for their own victimization. We ought not underestimate the enduring power of a Jewish religious outlook that understands Jewish suffering as solely the result of Jewish misdeeds. For some ultra-Orthodox Jews, such as a former Ashkenazic chief rabbi of Israel, there is no better way to explain the catastrophe that befell European Jewry than to blame it on sinning Jews—and who were the greatest sinners if not German Jews, who introduced *Haskala* (Jewish Enlightenment) and religious reform? To more religiously liberal Jews, particularly their rabbis and teachers, the experience of German Jewry is tailormade to serve as a cautionary tale about the consequences of assimilation. And to Zionist educators, the German-Jewish experience provides a perfect illustration of the futility of diaspora existence and the corrosive impact such an existence has upon Jewish solidarity. Whereas other westernized and acculturated Jews were also decimated, French and Italian Jewry for example, the fact that the Nazis originated in Germany places the spotlight on German Jews. They must have done something to set off the Final Solution.

These explanations are important, but they omit the manner in which German Jews contributed to the sullying of their reputation. The crucial element here is the long history of intergroup tensions between German Jews and their coreligionists in Eastern Europe. Within Germany this manifested itself in the popularization of stereotypes that portrayed the culture of East European Jews as backward and uncouth. Not surprisingly, such contempt was reciprocated: negative stereotypes of German Jews were widely disseminated in Eastern Europe—especially the images we have encountered in our cautionary tale of German Jews obsessed with assimilation and eager to disassociate themselves from the rest of world Jewry. In the post-Holocaust era, a set of ready-made stereotypes was available for exploitation by those who wished to draw lessons from the European catastrophe. To put matters bluntly, today's negative image of German Jewry represents the revenge of the *Ostjude*.

Beyond the cautionary tale, what more is known by American Jews about the German-Jewish experience? Two small sub-groups within the American Jewish community continue to enshrine some German Jews in their pantheon of heroes. For intellectually oriented, highly literate Jews, there is a continuing fascination with Freud, Kafka, Marx, and Einstein—and with the cultures that produced such geniuses. And for a small religious and scholarly elite, the theological concerns of Buber and Rosenzweig, Baeck and Hermann Cohen, and the *Wissenschaft* of Zunz and Graetz, Geiger, and Frankel continue to resonate. But even within these circles, it is difficult to measure the enduring impact of German-Jewish cultural heroes. It is ironic that German Jewry, which prided itself on its religious self-definition (as in the formulation, "German citizens of the Jewish faith"), has so little impact upon the religious concerns of most contemporary Jews.

This stands in marked contrast to the influence of another group of Jewish immigrants which also arrived in America during and after World War II—the population of religiously observant Jews from Eastern Europe. It is this immigrant wave that gave new life to Orthodoxy, built a vast network of Jewish day schools, and shaped Jewish popular culture with its spirited *nigunim* and swirling dances. The continuing influence of this group may be measured by the fact that during the past year, perhaps the best-selling Jewish book was a biography of Rabbi Moshe Feinstein, a leading member of this immigrant population. And within all of the Jewish movements in America, especially Reform and Reconstructionism, there is today a fascination with neo-Hasidism—another import from Eastern Europe. The impact of German-Jewish culture is negligible by comparison: Lewandowski is unable to compete with *klezmer*, and Franz Rosenzweig cannot outsell Artscroll.

I trust that the foregoing remarks clarify why I regard questions about the "German-Jewish legacy" as unattuned to American Jewish circumstances—both the reality of the lives lived by Jewish immigrants from Germany, as well as the standing of such Jews in the minds of American coreligionists. I do believe, however, that an examination of the German-Jewish experience could enrich American Jewry, and not coincidentally improve the image of German Jews. It is an ongoing source of wonderment to me that American Jews project some of their own worst vices upon German Jewry, rather than seek understanding and perhaps even solace in the history of that Jewry. To cite two glaring examples: I am often informed during adult education lectures that German Jews were prototypical assimilators who intermarried at a staggering pace. It requires much effort for me to convince my auditors that American Jewry's present rate of intermarriage dwarfs that of virtually any other Jewry. Additionally, when American Jews dismiss German Jewry for its assimilation, they ignore important models of religious adaptation, which produced at their finest an Orthodoxy that attempted a genuine reconciliation of Judaism with Western culture, and a liberal Judaism that promoted the observance of rituals and only moderate reforms. In an age when much of organized Judaism in America is careening toward ever more radical or reactionary extremes, there is much to learn from the religious syntheses produced by German Jewry. If nothing else, an examination of the German-Jewish experience might help American Jews place their own struggles with acculturation and westernization into perspective.

It is this shared experience of modernization, rather than a unique legacy, that I find compelling in the saga of German Jewry. More than any other Jewry, the Jews of Germany struggled with issues that are of vital concern to the American Jewish community in which I live: How can Jews sustain a distinctive culture in the face of a powerful and attractive majority culture? How can a Jewish community cope with high rates of intermarriage and defection? How does one forge a modern Judaism within a Western society? And above all, is it possible for a diaspora Jewish community to withstand the allure of assimilation in the modern era? The history of German Jewry warrants the attention of American Jews because for over a century and a half, articulate and thoughtful Jews in Germany grappled with questions that continue to challenge American Jews today.

## Contributors

Carol Ascher divides her time between writing fiction and analyzing research on minority education at Teachers College, Columbia University. She is the author of *Simone de Beauvoir: A Life of Freedom* (1981) and co-editor of *Between Women: Biographers, Novelists, Critics, Teachers and Artists Write About Women* (1984). She is also the author of a novel, *The Flood* (1987).

Steven E. Aschheim received his Ph.D. in 1980 from the University of Wisconsin-Madison and is Lecturer in German Cultural and Intellectual History at the Hebrew University. He is the author of *Brothers and Strangers: The East European Jew in German and German Jewish Consciousness, 1800 – 1923* (1982). Prof. Aschheim is currently working on a study dealing with the impact of Nietzsche on German political culture.

Renate Bridenthal is Professor of History at Brooklyn College, the City University of New York. She is co-editor of *Becoming Visible: Women in European History* (1987,2nd) and of *When Biology Became Destiny: Women in Weimar and Nazi Germany* (1984). She is currently writing a book on German housewives' organizations between the two World Wars.

Henry L. Feingold is Professor of History at Baruch College of the City College of New York. Among his many publications are *The Politics of Rescue* (1970) and *Zion in America* (1974).

Tom L. Freudenheim was educated at Harvard University and New York University where he was a student of Erwin Panofsky and Richard Ettinghausen. He has been the Director of the Baltimore and Worcester Art Museums and currently serves as the Assistant Secretary for Museums of the Smithsonian Institution.

Peter Gay is Durfee Professor of History at Yale University. He is the author of numerous works on European history including *Weimar Culture: The Outsider as Insider* (1968), *Style in History* (1974), *Freud, Jews and Other Germans* (1978) and, most recently, *Freud: A Life for Our Times* (1988).

Alfred Gottschalk is the President of Hebrew Union College – Jewish Institute of Religion and Professor of Bible and Jewish Thought. He is a member of the Executive Committee of the United States Holocaust Memorial Council and chairs its education committee. He has recently delivered the Thirty-Second Leo Baeck Memorial Lecture entitled "The German Pogrom of November 1938 and the Reaction of American Jewry."

Atina Grossmann is Assistant Professor of History at Columbia University. She is co-editor of *When Biology Became Destiny: Women in Weimar Germany* (1984). Her book on population policy and sexual politics in Weimar Germany is to be published by Oxford University Press.

William W. Hallo is Willam M. Laffan Professor of Assyriology and Babylonian Literature at Yale University. He also serves as Curator of the Yale Babylonian Collection. He is the author or co-author of, among other works, *Early Mesopotamian Royal Titles* (1957), *The Ancient Near East: A History* (1971) and *Heritage: Civilization and the Jews (1984)*.

Anthony Heilbut is a free-lance writer and author of the highly-acclaimed study of German-Jewish refugees in America *Exiled in Paradise* (1983). He has also published *The Gospel Sound: Good News and Bad Times* (1985) and is now completing a critical biography of Thomas Mann to be published by Alfred Knopf.

Frances Henry is a Social Anthropologist at York University, Toronto, Canada. Her interest in ethnic relations and her German-Jewish background led to the writing of a book on Jewish-Gentile ethnic relations in a small town in Germany entitled *Victims and Neighbors: A Small Town in Nazi Germany Remembered* (1984).

Uri D. Herscher is executive vice-president of the Hebrew Union College-Jewish Institute of Religion and Professor of American Jewish History. Among his publications are *Jewish Agricultural Utopias in America 1880-1910* (1981), *The East European Jewish Experience in America 1882-1982* (1983), and (with Abraham J. Peck) *Queen City Refuge. An Oral History of Cincinnati's Jewish Refugees from Nazi Germany* (1989).

Wolfgang Holdheim is Professor of Comparative Literature and Romance Studies and Frederic J. Whiton Professor of Liberal Studies at Cornell University. Among his publications are *Theory and Practice of the Novel: A Study on André Gide* (1968) and *The Hermeneutic Mode: Essays on Time in Literature and Literary Theory* (1984). He has also published *Die Suche nach dem Epos: Der Geschichtsroman bei Hugo, Tolstoi und Flaubert.*

Henry R. Huttenbach is Professor of History at the City College of New York. He has published *The Life of Herta Mansbacher: A Portrait of a Jewish Teacher, Heroine and Martyr* (1980) and *The Destruction of the Jewish Community of Worms* (1981).

Georg G. Iggers is Distinguished Professor of History at the State University of New York at Buffalo. He is the author, of among other works, *The German Conception of History* (1968), *New Interpretations in European Historiography* (1984, 2nd) and editor of *The Social History of Politics* (1985).

Walter Jacob is the senior rabbi of Rodef Shalom Congregation in Pittsburgh, Pennsylvania. He has authored or edited eleven volumes including *Christianity through Jewish Eyes* (1974), *The Changing World of Reform Judaism* (1958) and *Contemporary American Reform Responsa* (1987).

Manfred Jonas is John Bigelow Professor of History at Union College. He is the author or editor of, among other publications, *American Foreign Relations in the Twentieth Century* (1967), *Roosevelt and Churchill: Their Secret Wartime Correspondence* (1975) and *The United States and Germany: A Diplomatic History* (1984).

Hans Juergensen is Professor of Humanities at the University of South Florida at Tampa. He has served as a consultant to the Nobel Prize Committee on Literature and to the United States Holocaust Memorial Council. He has published numerous volumes of poetry including *Existential Canon, and Other Poems* (1965), *Sermons from the Ammunition Hatch of the Ship of Fools* (1968), and the forthcoming *Testimony: Selected Poems, 1954 – 1986.*

Marion Kaplan is Associate Professor of History at Queens College, the City University of New York. She is the author of *The Jewish*

*Feminist Movement in Germany: The Campaigns of the Juedischer Frauenbund, 1904 – 1930* (1979). She is the editor of *The Marriage Bargain: Women and Dowries in European History* (1985) and co-editor of *When Biology became Destiny: Women in Weimar and Nazi Germany* (1984). She is currently writing a social history of Jewish women in Imperial Germany.

Robert Liberles is Senior Lecturer in Jewish History at Ben Gurion University, Beersheva, Israel. He is the author of *Religious Conflict in Social Context: The Resurgence of Orthodox Judaism in Frankfurt am Main, 1838 – 1877* (1986) which was awarded the 1986 National Jewish Book Award in History.

Steven M. Lowenstein is the Isadore Levine Professor of Jewish History at the University of Judaism in Los Angeles. He is the author of *Frankfurt on the Hudson: The German Jewish Community of Washington Heights, 1935 – 1983* (1988).

Joseph B. Maier is Emeritus Professor of Sociology at Rutgers University. He is currently the president of the Rashi Association for the Preservation of Jewish Cultural Monuments in Europe. Professor Maier is the author of several volumes, among them *On Hegel's Critique of Kant* (1939, 1966), *Politics of Change in Latin America* (1964), and *Ethnicity, Identity and History* (1982).

Henry Meyer is Professor of Violin at the College Conservatory of Music at the University of Cincinnati and a member of the internationally-acclaimed LaSalle Quartet.

Michael A. Meyer is Professor of Jewish History at Hebrew Union College-Jewish Institute of Religion, Cincinnati. He is the author of *The Origins of the Modern Jew: Jewish Identity and European Culture in Germany, 1749 – 1824* (1967), which was named the best book on Jewish thought in 1967 by the Jewish Book Council of America, *Ideas of Jewish History* (1974) and *Response to Modernity. A History of the Reform Movement in Judaism* (1988).

George L. Mosse is Weinstein-Bascom Professor of History at the University of Wisconsin – Madison and Koebner Professor of History at the Hebrew University, Jerusalem. His recent publications include *Towards the Final Solution* (1978), *Nationalism and Sexuality* (1985), and *German Jews beyond Judaism* (1985).

Aryeh Neier is the Executive Director of Human Rights Watch (Americas Watch, Asia Watch, Helsinki Watch). From 1970 to 1978 he was the National Executive Director of the American Civil Liberties Union. He is the author of, among other works, *Crime and Punishment: A Radical Solution* (1976), *Defending My Enemy* (1979), and *Only Judgement* (1982).

Gert Niers is the editor-in-chief of *Aufbau*. He holds a Ph.D. from Rutgers University and is the author of *Frauen Schreiben im Exil* (1988).

W. Gunther Plaut is the Senior Scholar of Holy Blossom Temple, Toronto and the former senior rabbi of the congregation. He is the author of many volumes which include *The Jews in Minnesota* (1959), *Judaism and the Scientific Spirit* (1962), *Germany Today* (1962), and *The Rise of Reform Judaism* (1963).

Herbert Pierre Secher is Professor of Political Science at Memphis State University. He is the editor of *Basic Concepts of Sociology (Max Weber)* (1962) and has written widely on German and Central European politics.

Curt C. Silberman has practiced law in the United States since 1948. He is the former president of the American Federation of Jews from Central Europe and the Jewish Philanthropic Fund of 1933 as well as a trustee of the Leo Baeck Institute. He is the author of several articles dealing with international law.

Diane R. Spielmann holds a doctorate in German literature/Jewish writers and is the archivist of the Leo Baeck Institute. She is the sister of Lee A. Spielmann.

Lee A. Spielmann is a practicing attorney in New York who, as a law student, worked with the Department of Justice, Office of Special Investigations. His parents are survivors of the Holocaust.

Hans J. Steinitz is an editor and journalist and the former editor of *Aufbau*, (1966 – 1985). Among his publications are *Regierungs-und Verfassungsformen des Auslands* (1947), *Mississippi, Geschichte eines Stromes*, and *Aufbau, Dokumente einer Cultur in Exil* (1972).

Lucy Y. Steinitz holds a doctorate in social work and is the Executive Director of the Jewish Family Services of Baltimore. She is the editor (with David M. Zyoni) of *Living After the Holocaust: Reflections by Children of Survivors in America* (1976). She is the daughter of Hans J. Steinitz.

Guy Stern is Distinguished Professor of Romance and Germanic Languages and Literatures at Wayne State University in Detroit. He is the author of, among other works, *War, Weimar and Literature: The Story of the "Neue Merkur," 1918 – 1925* (1971), and *Alfred Neumann* (1979).

Herbert A. Strauss is director of the Zentrum fuer Antisemitismusforschung at the Technische Universitaet, Berlin. He is the founder of the Research Foundation for Jewish Immigration. He is the foremost interpretor of the German-Jewish refugee experience in the United States and was the project director of the three-volume *International Biographical Dictionary of Central European Émigrés, 1933 – 1945* (1980 – 1983).

Werner Weinberg is Professor Emeritus of Hebrew Language and Literature at the Hebrew Union College – Jewish Institute of Religion, Cincinnati. His most recent publication is *Self-Portrait of a Holocaust Survivor* (1985).

Jack Wertheimer is the Joseph and Martha Mendelsohn Associate Professor of American Jewish History at the Jewish Theological Seminary of America, New York. He is the author of *Unwelcome Strangers: East European Jews in Imperial Germany* (1987) and editor of *The American Synagogue: A Sanctuary Transformed* (1988).

Theodore Wiener received his rabbinic ordination from the Hebrew Union College in 1943. He is Judaica subject cataloguer at the Library of Congress and the author of numerous scholarly publications.

Norbert Wollheim is a survivor of the Holocaust and was instrumental in the founding the Bergen-Belsen DP camp and of the Jewish communal organizations in postwar northern Germany. He was also instrumental in bringing legal action against the German firm of I.G. Farben for its use of slave labor during the Holocaust.

Harry Zohn is Professor of German at Brandeis University, Waltham, Massachusetts. He has translated numerous German and Austrian writers including Theodor Herzl, Walter Benjamin, Gershom Sholem and Martin Buber. His published works include *Wiener Juden in der deutschen Literatur* (1964) and *Der Farbenvolle Untergang* (1971).

# Index